D0975228

Job

INTERPRETATION
A Bible Commentary for Teaching and Preaching

INTERPRETATION
A BIBLE COMMENTARY FOR TEACHING AND PREACHING

James Luther Mays, *Editor*
Patrick D. Miller, Jr., *Old Testament Editor*
Paul J. Achtemeier, *New Testament Editor*

J. GERALD JANZEN

223

Job

INTERPRETATION

A Bible Commentary
for Teaching and Preaching

John Knox Press
ATLANTA

Library of Congress Cataloging in Publication Data

Janzen, J. Gerald, 1932–
 Job.

 (Interpretation, a Bible commentary for teaching and preaching)
 Bibliography: p.
 1. Bible. O.T.—Commentaries. I. Title. II. Series.
BS1415.3.J36 1985   223'.107   84–48512
ISBN 0–8042–3114–1

© copyright John Knox Press 1985
10 9 8 7 6 5 4 3 2
Printed in the United States of America
John Knox Press
Atlanta, Georgia 30365

SERIES PREFACE

This series of commentaries offers an interpretation of the books of the Bible. It is designed to meet the need of students, teachers, ministers, and priests for a contemporary expository commentary. These volumes will not replace the historical critical commentary or homiletical aids to preaching. The purpose of this series is rather to provide a third kind of resource, a commentary which presents the integrated result of historical and theological work with the biblical text.

An interpretation in the full sense of the term involves a text, an interpreter, and someone for whom the interpretation is made. Here, the text is what stands written in the Bible in its full identity as literature from the time of "the prophets and apostles," the literature which is read to inform, inspire, and guide the life of faith. The interpreters are scholars who seek to create an interpretation which is both faithful to the text and useful to the church. The series is written for those who teach, preach, and study the Bible in the community of faith.

The comment generally takes the form of expository essays. It is planned and written in the light of the needs and questions which arise in the use of the Bible as Holy Scripture. The insights and results of contemporary scholarly research are used for the sake of the exposition. The commentators write as exegetes and theologians. The task which they undertake is both to deal with what the texts say and to discern their meaning for faith and life. The exposition is the unified work of one interpreter.

The text on which the comment is based is the Revised Standard Version of the Bible. The general availability of this translation makes the printing of a translation unnecessary and saves the space for comment. The text is divided into sections appropriate to the particular book; comment deals with passages as a whole, rather than proceeding word by word, or verse by verse.

Writers have planned their volumes in light of the requirements set by the exposition of the book assigned to them. Biblical books differ in character, content, and arrangement. They also differ in the way they have been and are used in the liturgy, thought, and devotion of the church. The distinctiveness and use of particular books have been taken into account in decisions about the approach, emphasis, and use of space in the commentaries. The goal has been to allow writers to develop the format which provides for the best presentation of their interpretation.

The result, writers and editors hope, is a commentary which both explains and applies, an interpretation which deals with both the meaning and the significance of biblical texts. Each commentary reflects, of course, the writer's own approach and perception of the church and world. It could and should not be otherwise. Every interpretation of any kind is individual in that sense; it is one reading of the text. But all who work at the interpretation of Scripture in the church need the help and stimulation of a colleague's reading and understanding of the text. If these volumes serve and encourage interpretation in that way, their preparation and publication will realize their purpose.

Series Editors

PREFACE

It has been said that poems are not so much finished as abandoned in despair. The attempt to write this commentary has brought me to the same place. Any claim to offer here a definitive reading of Job is undermined (for example) by my own experience of the past two weeks: The manuscript was sent off to the editors in mid-semester—a week after it was "finished;" two days after a change in understanding one verb led to a complete revision of the section in which the verb occurred before further classroom work could necessitate more drastic changes. If it is hereby abandoned to the printed page, however, despair is tempered with the hope that it, like other such efforts, will help the reader to make further progress with Job.

In addition to those studies acknowledged in the notes and the Bibliographies (by no means complete), I am indebted to many people. First I must acknowledge James Dunn Fleming Beattie, who assigned me a paper on Job almost thirty years ago. He knows in what sense I owe this book to him. Generations of seminary students have helped me both to understand Job and to appreciate how provisional that understanding must remain. Two former students gave special help: As my student assistant, Jeanne Groom worked closely with me in laying out some of the basic lines of interpretation; Jay Southwick, in the same capacity, gave detailed critique of the first two drafts. James S. Ackerman of Indiana University read portions of the manuscript and contributed significantly (as did my colleague, Edgar A. Towne) to the hermeneutical atmosphere in which I wrote. Several Episcopal congregations in Indianapolis, through study groups and opportunities for interim ministry, helped me to read Job in its contemporary human as well as its ancient textual version: St. Christopher's, St. Paul's, The Church of the Nativity, and St. Matthew's. The editors of this series, Patrick D. Miller and James Luther Mays, have given much help at every stage; Arlene Jones and Joan Crawford deserve the readers' gratitude as well as my own for their work in preparing the manuscript for the press. Christian Theological Seminary underwrote the cost of manuscript reproduction.

Note on the citation of others' views. Other works are generally cited in accordance with the style established for commentaries in this series. A departure from this style occurs in

connection with two other commentators. Though many studies of Job contributed in one way or another to the understanding which lies behind the present work, the commentaries of
Marvin H. Pope and Robert Gordis proved to be working com-
panions to every verse. Since they are referred to frequently,
their commentaries are referred to only by the authors' names.
Where no page number is given, it is to be assumed that reference is to their discussion of the passage in question.

J. Gerald Janzen
Christian Theological Seminary

CONTENTS

INTERPRETATION

ABBREVIATIONS
used in this volume

JAAR Journal of the American Academy of Religion

Interp Interpretation

VT   Vetus Testamentum

JBL   Journal of Biblical Literature

RSV   Revised Standard Version

NIV   New International Version

AV   Authorized Version

JB   Jerusalem Bible

JPS   Jewish Publication Society of America: The Holy Scriptures (1917)

NEB   The New English Bible

To my wife Eileen
and to all the
brothers, sisters, and acquaintances
of Job

". . . provided we suffer together . . ."
(Romans 8:17)

Introduction

The Book of Job has to do with the most painful and unavoidable questions which can arise in human experience. These questions arise in connection with experiences of arbitrary suffering. The questions begin by asking after the meaning of such suffering, but in their most extreme form they go on to call into question the meaningfulness of life and of existence as such. The sufferer begins to suspect that the fabric of meanings and the pervasive and undergirding sense of worthwhileness which normally attends our days are only something we have fabricated to mask from ourselves the pointlessness of all our days.

Focusing as it does on issues of suffering and the questions it raises, the Book of Job has a universal appeal, in some respects unique in the Scriptures of the Judaeo-Christian tradition. One practical evidence of this may be offered from many years' experience in the study of this book with seminary students and lay people: Of all the books of the Bible, this one requires the least by way of pre-requisite knowledge and information to make a beginning. There is hardly a person who does not have personal acquaintance with the questions to which the book is addressed. Another evidence of its universal appeal lies in its grip on the imagination of writers and thinkers who otherwise find the biblical tradition uncongenial and unhelpful.

Yet the Book of Job does not stand on the margin of the biblical tradition, a citizen of world literature unsure of its home country. Thematically and perspectivally it stands squarely within the Bible. Indeed, it may be said to stand astride the whole of the biblical tradition at one critical juncture and to raise the universal questions in such a way specific to Israel that, depending on their resolution, the centuries-old tradition as a whole is faced either with its own dissolution or with a call to transformed self-understanding. In this respect, the deepest understanding of this book presupposes an intimate knowledge and appreciation of the formative existential energies of ancient Israel as articulated in the central meta-

phors and themes of the Old Testament. In this connection
we may note that the universal human question, "Why do the
righteous suffer?" is posed in Job within the context of a prior
and (at least for the narrator) deeper question posed by God:
"Why are the righteous pious?" These two questions are
posed, explored painstakingly in their specific dimensions and
for their implications, and then resolved, all in a manner
which is characteristic of—and at the same time transforma-
tive of—the very traditions which the questions call into
doubt. These traditions have to do with the character of God
and the status and vocation of humankind in the world, as set
forth in Israel's classic expressions concerning creation, redemption, and the covenant relationship.

Later in this introduction, and at various points in the commentary, an attempt will be made to indicate some of the leading features of the Old Testament tradition in relation to which
the Book of Job is here interpreted. Also, though more briefly
and tentatively, some suggestions are ventured as to how the
thematics of Job relate to the thematics central to the New
Testament. The latter attempt is fraught with danger. It is all
too easy for Christians simply to interpret Job in terms of Jesus
and his cross, and thereby to impose upon Job perspectives and
categories of understanding that are anachronistic and that may
obscure what Job has to teach us. It has been the experience of
this commentator, both in private study and in the classroom,
that the Old Testament is most fruitfully read when it is read
in the first place within its own terms. Part of that fruitfulness
consists in the emergence of perspectives on existence of great
power and illumination. Another part consists in the capacity of
such perspectives to deepen, broaden, and refresh perspectives
presented in the New Testament but which, through centuries
of subsequent devotional and homiletical exploration and theological formulation, have become blunted by familiarity and
hardened into narrow creeds. If we can prescind from our
knowledge of the New Testament and the Jesus story to read
the Book of Job in and for itself, it may be that Job will offer us
a key to what the vocation of Jesus may have been like, as it
were, "from the inside." For these reasons, connections between Job and the New Testament are deliberately only indicated for further pondering (preferably in the context of the
study of the New Testament) and are not developed further in
the context of this study of Job.

A Synopsis of the Book

The narrative opens on a man who is extraordinarily blessed and prosperous, upright, and pious. Such a man is of extraordinary interest in the divine realm. Then, in that realm, the question arises: *Why* is the man so pious and so upright? Is it only because he is so blessed and so prosperous? The question which is raised in heaven is not answered there but is given into the hands and heart of the man to answer in the context of manifold suffering. At first he responds to his calamity with steady trust and acceptance. Then his response begins to betray traces of ambiguity. A first attempt at help on the part of his wife is followed by the arrival of three friends who come to condole with him and to comfort him. The so-called prologue (chaps. 1—2) ends on this latter scene.

After seven days of silent suffering and silent condolence, the man at last erupts into speech and curses the day of his birth, using the language of creation in the first chapter of Genesis and standing the latter tradition on its head. One of his friends responds, diffidently, offering Job the accumulated wisdom of the community concerning such calamities, a wisdom which Job himself apparently had often formerly offered to other sufferers. Job's response to this counsel is no less vehement than his initial outburst. Thus is set in motion a series of poetic exchanges between Job and his three friends, in a pattern which proceeds as follows: Job, Eliphaz, Job, Bildad, Job, Zophar, Job, Eliphaz, and so on, until three cycles are all but completed (chaps. 3—27). At this point, Job reverts to speech in the mode of soliloquy and addresses himself to the enigma of wisdom, and its apparent inaccessibility to humankind (chap. 28), before summing up his own life in a retrospective affirmation of his past life (chap. 29), an unblinking recognition of his present condition (chap. 30), and an integrative oath before God (chap. 31).

Now a newcomer enters the picture. A youth, Elihu, perhaps a member of the retinue of one of the three friends, claims to speak not from observation and experience, as his three superiors have largely done, but by divine inspiration. Thereby he claims also to offer new (divine) perspectives on the issues which the four primary speakers had canvassed in such detail but to no satisfactory resolution. Yet even his utterances (chaps. 32—37), lengthy as they are, do not conclude the matter. At

3

long last Yahweh, who has remained silent all the while (as, for instance, in Isa. 42:14), speaks and addresses Job directly (chaps. 38—41). Such "answer" as Yahweh gives to Job, however, comes only in the form of further questions. To these divine questions (which, we may suppose, are a continuation of the original divine question posed in heaven, as in 1:9), Job at first offers his own contrite (or self-masking) silence (40:3–5). Finally he offers his full confessional agreement to what the divine questions imply (42:1–6). In a manner which eludes propositional statement, but which works to invite readerly participation, both the divine questions to Job and his own questions to God are resolved in a covenanting convergence which implies transformed perspectives on the character of God and on the status and vocation of humankind in the world.

The book concludes as it began, with a prose narrative (42:7–17) in which Job is restored to his former estate and more. What has been gained through this terrible ordeal? The restoration is narrated in such a way as to suggest that Job is no longer the person he was in the beginning. As so often happens in this book, there is an unintended and ironic truth in what one of his friends had said: His end makes his beginning small by comparison (8:7).

The book, then, moves from idyllic *beginning* through catastrophe and a vast dialectical terrain back to an *end* which is a transformed version of the beginning. The dialogues traverse the landscape of human experience in all its shifting lights and topographic variety, along with similar varieties of human opinion both orthodox and heterodox, conventional and novel, prudential and reckless. The shape of the book thus corresponds to the shape of the Christian canon, which *begins* with an idyllic creation story suffused with light and charged with blessing (Gen. 1—2), moves through catastrophe and along a vast canvas of universal and particular history, and arrives finally at an *end* imaginatively envisaged as a transformed version of its beginning (Revelation 21—22). This same shape, differently presented yet thematically and metaphorically similar, may be discerned already in the Old Testament itself, if we attend carefully to such eschatological envisagements as are presented in Deutero-Isaiah and Trito-Isaiah, the latter chapters of Ezekiel, and so on. In its format, then, as well as in its thematics, the Book of Job is both entirely at home within the Bible and an epitome of it.

**The Setting of the Book of Job in the History
of the Religions of the Ancient Near East**

The story of Job is set "long ago and far away." It is as
though a deliberate effort had been made to pose the problems
raised in the book in general human terms, by removing the
story from a specifically Israelite setting. Of course, the precise
effect achieved by this removal and "distancing" of the story
presupposes readers who in fact or in imagination are situated
in Israel at a specific time in that people's history. Scholarly
efforts to date and to place the author, however, have not yet
achieved a consensus. The conclusion adopted in this commentary for working purposes is that the Book of Job was written
in the exile and that the problems with which it deals arose in
the existential tension between that historical upheaval and
Israel's religious traditions.

When the Book of Job is read in the specific context of
Israel's religious traditions, it is often contrasted with the Book
of Deuteronomy and the latter's theology of consistent reward
and punishment. The widespread popularity of such an approach is reflected in the words of thanks which Robert Frost
has God offer to Job for the part he has played to ". . . stultify
the Deuteronomist / And change the tenor of religious
thought" ("A Masque of Reason"). Though there is some truth
in such a view, the contrast between Deuteronomy and Job
provides much too narrow a frame of reference within which
to read the book even in its Israelite setting. Recently, two
historians of religion, Thorkild Jacobsen and Frank Moore
Cross, have attempted to locate the Book of Job within the
history of the religions of the ancient Near East. A summary of
their relevant comments will provide a basis for the reading of
the Book of Job offered in this commentary.

Thorkild Jacobsen, in his history of Mesopotamian religion
(*The Treasures of Darkness*), characterizes three millennia of
religious understanding in terms of three fundamental metaphors for the gods. In the fourth millennium the gods were
powers immanent in the phenomena of nature, powers willing
to come to specific form as the phenomena. In the third millennium the gods transcended nature and society, as royal, divine
figures who had created nature as a complex artefact and who
had created humankind to be slaves to serve the gods by work-

5

ing on the earth, the divine estate. In this understanding, the gods were set free from further toil. In the words of the creation epic "Enuma Elish," the high god Marduk ". . . formed mankind, / imposed toil on man, set the gods free" (quoted in Jacobsen, p. 181). Another myth, The Story of Atrahasis, presents a similar picture of the gods and humankind. Jacobsen comments:

> . . . the myth views absolute power as selfish, ruthless, and unsubtle. But what is is. Man's existence is precarious, his usefulness to the gods will not protect him unless he takes care not to become a nuisance to them, however innocently. There are, he should know, limits set for his self-expression (p. 121).

In the second millennium, among some Mesopotamians, the gods became viewed, in part, as "personal" deities standing in direct relation to the individual family or clan head and understood to be as divine parents of their human children, responsible for their birth, nurture, protection, and guidance. Within this metaphor the god was said to be with the human devotee as the power within the individual for enabling success. In such an understanding, persons could approach their personal god with all the trust and confidence—in the root sense, with all the familiarity—with which they approached their own human parents. This "personal religion" gave way in the first millennium in Mesopotamia before the resurgence of older modes of perception of divine nature and activity. However, first it entered into the religious experience of Israel's ancestors (Abraham and Sarah and descendants); and indeed, it formed the basis of Israelite Yahwism. Jacobsen writes:

> As far as we can see, it is only Israel that decisively extended the attitude of personal religion from the personal to the national realm. The relationship of Yahweh to Israel—his anger, his compassion, his forgiveness, and his renewed anger and punishment of the sinful people—is in all essentials the same as that of the relation between god and individual in the attitude of personal religion. With this understanding of national life and fortunes as lived under ultimate moral responsibility, Israel created a concept of history as purposive—one which in basic essentials still governs conceptions of meaningful historical existence (p. 164).

6

Nevertheless, in commenting on the implications of this personal religion in its Mesopotamian form, Jacobsen draws attention to what he considers

... the paradoxical character of personal religion, with its conspicuous humility curiously based on an almost limitless presumption of self-importance, its drawing the greatest cosmic powers into the little personal world of the individual, and its approach to the highest, the most awesome, and the terrifying in such an easy and familiar manner (p. 161).

This paradox issues eventually in a religious crisis, in the tension between belief in the gods as encountered in the way things really are (third millennium cosmic lords) and belief in the gods as humans would like them to be (second millennium personal parents). The crisis comes to a focus in the problem of the righteous sufferer. In Mesopotamian religion, the problem is dealt with in two works, *Ludlul bel nemeqi* and the Babylonian Theodicy, in both of which the ways of the gods are acknowledged to be incomprehensible. It is in such a context that Jacobsen then comments on the Book of Job:

> The personal, egocentric view of the sufferer—however righteous—is rejected. The self-importance which demands that the universe adjust to his needs, his righteousness, is cast aside, and the full stature of God as the majestic creator and ruler of the universe is reinstated. The distance between the cosmic and the personal, between God in his infinite greatness and mere individual man, is so great and so decisive that an individual has no rights, not even to justice (p. 163).

Jacobsen analyzes and comments on these ancient Mesopotamian and Israelite texts not only with scholarly authority but with deep and humane sympathy. The conclusions to which he comes—both in his reading of Job and in his reading of the general human situation—are paralleled remarkably, from a contemporary point of view, in the recent work of the theological ethicist James M. Gustafson (see Gustafson, 1981). The latter work thereby offers a ready means of translating Jacobsen's reading of the Book of Job into a contemporary setting and idiom for ethical and religious purposes. Nevertheless, this reading of the resolution arrived at in Job will be questioned below and implicitly throughout the commentary.

Frank Moore Cross, in his history of Israelite religion (*Canaanite Myth and Hebrew Epic*), picks up the analysis where Jacobsen leaves it. Cross connects the religion of Israel's ancestors with the personal religion of second-millennium Mesopotamia (p. 75 and note). Then, as the title of his book

7

suggests, he traces the history of Israel's religion in comparison with that of Canaan, from the ancestral period to the exile. His comments on Job come in his concluding chapter entitled "Exile and Apocalyptic," under the heading, A Note on the Study of Apocalyptic Origins.

As Cross observes, the sixth century (the century of the exile) was rich in literary and theological activity. The epic traditions of early Israel and the traditions of Israel in the land were given final form, respectively by the Priestly traditionists and the final editor of the Deuteronomic History. The result was the Hebrew Bible in basically its present form from Genesis through Second Kings. In all this material, one may say, the implications of the originating metaphor of personal religion were drawn out and elaborated by means of the details of Israel's life and history. However, Cross argues, "these attempts at the interpretation of history ultimately were inadequate" (p. 343). They were inadequate insofar as they suppressed the ambiguities of history. The Book of Job has its significance in exposing these inadequacies:

> The argument of Job attacked the central theme of Israel's religion. It repudiated the God of history whose realm is politics, law, and justice, whose delight is to lift up the poor and to free the slave. The God who called Israel out of Egypt, who spoke by prophet, the covenant god of Deuteronomy, did not reveal himself to Job. It is true that God spoke, but note that he spoke from the storm cloud. It is true that he revealed transcendent wisdom and power, but they were revealed in thunder and lightning, in the language of Ba'l. He was revealed in the defeat of the dragon of chaos, in the myths of creation. There is a sense in which Job brought the ancient religion of Israel to an end. History to Job was opaque. Job viewed the flux of history in despair; he detected no pattern of meaning there. History was a riddle beyond man's fathoming. The Lord of history failed to act. 'El or Ba'l, the transcendent creator spoke. Only He lived. Job saw Him and bowed his knee (p. 344).

It is important to note Cross's qualification, when he writes "... Job brought the *ancient* religion of Israel to an end" (italics added). For he goes on to observe that "Job belongs in the main line of the evolution of Israel's religion," noting that "Job's importance was not forgotten in apocalyptic circles." Nevertheless, he concludes, "the creation of the new faith of Israel fell on shoulders other than those of the author of Job;" and he goes on to identify those others as Second Isaiah and other sixth-

8

century prophetic materials in the Isaianic tradition, as well as Ezekiel. We shall have occasion often in the commentary to draw attention to points of close connection between Job and Second Isaiah.

The above-outlined history-of-religion perspectives of Jacobsen and Cross provide us with a much more clearly delineated setting for the study of Job than was hitherto available. Their achievements in general are magisterial, and the issues which they identify in the Book of Job must be acknowledged to be largely correct. Yet, in our judgment, their assessment of the Joban resolution of those issues is off the mark. A few brief and unelaborated remarks are in order, both by way of indicating our points of divergence and by way of introducing our own view of Job.

Critique of Jacobsen and Cross. In response to Jacobsen, it is to be observed that his reading of Job focuses entirely on the questions which Job addresses to God, in the dialogues, and ignores completely the question raised in heaven concerning Job, in the prologue. Such an approach cannot but skew one's analysis and one's conclusions. Secondly, one cannot simply move laterally from the views presented in the Mesopotamian *Ludlul bel nemeqi* and the Babylonian Theodicy to those presented in the Book of Job. The views presented in the two Babylonian works arose at a certain point in Mesopotamian religious history, a history which was quite different from the thousand-year Israelite religious history which preceded the writing of Job. In Mesopotamia, by the second millennium, two religious metaphors co-existed and vied for credibility. Moreover the more recent of the two, the "personal" metaphor, was the newcomer and interloper, whereas the older "lordly" metaphor enjoyed the sanction (in religious matters always a weighty sanction) of more ancient tradition. Under the stress of the vicissitudes of history, the relatively tender religious and existential consciousness which budded in the form of personal religion was not hardy enough to survive, so that older and more deeply rooted views seemed, if not more hopeful, at least more realistic.

With Israel matters were different. As the ancestral traditions of Genesis attest, the metaphor of personal religion was no late interloper or tentative newcomer in Israel's experience or traditions of God, but rather, this metaphor named the charac-

9

ter of Israel's founding experiences. (See, for instance, Deut. 32:6 and Exod. 4:22–23; and note the meaning of the name Abram: "the [divine] father is exalted.") It was the gods of the *other* nations who subsequently were identified by loyal Yahwists as interlopers (e.g., Deut. 32:16–18). Whereas in second-millennium Mesopotamia two metaphors *internal* to the culture vied for survival, in Israel the struggle was between the personal metaphor internal to Israel's tradition from the beginning and that other ancient, "lordly" metaphor, which, for all its appeal, was viewed by the leading figures and by the traditionists as an idolatrous temptation coming from the outside. The fact is that Israel's religious history taken as a whole did not, as did that of Mesopotamia, end in a dark age. Rather, the descendants of Abraham and Sarah emerged from the exile with a faith which, however re-formulated and transformed, continued to ground itself firmly in the traditions of those ancestors and the traditions of the Exodus and Sinai. If Cross's comment concerning Job's position along the main axis of Israel's religious history has any merit, then it is difficult to see how the book can at the same time be viewed as a retrograde movement to re-affirm third-millennium religious sensibilities.

Cross's placement of Job "in the main line of the evolution of Israel's religion" is here accepted. For that very reason, the data which he interprets as in the passage quoted above at length are interpreted differently. One may indeed acknowledge the fact that under the pressure of events in the late seventh and early sixth centuries many Israelites turned to the gods of Canaan and Mesopotamia for help and guidance. Can we really suppose, however, that a book written out of such impulses would be capable of influencing the main line of development of Israel's religion? Where Cross reads disjunction from the "ancient religion," we read critique, deepening, and even transformation, but in any case fundamental continuity. The ancient religion was not wrong; rather, it had not yet fully confronted its own implications. While the whole of the commentary itself is only a partial response to the view of Cross, the following items will indicate where we see points of continuity between Job and the Israelite tradition in contrast to Cross's arguments for discontinuity.

10

(1) Is it correct to say that "'El or Ba'l, the transcendent creator spoke"? The prologue and the epilogue of Job refer to the deity as Yahweh or Elohim; by contrast, the dialogues use

the terms *Eloah, El,* and *Shadday,* but never Yahweh. Yet the rubrics in chapters 38:1—42:6 consistently use the name Yahweh (38:1; 40:1, 3, 6; 42:1), as though the narrator were presenting the same God who spoke in 1:7–12 and 2:2–6 and who will speak in 42:7–8. Moreover, it is arguable that Genesis 1 provides at least as good a background for the interpretation of the creation theology of the divine speeches as do the creation traditions of Canaan.

(2) The fact that Yahweh speaks in storm and cloud, thunder and lightning does not establish the divine speeches as Baalistic. It may be claimed with equal plausibility that such imagery indicates the continuity in Job of such classic Israelite usages as may be found, for example, in Exodus 19—20, Psalm 8, and Ezekiel 1:4.

(3) The God who is revealed in the defeat of the dragon of chaos is not thereby divorced from involvement in the concerns of history, as is clear from Job's near-contemporary and (according to Cross) close successor, Second Isaiah (see Isa. 51:9–11).

(4) The God who called Israel out of Egypt is a God whose habitation is Mount Sinai in the wilderness (sometimes called by Israel *tōhû,* "formlessness"). This God who acts in justice to lift up the poor and the slave also acts in the wilderness to try the liberated ones to know what is in their heart; specifically, to know whether they serve God for bread alone (Deut. 8:2–3). The Book of Job falls well within such a tradition.

(5) Similarly, the God who spoke by prophet at times apparently spoke through conflicting prophetic agencies, by way of testing the hearts of kings. As we shall argue, the Book of Job is in part a critique of prophetic religion (see below, commentary on the Elihu speeches); but it stands within that tradition and does not repudiate it.

(6) The address of the covenant God is not identified in the Old Testament by the presence or absence of covenant terminology or covenant forms alone, but at a much deeper level, by the presence of fundamental conceptions of the divine-human relationship. Thus, for example, that relationship is presented in a thoroughly covenantal manner in Genesis 2—3, though, as befits the universal human setting of the story, the terms in which it is presented are for the most part more general. So, too, in Job—which is set outside of Israel and therefore outside the explicit frame of reference of covenant—the divine-human relation is explored in such a way as to engage, and at

11

the same time to satisfy and to re-educate, the covenanting religious consciousness.

(7) The assertion that "the Lord of history failed to act" assumes that the epilogue formed no original part of the Book of Job. That assumption, for all its widespread acceptance, is here challenged. The assertion also implies a certain reading of the divine speeches. In the present commentary Job 38—41 is read as a renewed "speech from the burning bush" which, in the tradition of Moses, calls Job to a worldly task supposedly impossible yet crucial to the divine purposes. Granted, the reading of the divine speeches in part as a new speech from the bush implies a transformation of that famous scene in Exodus 3.

The Place of Job in the History of Israel's Religion

The above comments on the views of Cross and Jacobsen have already begun to indicate the views on which this commentary is based. These views may now be elaborated briefly as follows. Though a full elaboration would require a survey of the whole of Israel's tradition leading up to Job, we here select those representative traditions which are relevant. The following traditions are especially prominent:

(1) *Genesis 1*, with its twin focus in God as cosmic creator and in humankind as the divine image, *'adam* from the *'adama* (ground) yet given dominion over the earth and specifically over the denizens of sea, air, and land; (2) *Psalm 8*, with its twin emphases on the finitude of mortal earthlings and on the royal vocation to which humankind has been called by the creator, a vocation including, again, dominion over the denizens of earth, sky, and sea, a dominion specifically including "the beasts of the field" and "whatever passes along the paths of the sea;" (3) *Genesis 2—3*, with its portrayal of a human vocation to live loyally before God on earth in the face of a temptation to interpret that vocation otherwise through a "wisdom" indicated by the agency of a divinely given tempter; (4) the traditions of *Exodus* and *Sinai* (and therefore, to be sure, Deuteronomy), including the call of Moses at the bush, the covenanting claims of Sinai and the testing in the wilderness; (5) *Second Isaiah* (Isa. 40—55). Job and Second Isaiah arose as mirror opposites from one emergent Israelite consciousness. An analogy that comes to mind is the twin products of the poetic maturity of Rainer Maria Rilke, written within weeks of one another: first his "Duino

12

Elegies" and then his "Sonnets to Orpheus;" the one a group of elegies verging on praise, the other a series of sonnets of lyric praise arising in the face of death and loss. Just so, one may view the rise of Job and Second Isaiah in the exile. The myriad connections between these two flowerings of the exile remain yet to be fully traced. They range from vocabulary usage peculiar to these two books, through preoccupation with common themes and motifs, to the fundamental issue of the nature of human vocation and hope under the conditions of the suffering and calamity which stalk the path of history.

The Book of Job constitutes a critique and an implicit deepening and transformation of Israel's understanding of creation, covenant, and history. What does it mean to be *'adam*— to be an earthling, made from dust? What does it mean to be the divine image, and therein a royal figure in the earth? What does it mean to affirm at one and the same time that to be human is to be dust and the royal image of God? Can these two metaphors for humankind be sustained together? Indeed, may these two metaphors be so conjoined as to constitute a new complex metaphor? Or does human experience honestly attended to drive us to one metaphor at the expense of the other? If these two metaphors of human existence—dust and royal image—are conjointly sustainable (dust *as* royal image; royal image *as* dust), does not the human experience invite us to transformed understandings of what it means to be dust and to have royalty stamped on the forehead of that dust? (And what, then, is the import of the Book of Job for the deeper significance of Ash Wednesday?) Does not dust itself, without ceasing to be dust, begin to become aware of an unimaginable destiny? And does not royalty, without ceasing to be royalty, begin to become aware of the conditions under which and the modes in which its royal power is to be exercised?

In spite of his preceding comments on Job, Thorkild Jacobsen concludes his exposition of Mesopotamian personal religion with a paragraph (quoted above) on Israel's adoption of that religious metaphor. He concludes the paragraph with these words: "With this understanding of national life and fortunes as lived under ultimate moral responsibility, Israel created a concept of history as purposive—one which in basic essentials still governs conceptions of meaningful historical existence" (p. 164). Similarly, in spite of his preceding comments on Job (quoted above), Frank Cross goes on to assert that "Job

13

belongs in the main line of the evolution of Israel's religion" (p. 345). It is now widely recognized that the New Testament arose within a religious matrix pronouncedly apocalyptic in character. The centrality of the divine-parent metaphor is a commonly acknowledged feature of the Gospels as well as the other New Testament documents. Passages abound in which the conjoint metaphors of *creaturely* vocation to *royal* status and function are thematized. (Noteworthy are Mark 10:35–45; Matt. 16:13–28; Luke 23:32–43; I Cor. 1:18—2:13; II Cor. 1: 3–7; Philipp. 2:5–13, and Rom. 8:15–30.) In the last-mentioned passage, it is emphasized that suffering under the vicissitudes of history (Rom. 5:1–5; 8:31–39) leads to an affirmation of human vocation to be the children of God, a vocation which on the one hand involves suffering together and on the other hand being glorified together. In addition, this vocation is to be fulfilled within the setting of cosmic creation (Rom. 8:19–21). In the New Testament this question and these themes gather pre-eminently around the figure of Jesus, then broaden out to draw others into a like vocational self-understanding. But the question and the themes take shape already in Job and in Second Isaiah.

One aspect of the general historical setting of Job has not yet been mentioned, and that has to do with what we may call the evolution of human consciousness. According to the eccentric but seminal thesis of Julian Jaynes (*The Origin of Consciousness*), the period 1500–800 marks the rise of individual consciousness in the ancient Near East. In broad terms, this period marks the rise of individuated consciousness *vis-à-vis* both the social group and the divine realm. One may suggest a correlation between this thesis of Jaynes's and the analysis which Jacobsen has offered of the rise and the character of personal religion (see further Janzen, *Interp.* 37:178–83). In this commentary the Book of Job is viewed as one exploration of the vocational implications of the gift and the burden of consciousness. What does it mean to be a sentient, suffering, solitary consciousness before God and in the world? What is the nature of the claims laid upon such an individual by others, by tradition, by God, in the face of experiences which isolate oneself within a self-awareness which at the same time is being called in question? What becomes of the nature of covenant and community when consciousness takes on such a solitary dimension?

14

Approach to the Interpretation of the Text

A Literary Reading. In this commentary the approach to interpretation proceeds under the conviction expressed by David J. A. Clines in the following words: "The distinction between the Bible as literature and the Bible as scripture is largely artificial. The church can properly hear its Bible as Scripture only when it reads it as literature" (*Interp.* 34:115). This is not to say that the Bible is devoid of reference to historical events or indifferent to theological realities! However, it is to suggest that the proper approach to the historical events and the theological meanings to which the Bible testifies is through careful prior attention to the text in its literary character. John W. Dixon, Jr., writing of art, distinguishes between matter, form, and content. In the case of art, *matter* is "any and every physical material used in the making of the work of art," *form* is "anything done to the material by the hand and mind of the artist," and *content* is "everything that is communicated through and by means of the form. . . . what is often called 'meaning'" (JAAR 51:24). John Ciardi addresses the relation between form and content in the title of his introduction to poetry by asking, *How Does a Poem Mean?* In our view, the interpretation of Scripture has tended to move prematurely to questions of historical fact and literary pre-history ("matter"), and/or to questions of theological meaning ("content"); it has moved too quickly to *what* Scripture means apart from *how* it means. The present commentary no doubt often suffers from these faults of impatience, but the attempt is made, under the limitations of space and the writer's competence (and patience!), to move in the direction of greater attention to *how* the Bible means.

The aim, then, of the interpretive approach here undertaken is not to extract ("exegete" or lead out) from the text and to place into the waiting hands or mouths of readers a meaning which they are to be supposed to be incapable of finding for themselves in the text. The aim, rather, is to "eisegete" the reader—to lead the reader into the text, to invite the reader to enter into the text and to entertain its meaning from within the text, according to the perspective and the entry which this commentator has so far gained. Some further words of Dixon are to the point here:

> Content [or meaning] is not form, but it is inseparable from form. It has no existence without form. It emerges from the form. There is no statement of it other than the work itself; any verbal statement is a translation, a pointing finger, a way of saying "It is something like this" in hopes that verbal statement helps the hearer to see what exists *only* in the formed material and what can be apprehended *only* by the intelligent eye, not carried over into any verbal formula (p. 24).

The many so-called interpretive passages in this commentary are not, then, to be taken as so many "syphonings-off" of the meaning of the text, as though the meaning in the text could after all satisfactorily be "carried over into any [other] verbal formula." Rather, the so-called interpretations are attempts to position the reader for ways of entering into the text itself. (It may be suggested that such aims might profitably inform the reading and exposition of Scripture in the context of the liturgy.)

If the aim of this commentary is to lead the reader into the text, or to position the reader for such an entry, what should be the corresponding aim of the reader? How may this commentary best be used? The aim should not be to find out from the commentator what the Book of Job means, but rather to attend sensitively and with sympathetic imagination to the concreteness of the text, to what Archibald MacLeish in his poem "Ars Poetica" calls the *being* of a poem rather than its *meaning*. In that particular poem, we may recall, he insisted on the character of any poem as "mute . . . , dumb . . . , silent . . . , wordless." The text offers images, metaphors, tones of feeling, perspectives, transitions, and clashes of view which are to be appropriated and stored or (as in the case of Jacob and of Mary) "hid in the heart," where the meaning which is implicit in their being or their form may mingle hiddenly with already acquired images, tones of feeling, and so on, or may lie dormant awaiting further experiences in conjunction with which they will then occasion insight and understanding. This commentary, then, will best be used as an instrument by which the reader may disengage from distracting concerns and obfuscating agendas and take up one's position before the text; and it may be used as a guide to some likely points of entry into the text. Such a way of reading—in the first instance of the Bible itself or any literature, but also of a commentary such as the present one—involves patience and a trust in the efficacy of implicit meaning.

16

The discipline of the literary reading of the Bible has by no means yet reached a stage of maturity. Even such features of the discipline which have already been established are here used only in *ad hoc* fashion. A few items which enter frequently into the analysis of Job should be mentioned in this Introduction. A prominent feature of biblical literature is the repetition of *key words,* whether within a short unit of text or across a considerable textual interval. The frequent indication of Hebrew words (in transliteration) is meant to enable the reader of the English text to appreciate this feature somewhat more fully. Another prominent feature is the fondness for what is variously called *chiasmus* or envelope construction or inversion, wherein units of the text (words, images, themes) occur in sequences such as *abb'a'* or *abcb'a'.* Somewhat related to this feature is a tendency to open and close passages with the same word, image, or other means. This "bracketing" or marking-off device is called an inclusion.

Irony. It is widely acknowledged that the Book of Job abounds in irony. Most simply put, the recognition of irony in a text is the recognition that ". . . some statements cannot be understood without rejecting what they seem to say," that is, without taking them to mean something else than what they seem to say, a something else which undercuts their apparent meaning (Booth, *A Rhetoric of Irony,* p. 1). Since the present commentary arrives at its understanding of the meaning in the Book of Job largely on the basis of the ironies here identified in the book (that is, since the *content* is dependent upon this particular rhetorical *form*), it is appropriate to apprise the reader of the understanding of irony employed in the interpretation. That understanding is derived largely from Wayne Booth, the relevant features of whose study of irony may be summarized as follows.

Irony can be said to serve the purposes of "reconstruction." This latter metaphor, drawn from the building trades, implies "the tearing down of one habitation and the building of another one on a different spot" (p. 33). Instead, however, of attacking the first habitation (an attitude, a conviction, a set of beliefs) directly, by plain frontal attack, irony is a way of subverting it indirectly and from within. The ironist appears to share the place being described, but inhabits it—talks about it or represents it—in such a way as to expose its uninhabitability. Usually

17

(but not necessarily) the ironist at the same time implies another place, a superior place, on which to stand or in which to dwell. Whereas the direct frontal attack and a similar advocacy of a preferred alternative may have the character of verbal or logical coercion, ironic "reconstruction" tends to operate in a more persuasive and invitatory mode. The persuasive and invitatory rather than coercive character of irony is seen in the fact that some readers may well miss the irony and choose to "dwell in happy ignorance in the shaky edifice, thus adding to its absurdity" (p. 36). Precisely because of this invitatory character, irony implicates the willing reader actively in the affirmation of the new position. Booth writes of "a kind of morally active engagement [that] is invited by the irony . . ." (p. 66). And he writes, "having decided for myself that the ostensible judgment [reflected in the apparent meaning of the text] must be somehow combatted, I make the new position mine with all the force that is conferred by my sense of having judged independently" (p. 41).

This last feature of irony, its invitation to morally active engagement, in our view is one of the keys to the reading of the divine speeches to Job in chapters 38—41. Indeed, if our interpretation is at all near the mark, the divine speeches provide a parade example of how *content* (or meaning) is conveyed in and through *form*, in this instance the use of rhetorical questions ironically. For, in our view, the divine speeches come not as a rebuff to Job's presumption, but as a challenge and an invitation (much in the spirit of Jer. 12:5) to move beyond the creatural theology which he still inhabits to a theology of morally active engagement and participation in the making of meaningful form.

Existential Questions. In addition to irony, and closely related to it in function, another rhetorical feature which pervades the Book of Job is the use of questions. From 1:7 through to the end, all that is narrated or said either moves toward or proceeds from questions of the deepest import. The approach to questions which is undertaken in this commentary has been developed and employed hermeneutically elsewhere (Janzen, *Semeia* 24, see esp. 12–18). This approach may be summarized for present purposes as follows.

We may distinguish several sorts of questions. One sort poses a *request for information* about an already existing state

18

of affairs which happens to be unknown to the questioner. Another sort, the *rhetorical question,* involves that which is well known by the questioner, but is posed as a question for the purpose of enlisting the hearer's own energies of affirmation (or, to use Booth's words, the hearer's "morally active engagement") in drawing the hearer toward what is already known by the questioner. A third sort, the *impossible question,* has the effect of heightening the sense of human frailty, inasmuch as it calls attention to limits imposed upon human intellectual and physical ventures (Crenshaw, *Semeia* 17:19).

A fourth sort we may call an *existential question.* As this phrase is here used, an existential question has to do with the fact of being alive and of finding oneself in a process of personal growth and becoming. This process occurs through the power of decision exercised in active response to possibilities which stand before one. Such presented possibilities pose themselves as the question of one's existence. An existential question is not posed to be answered, if by answer we mean some piece of information foreign to the questioner which is brought or drawn toward the questioner who remains stationary. Rather, such a question poses a goal to be lived toward, in such a way that, in time, the questioner becomes a self which is then the "answer." Moreover, the power to live toward such a question arises from the question itself, and this power arises within the person as the question is taken in and entertained attentively. For the power lies, and is experienced, in the tension between who and what one *is* at a given point and who and what one vaguely but importantly senses one may *become.* One name for this tension and this power is hope. The power is entertained as hope. It is appropriated and exercised in the mode of patient and active faith. But, like literary meanings which reside inextricably within literary forms, the power of the question cannot be abstracted and appraised apart from the question; for the power resides in the question until the questioner has become the answer (or perhaps, until the question has been discovered to be an impossible question; such is the risk which attends existence in faith).

As forms of power, existential questions may be dissipated through premature and indiscriminate disclosure. For this reason they are to be discreetly husbanded and narrowly channeled in acts and commitments and intentions which are consonant with them. For the disclosure of one's own question

19

to others admits those others into the sphere of power of one's own becoming. Those others, who thereby come to share in the power of the question, themselves become, by the way they appropriate and act in that power, partners with one in shaping and determining the eventual answer. Such a relationship, in which existential questions are shared toward a shared outcome, is of the essence of covenant, whatever the specific terms and forms of covenant language may be. A covenant relation, in this view, is one in which the participants in the covenant share their existential questions toward a shared outcome. Considered in this way, covenant relations are a form of historical existence in which, to use some terms of Thorkild Jacobsen, the history is purposive and lived under ultimate moral responsibility.

Considered in terms of the biblical thematics of vocation, human existential questions may be said to be posed to us by God. The matter is perhaps more radical than this. In a number of essays we have attempted to suggest the biblical-exegetical credibility of a view of God as dynamic and self-creative process of becoming, named in the self-designation "I will be who I will be" (Janzen, see Bibliography). In this view, the divine-human covenant is grounded in the divine creation of the world. The significance of the creation, viewed as a covenanting act, lies in the fact that the aboriginal life of God, purely self-determining, by an act of decision brings into being derivative yet finitely originative centers of life, with whom then God freely shares the power of the divine existential eros or question. This shared question eventually takes on the contours of eschatological symbolism in the biblical tradition (Janzen, *Semeia* 24).

It is in the framework of such an understanding of existential questions that we approach the questions which loom so prominently in the Book of Job in both its narrative and its dialogical sections. Two questions are primary: From the human side arises the question as to the meaning of innocent suffering for one's understanding of one's own life and of human existence in general, and for one's understanding of the divine character and purposes. However, this human question is correlative to—and in Job is presented as arising within the context of—the divine question as to the motivation and character, and therefore the meaning, of human piety and rectitude.

20

This divine question, in turn, may be viewed not only as a question about humankind but, ultimately, as a question posed by God about God. Apart from the existence of the world, divine existential questions might be imagined to characterize the divine life as a completely self-determining voyage of eternality through the mysterious primordial seas of non-being. In the face of the existence of the world, but apart from covenanting with the world, the classical doctrines of the absoluteness and the impassibility of God would mean that God continues to be completely self-determining, keeping the divine existential questions a total secret from the world. But if Job's question about God is embedded in God's question about Job, and if those questions imply an even deeper question in God as to God's intrinsic worthiness to be worshiped; and if Job has an irreducible part to play in "answering" these questions; then the Book of Job may be seen as contributing to a deepening of the bases, a re-casting of the nature, and a renewal of the viability of the divine-human covenant relation.

The resolution of the Joban drama is understood here to come in the divine speeches of chapters 38—41 and in Job's answering response in 42:1–6. As is commonly noted, the address of God largely takes the form of questions posed to Job. These questions are as commonly taken to be rhetorical in character. James L. Crenshaw (see above) identifies them as a special instance of rhetorical question—that is, as an instance of the posing of impossible questions. Such a reading, of course, is a distinct not to say likely possibility. In such a case, the divine speeches are an abasement of Job. Such readings take the questions at face value as being straightforwardly rhetorical, re-asserting divine majesty and wisdom and human frailty and ignorance, and inviting Job to acquiesce in such views. If, as we believe, the rhetorical questions are to be taken ironically, then a quite different possibility is opened up for Job's—and for the reader's—self-understanding.

Among other indications that these rhetorical questions in chapters 38—41 are to be taken ironically—and therefore to be taken as genuine questions—is the frequency with which the reader encounters ironically functioning rhetorical questions earlier in the dialogues, and indeed already in the prologue. When the questions in the divine speeches are so read, a number of fresh perspectives are opened up. For instance, a conventional view of things divine and human (a view reflected also in Crenshaw's analysis in terms of impossible questions) is "deconstructed," and a new view is constructed in its stead. This

21

befits the Book of Job as an essay in the reversal of long-held views. Again, the "energy for morally active engagement" (Booth) which irony offers, combines with the energy offered in the posing of a truly existential question, to place before Job and before the reader a calling and a vocation to a task hitherto only implicit, not to say hidden, in the metaphor of God as parent and humankind as image of God. Further, when Job is read in this way, the book dovetails with such visions as that of Second Isaiah, not to speak of that presented in the Gospels and in, for example, Romans 8.

Matters of Text: Translation and Integrity

Two matters remain for introductory comment. The first has to do with the translation of the Hebrew text, which is notorious for its difficulty. No one translation provides an adequate basis for study and interpretation. A problem which besets the translator's task generally is that one's choice among possible renderings will depend upon how one construes the wider context and, ultimately, the book as a whole. On a number of occasions our own translation is introduced as the basis for further comment. There is no space, nor is it appropriate to the conception of this commentary series, to give detailed technical justification in every case. Such arguments will perhaps be offered elsewhere. It is hoped that enough discussion is offered to forestall the impression of arbitrariness or manipulation of the evidence.

The second matter has to do with the literary integrity of the book. Frequently chapter 28 is considered secondary, along with the Elihu speeches and sometimes one or another portion of the divine speeches. Likewise, it is often argued that the prose prologue/epilogue and the poetic dialogues arose separately from one another and, therefore, should be separated for purposes of ascertaining the meaning of Job.

One should note, however, that the primary basis for these judgments is the supposed incompatibility in the meaning which the respective parts of the book are believed to contain, or the lack of any coherent contribution which a supposedly "secondary" section makes to the dramatic progress and the final meaning of the whole. Such judgments too often are arrived at largely on the basis of analytical methods which divert attention from the literary character of the text. *Meanings* are arrived at in specific contexts in disregard of the place of those contexts in the book as a whole. These meanings are then abstracted from even their immediate contexts and formulated propositionally in theological or ethical terms. Then the disembodied propositional meanings of various passages are compared with one another for compatibility. It is then overlooked that poetic/literary modes of expression can tolerate larger degrees of dissonance and tension among component parts of a literary whole than is possible in more abstract forms of thought and expression. *Matter* (in this instance the pre-history of oral or written traditions) is likewise identified in specific segments and then attributed to diverse origins, as though the employment of a diversity of materials were not to be interpreted within the context of a study of overarching form. Meanwhile, literary *form* is neglected, along with the subtle shifts in nuance and the transformations of meaning by means of which the diverse thematics of various parts of the text (like the diverse and turbulent thematics of existence itself) are held together in an organic and living whole.

It is impossible, for example, to strip away the prologue and the epilogue and to read the dialogues by themselves. The poetry cannot be supposed to have existed in such a form, for it requires the prologue to set the scene for its own intense dialogical questioning. Either the prose sections were composed for specific literary effects by the author of the poetry or, what amounts to the same thing, the poet adopted (or adapted) for fresh purposes a story already extant in some form. Even if the latter be the case, it will not do to say, as Marvin Pope does, that "The author was naturally limited by the prefabricated materials with which he had to work and could not have taken a great deal of liberty with a familiar story" (p. xxviii). For one thing, any poet capable of bringing the iconoclastic dialogues to a custom-bound audience cannot be supposed to have labored under any sense of the sacrosanct character of the text of an already existing prose story. In the commentary we will show that nothing in the prologue is incompatible with what we find in the dialogues—not even the figure of Job in response to his calamities. As for the epilogue, the question is whether one is able to bring to the reading of it the results of all that has gone before, and in that light to read its supposedly conventional ending with nuanced appreciation; or whether one reads it in forgetfulness of that series of speeches which it brings to a conclusion. For another thing, Pope's words fly directly in the

23

face of fifty years of biblical scholarship which has proceeded under the name and by the methods of "tradition-history criticism." In this approach to the text it is assumed that, until the final stages of the fixing of the text, the community's traditions are always open to revision.

Finally the issue comes down to how one reads the book. *Can* it be read as a whole? Can it be read as a whole inclusive of much tension and turbulence between its parts, such that the very *form* of the book itself contains part of its *meaning* (so that neglect or tampering with the form distorts the meaning)? Such is the conviction toward which many years of repeated close study have led this commentator. Such is the reading here offered. The two questions remain: Does this meaning make sense of the text? and Does the text, so read, make sense of life?

OUTLINE OF THIS COMMENTARY

INTERPRETATION

INTERPRETATION

PART ONE

Prologue
A Dialogue of Heaven and Earth

JOB 1—2

The prologue begins (1:3) and ends (2:13) on the theme of Job's greatness. Whereas his earlier greatness is one of moral stature and material prosperity, his latter greatness is measured in terms of physical and existential anguish. Job's earlier condition has arisen through the fact that he has been cradled and nourished within the life-giving orders and structures of the natural, social, and religious-symbolic world; and his piety and uprightness are his grateful response to God for life within such a "hedge." Then the question arises in heaven: Is Job's piety tied to the cradling and nourishing conditions of his life? Is it only a conditioned response? Or may it be that he is capable of a piety freely given? The question which arises in heaven is not answered there (for that would keep him within the hedge) but is given into Job's hands to answer (thereby conferring upon him a terrible dignity). The hedge is breached through a succession of calamities. His first response takes the form of conventional actions and words, those symbolic means by which one's world remains hedged about when calamity strikes one physically and socially and materially. Gradually, however, even the hedge and cradle of his inherited belief-structure shows signs of stress and strain, and by the end of the prologue he is entering silently into a strange realm of naked and solitary suffering.

* * *

On the Structure of the Prologue

It is commonly observed that the Book of Job comprises a series of poetic dialogues preceded and followed by prose narratives. The book may thus be said to exemplify Robert Alter's generalization that biblical literature manifests a pronounced preference for dialogue. Alter writes:

31

> The biblical writers, . . . are often less concerned with actions in themselves than with how individual character responds to actions or produces them; and direct speech is made the chief instrument for revealing the varied and at times nuanced relations of the personages to the actions in which they are implicated (*The Art of Biblical Narrative* p. 66).

The reasons for this preference he attributes to the Hebrew preoccupation with interaction of wills and with the role of language both in effecting and in disclosing the intentions of wills, human and divine. He writes again,

> Spoken language is the substratum of everything human and divine that transpires in the Bible, and the Hebrew tendency to transpose what is preverbal or nonverbal into speech is finally a technique for *getting at the essence of things* . . . (p. 70; italics added).

These generalizations are eminently applicable to the Book of Job. Yet we should not therefore suppose that the prologue may be read quickly in order to get to the "real meat" of the dialogues. For one thing, the prologue itself contains a good deal of dialogue; furthermore it displays a density of literary form and theological content which claims reflection and comment out of proportion to its comparative length.

One should note, first, that the prologue itself is emblematic of the structure of the book as a whole. An almost completely narrative introduction (1:1–5) is followed by several largely dialogical scenes (1:6—2:10), and these dialogues are followed by a narrative conclusion (2:11–13). The dialogical scenes in the prologue, however, transpire on two levels, heaven and earth. We may schematize the prologue as follows:

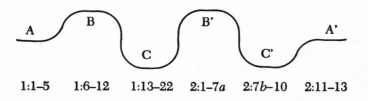

A	B		B'		A'
		C		C'	
1:1–5	1:6–12	1:13–22	2:1–7*a*	2:7*b*–10	2:11–13

32   Within each level the dialogue proceeds on a horizontal axis between inhabitants of that level (that is, between Yahweh and Satan; and between Job and messengers/wife). But insofar as each dialogical scene arises in response to something on the other level, the sequence *ABCB'C'A'* may itself be said to signal an implicit dialogue moving along a vertical axis. Elsewhere in the Bible, vertical dialogue between heaven and earth often is rendered explicitly. In Job such a rendering is given only at the end, in the divine speeches; yet it is present implicitly already in the prologue, as an inkling of the biblical vision generally. The importance of this last observation lies in the foreshadowing function of the structure of the prologue. Taken by themselves chapters 3—37 might be supposed to present simply a horizontal dialogue of the sort *C/C'*. Against the background of the prologue (and in view of the way in which, as we shall see, dialogue *C'* echoes elements of dialogue *B'*), chapters 3—37 are seen to present also the human pole of an implicit vertical dialogue with heaven. This observation is reinforced by 3:2 which says in Hebrew, "and Job *answered* and said," and by the frequency with which Job in chapters 3—31 addresses heaven directly. Divine silence and human verbal doubt too often in religious circles are taken to signal the deterioration or the breaking off of the vertical dialogue. Already through its structure the Book of Job presents both the silence and the verbal doubt as modes in which that dialogue continues unruptured and unabated.

We have observed that the dialogue transpires on two levels, heaven and earth, as though we should envisage a universe of at least two levels—or, with an eye to Job's frequent references to Sheol, of three levels. But (in the spirit of Robert Alter's remarks on the biblical preference for dialogue over narration for the sake of penetration to *the personal essence of things*) we suggest that this spatial imagery in Job is secondary to and elucidatory of a primary preoccupation with realms of personal presence. The actions and words of the prologue, like those of the rest of the book, center in two personal loci: the presence of God (e.g., 1:6 and 1:12*b*) and the presence of Job (e.g., 1:14*a* and 2:11). One may say that God is in heaven and Job on earth. But it is truer to say that the Joban drama is dominated by and played out within the realm of two personal presences and that terms like "heaven" and "earth" have their meaning as spatial ways of indicating those two presences. In such a perspective, of course, Sheol becomes a peculiar "realm" (see, e.g., 18:14), a realm of sheer negativity devoid of any presence human or divine, a "place" or rather "no-place" where, in the words of Dilys Laing, "all is solitary," a place where "I shall discover

33

forever my own absence" (Dilys Laing, p. 27). In such a view, the Book of Job may be taken as an exploration of doubt and silence, not only as modes of dialogue but also as modes of presence.

Job 1:1–5
Narrative Introduction to Job Himself

What's in a name? Job, *'iyyob*, seems to have developed from a well-attested second-millennium West Semitic name of a sort which fell into disuse in the first millennium (Marvin Pope). That name, *'ayya-'abum*, "Where is the (divine) father?" places Job within the ambience of Israelite ancestral personal religion with its reference to God as divine parent. In such a setting Job's name is a standing invocation of God's presence in his life. Robert Gordis, however, explains the name as a passive participial noun (from *'ayab*, "to hate") meaning "the hated, persecuted one." We may not have to choose between these two proposals. Word-plays through secondary etymology are a common device in biblical narrative. In the present instance we may have the combination of traditional meaning ("where is the [divine] father?") and novel association through sound-similarity ("the persecuted one") to achieve a word-play in which the very name *Job* poses the problem for the book and for Israel in exile. Does Job's experience not change the meaning of his own name? Does his sort of experience any longer justify the use of parental metaphors for God? The very name *Job*, which once was a confident invocation of God as divine father, now becomes an accusation against God as enemy and persecutor.

Modern commentators cannot be sure of the precise location of Uz. Nor do the places reflected in the biblical occurrences of this place name suggest that the Israelites were any clearer on the question. Was the name chosen for this reason? Narratively, then, the names "Job" and "Uz" introduce the story as happening "long ago and far away." Such distancing can serve many purposes. In this instance it may signal the writer's attempt to achieve (and it may invite the reader to enter into that achievement of) some perspective on a problem

34

which, considered in its present immediacy, would be so over-whelming as to render even clarity of questioning all but impossible. Prior to any provisional resolution of problems, prior even to specific lines of questioning, the capacity to distance and then to entertain the problem imaginatively already signals the emergence of elbow room within severe straits and thereby signals the mute presence and operation of grace.

This Job, who (as his name suggests) owes his birth and his idyllic prosperity (vv. 2–3) to the care of his personal God, makes exemplary response to God through his piety and his moral conduct. This exemplary response is described by two pairs of phrases: (1) he is (a) blameless [*tam*] and (b) upright [*yašar*]; (2) he (a') fears God and (b') turns from evil. *yašar*, commonly translated "upright," more precisely describes straightforwardness of conduct as along a straight path. Proverbs 4:25–27 shows how such straightforwardness can be placed in a poetically parallel relation with turning from evil. So also here in 1:1, such straightforwardness (b) is seen to be in a parallel relation with turning from evil (b') and thereby as synonymous with it. This means, then, that (a) "blameless" stands in a parallel and synonymous relation to (a') "fearing God" and so refers to the character of Job's piety. (For future reference, it should be noted that the adjective *tam*, "blameless," is cognate with the noun *tumma*, which RSV translates "integrity.") According to the general meaning of the word *tam*, piety so described is not nominal, flawed, or partial, but genuine, whole, and complete; and it constitutes the central principle of Job's individual integrity. Taken together, the two pairs of expressions in 1:1 sum up the Israelite conviction as to the distinguishable but inseparable relation between authentic piety and genuine morality.

It will remain for the speakers in the following heavenly scene to suggest, or rather to question, the precise nature of the causal relation between Job's piety/morality and his prosperity. For now one may note simply that in respect to both his piety/morality and his prosperity this man was without peer in his society. For verse 3b does not refer only to verses 2–3 (as implied by RSV punctuation) but to verse 1b as well. Formally, then, if the pairs of phrases in verse 1b express the connection between piety and morality, the structure of verses 1–3 expresses a sense of the connection between these two and prosperity.

35

By the way in which they set forth Job's exemplary piety and moral character, and his idyllic prosperity, verses 1–3 may give rise to a sense of the distance between Job and the circumstances of the reader; but that distance is immediately closed by the means which the narrator uses to solicit our sympathetic identification with this figure. Bearing in mind Robert Alter's comment on the use of dialogue to penetrate to "the essence of things," we note the effect achieved by concluding verses 1–5 with an interior monologue. Following an external portrayal of the man and his situation in life, we are taken inside his heart and mind, where we discover that he shares the common pathos of parental concern—a concern and a pathos which, for all that a parent may wish to do and may be able to do, in its helplessness finally can enact itself only in symbolic action heavenward—over what his children may do in the blithely heedless activities and spontaneous projects of youthful zest. Those youthful doings are set in the context of the children's celebrations "each on his day," a reference, in our view, to the celebration of birthdays (cf. 3:1, where Hebrew "his day" is correctly translated "the day of his birth").

As a birthday the feast is of great importance. For in celebrating a birthday one affirms not only an individual life but the generativity and general goodness of the world under the creative generosity of God; and one invokes the powers manifested on that day—its energies of blessing and its good auguries—by way of renewing one's life for another year. No other day has such a claim to be called "one's day." Indeed, it may be suggested that, while all other feasts are primarily communal in their focus, the feast of one's own birthday is a fitting component in the "personal religion" within which we have situated Job.

Now, construed as a day of birth, "on his day" resumes and advances the generative theme of verse 2. But in verses 18–19 the fourth and climactic calamity falls on just such a birthday feast, moreover the feast day of the eldest or, as the Hebrew puts it, the "firstborn." The catastrophic intersection of such a reality-affirming feast and such a calamity in the sharpest manner challenges creatural piety toward God as divine parent and giver of generativity and protection. The depth and the severity with which Job feels this challenge are registered in the words with which he breaks his long silence in chapter 3, words with which he curses "his day" (3:1). But in the first instance he meets this challenge with an affirmation couched in the imagery appropriate to the piety of personal religion (1:21) and its generative theme.

Job 1:6–12
First Scene in Heaven:
A Question Which Sets the Drama in Motion

It was suggested above ("On the Structure of the Prologue") that though the four scenes transpire alternately in heaven and on earth, yet each scene on one level arises in implicit dialogical response to the preceding scene on the other level. In the present instance, *B* (in heaven or, better, in Yahweh's presence) follows aptly from *A* (1:1–5) in a number of ways. For one thing, the relation between *A* and *B* exemplifies in sustained fashion Robert Alter's remark that

> the primacy of dialogue is so pronounced that many pieces of third-person narrative prove on inspection to be dialogue-bound, verbally mirroring elements of dialogue which . . . they introduce (p. 65).

In particular, the coming together of the "sons of Job" on a given one's "day" is matched by the coming together of the "sons of God" on "a day" or, as the Hebrew reads, on "the day." Jewish Targumic and Midrashic tradition identifies this as New Year's Day (Gordis). In Mesopotamian religion the gods assembled on New Year's Day to determine destinies for the coming year. Given that such a New Year's Day celebrated and renewed the creation of the cosmos with all its life-giving powers, the associations between verses 4–5 on the one hand and verses 6–12, 18–19 on the other are all the more effective as suggesting the full implication of Job's troubles.

In view of the strident monotheism (however "non-philosophical") of the Old Testament, the imagery of the divine council here and elsewhere is easily dismissed as merely a poetic and concrete way of portraying the divine governance of the world. Such a move should not be made glibly. In this instance at least the poetic imagery lends itself to the exploration of a profound theological—or rather, since the ques-

37

tion is posed from the divine perspective and about Job, a profound anthropological—question. That such anthropological questions can in Israel be attributed to God is evident from Hosea, where a series of divine questions gives expression to a struggle within God over Israel. James Luther Mays, commenting on Hosea 11:8–9, goes so far as to write of an "intense . . . impassioned self-questioning by Yahweh" (p. 156). We have argued elsewhere (Janzen, *Semeia*, esp. sections 1.11, 1.21, 1.31) that in Hosea those questions ought to be given great weight in our reflections on the nature of God and on the character of the divine-human covenant relation. Of course, in Hosea the questions arise over the covenant infidelity of Israel, whereas here they arise over Job's fidelity and have to do with its ground and character. In the latter instance the imagery of the divine council, with the Satan as a proper member, serves as a figural means to explore the possibility of the rise of a particular existential question within the life of God, a question which, shared with Job, becomes an existential question for Job and through him for humankind. The divine existential question is not resolved unilaterally or in solitary fashion within God. Rather, it is shared with Job through the import which his own experience has for his own questioning (see esp. the commentary on chaps. 9—10, the section 9:32–35). It is shared with him also through the Yahweh speeches and the epilogue. Also it is shared explicitly with the reader who, unlike Job, is given the privilege of access to the scene in the divine council. Furthermore, the question even for God is resolved only through the manner of Job's own response to his experience. If one views the shared exploration and resolution of existential questions as establishing one sort of covenant relation, then the Book of Job may be taken as one attempt to re-vision Israel's covenant relation with Yahweh, finding in that relation hitherto unsuspected implications and placing it on more deeply probed bases.

Classically in Israel the vision of the divine-human relation took as its point of departure the parent-child metaphor of Mesopotamian personal religion. That metaphor is reflected prominently in the ancestral narratives of Genesis. Even where the central metaphor was not so much natural-generative as historical-redemptive (after the Exodus and Sinai), the language of the parent-child relation and the ethos of filial piety continued to be appropriate (e.g., Exod. 4:21–23 and 19:4; Deut.

38

32:6 and 32:11; Hos. 11:1; Isa. 1:2–3; Prov. 3:11–12). Though Israel also employed other metaphors, the parent-child relation remained firmly in place. In the questions which arise in 1:6–12, one senses the exploration of the possibility that the human as child, while continuing to be filially related to God, finally passes out of wardship and into shared responsibility for the "inheritance" of the earth. We turn, now, to consider the text in closer detail.

Yahweh opens the heavenly dialogue with a question. Given the nature of the occasion (a formal assembly), given the Satan's proper role (the "eyes and ears of the monarch"), and given the sequel to the occasion (Yahweh's consent to and thereby complicity in the Satan's proposal), one suspects that this opening word is no casual conversation-starter, but rather a carefully chosen leading question, asking in effect, "Have you been doing your job?" The Satan's affirmative response is followed by another divine question which some have taken to be a piece of rash if innocent braggadocio. We take the question to have the purpose not only of directing the Satan's attention specifically to Job, but of sowing a seed in that investigative consciousness. This seed bears fruit as the Satan adopts the question form and brings Yahweh's implicit query concerning Job to explicit articulation.

What is this question? It is a question that has to do with Job's piety—its grounds and, therefore, its nature. That Job is pious (fears God), the Satan has no doubt. But the Satan attributes Job's piety to his sense of dependence upon and gratitude toward the divine creator who blesses, sustains, protects, and endows with good things. Job's piety arises as creaturely response to the divine goodness. In this connection the language of verse 10 includes an image that introduces a motif which will run through the rest of the book. The image of the hedge, here used with connotations of protection and safety from human and non-human marauders, sounds a motif which is heard also in Israel's language about its corporate and national existence in the land, safe from surrounding enemies (Ps. 80:12; Isa. 5:1–7; cf. also, e.g., II Sam. 7:1, 10). This motif is found also in language concerning cosmic realities where, as an analogue of a hedge, the firmament holds back the primal chaos waters to give space wherein humankind may enjoy the fruitfulness of the earth and may itself flourish in abundance (Gen. 1:6–9; Ps. 104:5–9; 148:6; and esp. Job 38:8–11). It is quite true: Job does not fear God

39

hinnām, "for nought" (v. 9); he fears God in grateful response for his creatural existence.

Some commentators have suggested that, as grounded in such a dependency and responsive to such material goodness— and as expectant also of such continued well-being—the piety which Job displays is suspect. True piety, in such a view, must be totally disinterested in causal considerations or in prospects of reward. Piety and uprightness must exist for their own sake, or purely for God's sake, or forfeit any claim to be called piety. Such a view, however, approaches issues of piety and morality in altogether too rational and intellectually abstractive a manner, divorced from the dynamics of human development. Does one convict a toddler of "less pure" filial piety because its bond of devotion and loyalty to the parent does not yet take the form which it may one day display? At three years old, a filial piety of gratitude and an "ethics" of largely imitative courtesy and expectation of mutual benefit may be as pure and worthy for its developmental stage as the unselfish act of a college student who, eager for a relaxing game of intra-mural volleyball after a hard day in the books, discovers that too many volunteers have turned up for the match and offers to drop out.

The issue of the nature of Job's piety, posed in the context of the parent-child metaphor, may be illuminated by reference to Bernard of Clairvaux on the stages of human growth in love toward God. According to Bernard, one begins by loving oneself for one's own sake. Not the highest degree of love, it is nevertheless the necessary starting point; for a sense of value which does not include a sense of one's own value indicates a state of alienation. Becoming aware that one is not sufficient unto oneself, but depends radically upon God, one begins to love God for one's own sake. This is the love of dependence and gratitude and expectation. The expectation need not be calculating or manipulative, but may take the form that the One who has given life may be trusted to nurture, sustain, and guide it and may be applied to for such needs. In the course of loving God for one's own sake, one may discover the intrinsic worthiness of God apart from all interested considerations; or, rather, the nature of one's interestedness begins to shift, so that one begins to discover an interest in the love of God for God's own sake. Finally, it may happen, one begins to love oneself for God's sake, in the awareness that one's own being is of importance to God and enters into the divine enjoyment. These modes of loving may arise developmentally; but they need not supersede one another, even though on a given occasion one or another may take the center of one's consciousness and intentionality. In such a view, not only can the earlier modes of piety be appreciated as praiseworthy or otherwise, within their own terms and relative to their own concrete circumstances, but they can and should persist alongside the latter modes (much as, in Transactional Analysis, one can be at once Child, Parent, and Adult). A piety which has arrived at one or the other of the last two stages, therefore, may also contain within it appropriate motives of gratitude and of expectation. If, now, the Book of Job may be said to trace the pedagogy of Job's piety toward God through the last two stages, then the assessment of the role and the theological understanding of Job's friends needs to be much more complex and nuanced than has been the case generally.

Let us consider, then, the dialectic of the question of 1:6–12. Now that God has found in Job an exemplary instance of creatural and dependent piety, the question arises as to whether there could be such a thing as independent and free *(ḥinnam)* piety on the part of humankind. This question, ostensibly about humankind, is also the implication of a prior question, one which is properly a divine existential question: Is the creator of the world and the divine benefactor of humankind worshipful only by virtue of what deity does for humankind? Or is God intrinsically worshipful? Is deity capable of creating a creature who, somehow, attains to such freedom and independence, such spiritual and moral maturity, as to be in a position to choose to offer God worship and service because of God's intrinsic worthiness to be loved? In other words, what sort of covenant is possible between God and humankind? In this way of viewing the prologue to Job, we may see how close it stands in its concerns to the story in Genesis 2—3, though with a different outcome.

In the nature of the question posed, the issue can be resolved only by the way Job responds to the question as posed through his ensuing experiences. The agony of Job, in body and in spirit, is his participation in the agony of God which is inaugurated through the questions in 1:6–12. Such participation in the divine life implies a new measure of the dignity of humankind as the image of God. (For such a reading of the Book of Job, it is significant that the Satan appears only in the prologue and is absent from the epilogue. Far from indicating the secondary

41

character of the epilogue, as some would have it, the Satan's absence there is one signal that the rift which has opened up in the divine consciousness through the rise of the question has been closed through Job's vocational response.)

Job 1:13–22
First Scene on Earth:
Job's Affirmative Response to His Calamity

Having arisen within God's presence, the question now goes forth to Job in and through his experience. Narratively the return to the human scene is effected by the resumption in verse 13 of the language of verse 5: day, brother's house, eating and drinking. Within chapter one the motif of the children's eating and drinking occurs at verses 4, 13, and 18, the repetition giving emphasis to the third occurrence. Within the scene in verses 13–22, the tenor of this "eating" motif is catastrophically intersected by the way it is echoed in the first three calamities: (1) asses *feeding;* the *mouth* of the sword; (2) fire fell and *ate* them; (3) the *mouth* of the sword. After verses 13–17, the reader is all too well prepared for the fourth servant's message. The repetitions have achieved an anticipatory effect known to all who have received terrible news, knowing one moment before its utterance what it will be, having time only to wish desperately that it might after all not really be so, and then, as across a great distance and with confused clarity, hearing the inevitable.

How does the presentation of the calamities dialogically instead of narratively help to "get at the essence of things" (Alter)? Usually dialogue (or, as in v. 5, interior monologue) gives access to the interior springs of the speaker. But in this instance the speakers seem merely to make reports. Yet perhaps the fourfold conclusion "I alone have escaped" is more than mere reportage and conveys something of the subjective immediacy with which the messengers themselves experienced the calamities. Moreover, in hearing with Job the actual reports of the messengers, the reader is placed alongside Job who hears. By means of the perspective in the reader through the sympathetic contract in verse 5, the reader's own response to the messengers' spoken reports give imaginative access to the interior springs from which Job will shortly make his response.

Before considering that response, we should note one further element of verses 13–19. The sources of the calamities are as follows: (1) the Sabeans (2) the fire of God from heaven (3) the Chaldeans (4) a great wind *(ruaḥ gedola)*. Job's enemies are, in origin, alternately earthly and heavenly (lightning and wind are phenomena of the heavens). This alternation echoes the alternation of the heavenly and earthly settings of the prologue's four scenes. It also foreshadows Job's identification, in the dialogues (especially in chap. 19), of both human and divine enemies as the sources of his affliction. Finally, by the way in which the heavenly phenomena in 38:25–38 are attributed to Yahweh's wisdom, the occurrence of such phenomena in 1:13–19 reinforces the fact that what on the one hand is attributed to the Satan (1:12) on the other hand is owned up to by Yahweh (2:3).

Job's response to the calamitous news is twofold. He reflexively makes the customary response of tearing his robe, shaving his head, and falling prostrate upon the ground. In such a state of shock, such social rituals display what Walter Brueggemann has called "the formfulness of grief" *(Interp.* 31:263–75), a phrase reminiscent of Emily Dickinson's title line, "after great pain a formal feeling comes." Such formal enactments of grief serve as a hedge against utter chaos of feeling and help to sustain a margin of sanity. Likewise, Job's utterance in verse 20 in all probability is to be taken as a conventional confession of bereavement, a verbal hedge against the primal waters. (A modern parallel may be found in the following account of one young Englishman's response to grievous news: Upon hearing of the death in action of his younger brother during the first World War, he automatically fell to his knees and, reaching for the familiar words of the Apostles' Creed which he as an Anglican had repeated so often in chapel, repeated several times, "I believe in God—I believe in God—.") The conventionality of Job's twofold response may lessen its moral and religious significance for some readers. Certainly it soon (much sooner than commentators generally recognize) will give way to other modes, and we will not have to wait until chapter three to begin to detect their inner springs. But this first response is of a piece, formally and materially, with the creatural piety which even the Satan recognizes Job to possess to this point.

We will attend more fully to the form and content of verses 20–21 when we are in a position to compare it with 2:10. For now a few observations will suffice. First, one notes that Job is the subject of the first two verbs in the utterance in verse 21

43

(came, shall return), while Yahweh is the subject of the second two (gave, took). The confession moves from experiential immediacy (I, I) to religious affirmation (Yahweh, Yahweh). Secondly, the confession begins on the generative theme to which we have already been introduced: "I came from my mother's womb." What Yahweh took away (children, possessions) is what Yahweh had given subsequent to Job's own naked birth and what in any case would be stripped from him in his own death. Thirdly, Job makes his submissive confession in the name of Yahweh, Israel's redemptive (Exod. 3:14–15) and covenant God. As in the formula for priestly blessing in Numbers 6:24–26, the threefold repetition of the divine name achieves intense emphasis. This threefold repetition gives specific point to the narrator's comment that in all this Job did not sin nor charge God with wrong *(tipla)*.

Job 2:1–7a
Second Scene in Heaven: The Heavenly Question Given Sharper Point

The second scene in Yahweh's presence transpires in words identical to those in the first scene (*B:* 1:6–12), varying significantly only to take account of what has occurred in *C* (1:13–22) and to advance the plot. Thus, Yahweh's opening question (2:3) exactly repeats 1:8, adding "he still holds fast his integrity *(tumma)*, although you moved me against him, to destroy him without cause *(ḥinnam)*." The key words *tumma* and *ḥinnam* have their force here because of the way they have previously been used. Yahweh began in *B* (1:6–12) by drawing attention to the fact that Job was blameless *(tam,* as in 1:1). Using the expression "feared God" which in 1:1 is synonymous with *tam,* the Satan in 1:6–12 *(B)* questioned whether Job's piety was free *(ḥinnam)*. Now in *B',* Yahweh owns responsibility for the calamity, whether or not the Satan acted as apparent instigator and executor. Yet Job maintains his integrity *(tumma)*. This latter quality characterizes neither merely Job considered in and by himself nor merely the relationship between Job and God. Rather, Job's own integrity or wholeness arises in and from his relation to God. Developmentally, Job's integrity up to now is causally grounded in his sense of dependency and gratitude which expresses itself in piety and straightforward conduct. Job is who he is because of Yahweh's benefits which, entering into him, have made him who and what he is; and his piety is his grateful acknowledgment of Yahweh as the ground of who he is. Yahweh now (2:3) appears to boast that that loyalty is unshaken despite Yahweh's uncaused (unprovoked) action toward Job. However (as in 1:8), given the office of the one to whom the boast is made, it is to be taken as veiling another incipient question. The Satan, expert in ferreting secrets and exposing what is hidden, gives the question its voice: How *deep* is this integrity? Does it go below the skin (v. 4)?

This figure with which the Satan opens is taken by many to be a folk-saying: "skin for skin." But its meaning is confessed to be unclear. Formal and contextual features, however, offer clues to the meaning of the saying as here used.

> Skin for (*beʿad*) skin; and all (*we-*) that a man has he will give for (*beʿad*) his life (*nepeš*).

Robert Gordis analyzes the conjunction "and" which joins the saying and the following clause as having an "epexegetical" grammatical function: It serves to indicate that the following clause "exegetes" the preceding saying. Such an interpretation is reinforced by the formal balance of both the saying and the clause, achieved by the presence of the same preposition "for" (*beʿad*) in the middle of each. According to the exegesis which the Satan offers of his own saying, then, the first "skin" of the saying is to be understood as a figure for "all that a man has."

Now it is to be noted that the phrase "all that a man has" is a resumption of the repeated phrase "all that he has" in 1:10, 11, 12. Further, in 1:10 we should note the three fold use of the preposition: "Hast thou not put a hedge about (*beʿad*) him and about (*beʿad*) his house and about (*beʿad*) all that he has, on every side?" The force of the preposition in this sentence is reinforced by the way in which the whole sentence is enclosed by the words "hedge . . . on every side." The preposition itself (which often indicates shutting or sealing up, fencing or hedging about, as in Lam. 3:7; Job 3:23) by its threefold repetition suggests a concentric and widening character of the hedge, moving out from Job to his house (family) and then to all he has. Whatever "skin for skin" may otherwise have meant as a folk-saying, by its literary connection with 1:10–11 through the repetition of the clause "all that he has" and the preposition *beʿad*, the saying is placed in a context which imparts to it fresh aspects

45

of meaning: One's family and one's possessions surround one and are attached to one like so many layers of skin.

Consciousness as Embodied and as Naked

The Satan's saying, as thus interpreted, touches upon a basic element in our awareness of being-in-the-world. We may assume that human consciousness twenty-six hundred years ago was not as sharply differentiated from its bodily basis, and from its wider life-world, as it is today. Yet even today, as recent phenomenological investigations have shown, we do not exist in clear independence of our bodies; nor does our embodied awareness end with our epidermis. Our embodied self, which enters most intimately into our awareness in the form of visceral feelings, and which localizes itself in the form of pains and pleasures specific to regions of the body, also extends itself beyond the epidermis through our sensory impressions, beginning with that extended skin called our home, our "house" (both our own family or "flesh and blood", and our artificially fabricated skin, the dwelling which shelters us), and extends even to our personal possessions. The artificiality of any absolute distinction between one's body and "all that one has" is disclosed in such experiences as the physical as well as inner existential shock of the death of a loved one. Our bodies feel that they have suffered a grievous wound. The same sense of our extended embodiment is disclosed in such experiences as the theft of an engagement ring, which leaves one feeling physically assaulted and stripped; the accidental loss or malicious destruction of a long-used fountain pen or other favorite tool leaving one with a sense of amputation; or the sudden alteration of a landscape through the razing of familiar buildings and the clearing of frequented woods, leaving one quite disoriented and denuded. The hedge —the complex structure of reality comprising valued materials and material embodiments of value, within which life arises and is sustained and has particular meanings along with a pervading undertone of worthwhileness—exists at many levels, or rather in concentric circles, reaching from the microcosm of one's own body through all manner of natural and social and symbolic orders to find its macrocosmic counterpart in that "firmament" which in material fact or symbolic conception is the outermost bound of our lived world. The poignancy of Job's first words of response now becomes clearer: "Naked I came . . . and naked shall I return (v. 21)." Job has been stripped of many of the

46

layers of his embodied existence, and this brings home to him in a new way his own nakedness, his finitude, as an individual. The hedge has been drastically thinned that stands between him and the chaos which lurks namelessly alongside the undertone of worthwhileness.

The Satan said, "touch his bone and his flesh;" and Yahweh said "only spare his life *(nepeš)*." Not just his extended body (in and through which his social existence is so largely realized), but his most intimately embodied self must be breached, to discover what Job will give for his life. What is the point of the Satan's charge? The Book of Job was written during a time (speaking in evolutionary terms) when humankind had not long emerged from a predominantly group consciousness only flickeringly and incipiently qualified by individual self-awareness and when the distinctions between self and world and between the diverse modalities of physical and mental existence were much less sharply drawn. By the time of Habakkuk and Jeremiah, Job and Second Isaiah and Ezekiel, one is able to discern in Israel an intensification of concern to explore and to assess the status of solitary self-consciousness in the community and in the world before God. (See further Janzen, *Interp* 37:178–83.) The Satanic charge in verse 5 articulates in provocative form the question, traceable ultimately to Yahweh, as to whether the rise and the entertainment of intense solitary and naked self-consciousness necessarily means a weakening of ties of wider loyalties or whether in fact the entry into such a condition does not pose a peculiarly intense challenge to covenanting loyalty, and a peculiarly promising opportunity, calling for a relational integrity *(tumma)* which is to be offered freely *(ḥinnam)* even when Job is reduced and stripped to his suffering naked self *(nepeš)*.

Job 2:7b–10
Second Scene on Earth:
Job's Ambiguous Response
to His Deepened Calamity

In chapter one, the heavenly scene opened with the Satan's entry into the presence of Yahweh, and it closed with the

Satan's departure from that presence. The Satan's subsequent action was not then narrated, but was presented indirectly through the messengers' speeches to Job. Here in chapter two, the heavenly scene likewise ends with the Satan's departure from Yahweh's presence. This time, without pause for change of scene, the narrative immediately and tersely describes the event of Job's new affliction. Our sympathetic identification with Job, inaugurated in 1:5, was secured in section C (1:13–22) by the manner in which we heard with Job the spoken reports. This time the narrator carries us swiftly to the object of our present concern: Job's response to the new affliction.

After the first series of calamities, Job's response was fully described both narratively and dialogically. No less than six verbs were used to portray his action (1:20–21): he arose, tore his robe, shaved his head, fell to the ground, worshiped and spoke—this last action taking us past his external behavior to his inner springs. Actions and speech united to show him exemplary in his use of the community's structures of piety (or symbolic "hedges") in the circumstance of distress. Job's response after the second calamity is presented in a quite different fashion, one which leaves us unsure of his attitude. There is no speech—at least not at first—to allow access to his mind or to interpret his behavior. And his behavior itself—very tersely described—is of uncertain significance, as a survey of commentary opinion shows. Does the scraping of his skin betoken a more extreme expression of grief than the shaving of the head —perhaps a form of ritual self-laceration? Or is it a pragmatic response to the itching pain of boils by application of a counter-irritant? One cannot be sure. The use of a common potsherd (a piece of refuse picked up from the surface of the village dump) would suit the latter type of action; but it would also suit an ironic portrayal of the former. Such an ironic portrayal itself, however, would constitute a rhetorical means by which to signal a rupture in the conventions of grief.

Likewise, sitting among ashes might be construed as an extreme use of ashes to express ritual mourning (cf. posture of Babylon in Isa. 47:1, 5, and of Jerusalem in Lam. 1:1; 2:10; 3:16 [ashes], 28–29). On the other hand, the town dump is the sort of place to which the community was wont to banish its lepers (Gordis). The uncertainty concerning these actions may be less a topic for scholarly solution than a narrative device by which Job's inner self is shrouded in ambiguity, in contrast to the open, straightforward and conventional response in 1:20–21. It is not until his wife speaks·that Job discloses something of his inner state; and, as we shall see, what is disclosed does nothing to relieve the ambiguity but rather intensifies it. First, however, we must reflect on the status and function of the wife's speech.

The Role of Job's Wife; Temptress or Loyal Partner?

In whose name does she speak? Whose question does she ask? Whose proposal for acted response does she voice? Her own? No doubt her own, yet not simply her own. For as we know from Genesis 2, she is bone of Job's bone and flesh of his flesh. In touching Job's bone and flesh, Satan (1:12; 2:6), or Yahweh (1:11a, 2:5a; and 2:3b), has touched her bone and her flesh. Conversely, just as the Satan has articulated Yahweh's incipient question, so (as we shall see) she articulates Job's. That it is his own question and his own possibility for action, which he is not yet ready to admit and to express, and to the recognition of which she fitly helps him, will be indicated by several features in Job's retort to her.

"Do you still hold fast your *tumma*—your integrity?" At one level, her question comes as part of the horizontal dialogue which we expect in *C'* (2:7b–10), arising from her perception of his behavior and, as bone of his bone and flesh of his flesh, from her sympathetic identification with something in him which he cannot or will not yet articulate. The way in which her question echoes both Yahweh's express words in 2:3 and the tenor of the Satan's following assertion, suggests that she is speaking in behalf of more than Job. Augustine's term for her was *adiutrix diaboli,* "the helpmeet of the devil." The narrative context of her speech supports that identification. Where Augustine erred was in his failure properly to assess the role of the Satan in Job (as well as the role of the snake in the garden). The role is the "helpmeet" one of asking the thankless question which already lies latent within a slumbering or semi-awakened moral and religious and existential consciousness. Not until that question, and the alternative for existence which it poses, has been felt in force deep within the soul as a real possibility for action is human existence ready for maturity before Yahweh in the community and in the world. Whether the alternative posed by this question is one that ought to be chosen or to be declined is something that the individual must decide. How one decides determines whether one affirms and participates in

49

establishing one's integrity at a new level or whether one denies one's integrity and implicates oneself in its deterioration and loss (as happened in the garden story). Parenthetically, we may remind ourselves that the Book of Job turns on two questions, one asked on earth and one in heaven: "Why do the righteous suffer?" and "Is there (disinterested) piety?" By the way in which the wife's question "Do you still hold fast your integrity?" voices both Job's incipient question and the question arising in heaven, the narrative invites us to see these two questions as two sides of one question, a question whose two sides are two sides of a covenanting relation re-assessing its own foundations.

For the wife's address to and for Job picks up the word integrity *(tumma)*, heretofore in Job relatively unambiguous in meaning, and places it in a new and questionable light. We have expounded the word as indicating (a) the quality of individual wholeness (b) arising in and from one's relation to God, and (c) expressing itself in acts of piety (such as blessing God) and straightforward conduct. One may read the wife's question as continuing that meaning of the word: Do you still hold on to your fear of God? Do you still bless God? [Cf. the synonymity between 1:8, 9a; 2:3a, 3b, 5b.] That is now a futile act. It does not pay. Give up your piety; curse God and die. But in a context in which the status of individual self-consciousness is being explored and assessed, one may also read the question another way: Do you still possess your own integrity as an individual? Are you not in danger, through your continuing piety, of denying the implications of your own experience, your own sense of what makes sense, your responsibility as a moral being? Are you not in danger of "bad faith" in alienating yourself from yourself by this disgusting display of fawning religiosity? If you really want to keep a grip *(maḥziq)* on your integrity, you will wake up to the fact that your integrity arises as your own self-grounded project and has nothing to do with God—and you will curse God, even if that means you die. (For other descriptions of such practical atheism, cf. Ps. 14 [the *fool*] and Job 21:14–16 as commented on below.)

We are inclined, uncertainly, toward the latter reading. Although it may be that the speech is irreducibly ambiguous, articulating for and with Job the question that now yawns before individuating consciousness: In view of this experience, is integrity maintained relationally through continuing submissive piety or is it sustained (insofar as it can be sustained) through the abandonment of all piety and the acceptance of the responsibility for independent self-affirmation? Or is there perhaps a third way? The ambiguity of the wife's speech comes fitly, helpfully, between the ambiguity of Job's behavior in verse 7 and the more pronounced ambiguity disclosed within him through his spoken response.

Job's Second Response (2:8–10), Compared with His First (1:20–22)

A close comparison between Job's two responses to his experience, in 1:20–22 and in 2:8–10, discloses that by 2:7 a pebble has been loosened within him which threatens to become an avalanche, and which, initially, he strives to prevent. We may note the following contrasts:

(1) "In all this Job did not sin *or charge God with wrong*" (1:22). "In all this Job did not sin *with his lips*" (2:10). The italicized words may simply be synonymous, signaling no shift in meaning. Yet, that they do so signal is implied in the words which we first hear Job speak, voicing his (pious) concern lest "my sons have sinned, and cursed God *in their hearts.*" By the way in which 1:5, 22 and 2:10 play off one another, we may suspect that by 2:10 a space has begun to open between what Job is saying and what he is thinking.

(2) In 1:22 Job utters a positive and declarative affirmation; in 2:10 Job couches his words in the form of a question. To be sure, the question has all the appearance of being rhetorical, and as such, an even stronger assertion couched as a question only in order to draw the hearer's own mind into active assent. But rhetorical questions are a tricky business. They provide a marvelous means whereby one who is uncertain or who is negatively certain may give the appearance of affirming what everyone knows and must acknowledge, while inwardly reserving judgment or entertaining other views. Such a use of rhetorical questions constitutes a particularly effective instance of irony. Since we shall have frequent occasion to argue for the identification of irony in the Book of Job, not least of all in the function of "rhetorical questions," and since all identifications of irony are debatable, turning upon the reader's construal of the literary context, it is important to note well this first instance.

(3) Job's self-hiding behind the question form is reinforced by the shift in his use of the first-person pronoun. In 1:21 he

51

spoke straightforwardly for himself, "I, my, I;" in 2:10 his individual "I" is hidden anonymously amongst the "we, we" (like
Saul amongst the baggage). The reader is invited to suppose Job
to be identifying himself with the "we;" but one suspects that,
so hidden within conventional group attitudes, Job is inwardly
free to locate his own "I" elsewhere if he wishes. Thus self-
consciousness begins to disengage itself from group-conscious-
ness, already before he and his friends come to a parting of
words.

(4) In 1:21 Job moved from a human existential affirmation
about his own independent finitude to a religious affirmation in
which both phases of his dependent experience of God were
stated positively: Yahweh has given; Yahweh has taken away.
The calamities took the form of a *privatio boni,* a taking away
of good things. In 2:10 there is a double shift: (a) the assured
declaration that Yahweh gave and took back in 1:21 assumed
the confident ability to speak, as it were, from the divine point
of view and reflected an attitude at home in periods in which
the community's life-world is intact and religious and theological affirmations take on a pronouncedly objectifying tone. The
question "Shall we receive . . . , and shall we not receive . . . ?"
in 2:10 signals the beginning of the loss of confidence in objectifying language, even in confessional contexts. The raw edges of
experience so challenge the traditional frame-of-reference that
religious utterances take on a more subjectivist character. One
speaks not "from above" toward the human scene, but from a
human stance outward, questioningly, toward God. (b) Along
with this shift comes an altered valuation of the texture of
experience. For Job, now, calamity is no longer the withdrawal
of once extended blessings and good things; it is the reception
from the divine realm of bad things alongside one's reception
of good things. To be sure, the phrase "at the hand of God" does
not recur after "evil" as it does after "good." But this again is
part of Job's newly-awakened, uncertain, questioning reti-
cence. Job, unlike the reader, knows nothing of what has transpired in heaven. Like his wife, who in the midst of her entirely
human concern inadvertently used the same language as was
used in heaven and thereby was shown to be caught up in the
heavenly dialogue and to be serving it, so Job uses the language
of heaven inadvertently in his using the word "hand" (cf. 1:11
etc.). In a polytheistic or dualistic religion, good may be thought
of as coming from one divine hand and evil from another.

52

Within Israel both good and evil can come from the same hand (Isa. 45:7; cf. Isa. 41:23 and Zeph. 1:12; also Jer. 18:7–10). That the narrative characters of Yahweh and the Satan ought not to be overly distinguished theologically is signaled, among other means, by the use of the word "hand" which, as it happens, occurs seven times in the prologue: 1:10, 11, 12 (RSV "power" and hand) 2:5, 6 (RSV "power"), 10. In the heavenly dialogue, the Satan's "hand" is mentioned three times while Yahweh's is mentioned only twice. The latter number is "completed" to three by the occurrence in 2:10, where the Satan's repeated "put forth thy *hand* now" is echoed in the inverse words "shall we receive . . . at the *hand* of God?" In heaven the ultimate correlation between Yahweh's hand and the Satan's hand is acknowledged in Yahweh's statement "you moved me against him, to destroy him without cause." Both preliminary alternation between the two pairs of hands and eventual identification of the two pairs of hands in 2:3*b* are reflected in Job's question in 2:10.

(5) In 1:21, as we have already observed, "I came from my mother's womb" continues the generative theme prominent in the preceding narrative and prominent in the personal religion which is the implicit context within which the problem of the book is set. The generative theme is absent from 2:10. The ground is being prepared for the contradiction of this theme in chapter three, where Job curses the day of his birth.

(6) Then there is the matter of the divine name. It is commonly observed that, whereas the name "Yahweh" occurs prominently in the prologue and the epilogue, it does not appear in the dialogues (except, of course, in the rubrics at 38:1; 40:1, 3, 6). Some have taken this difference as part of the evidence for diversity in the authorship of the dialogues and the prologue/epilogue. In this commentary the shifts in usage are differently interpreted (see commentary on 23:13). In any case, and allowing for the fact that the shift between "Yahweh" (the *Lord*) and "Elohim" (God) in the prologue is not always patient of meaningful interpretation, the shift in usage within the two responses is peculiarly suggestive when taken with the other features here being examined. In the first response, Job made his pious affirmation and blessed heaven by the use of the name Yahweh not once but three times, echoing perhaps the cultic conventions reflected also in Numbers 6:24–26. No less significant is it, then, that in the second instance Job confines himself

53

to a single, lapidary reference to—Elohim. Under circumstances which have torn away the "sacred canopy" of Job's faith (cf. the tent, or flimsy "hedge," under which Zeus and Nickles meet in Archibald MacLeish's play *J.B.*, as well as the closely related imagery in MacLeish's Joban sonnet "The End of the World"), it becomes questionable whether the ultimate efficacy attending our existence may any longer appropriately be named "Yahweh." Are the Exodus and its deliverance from oppression (as launched at the burning bush) and Sinai with its laws (received in the region of the burning bush) really a disclosure of the divine reality? The shift in names from "Yahweh" to pre-Mosaic terms for God, then, does not first begin with chapter 3, but occurs already in the prologue.

Elsewhere we have attempted to study the significance of the Israelite exegesis of the name Yahweh in Exodus 3:14 (Janzen, *Interp.* 33; *Journal of Religion* 60). There we have argued that in that inner-biblical exegesis Israel testifies to its experience of an ultimate reality not reducible to any specific actuality nor to the sum total of all actualities, with their patterns of necessity and coerciveness, but a reality which at its own heart is the power of free, self-determinate possibility. We have argued that in the further identification of Yahweh as "the God of Abraham, the God of Isaac and the God of Jacob (Exod. 3:15), God is affirmed to be not merely contrasted with the structures and powers of actuality, but also deeply and covenantally related to them. It is significant in the highest degree that, in resorting to terms like *El*, *Eloah*, and *Shadday* (The Almighty) in the dialogues, the agony and doubt of Job and the theology of the friends alike articulate themselves under the aegis of terms for God other than that name which above all other names celebrates the freedom of God. It is precisely *such* a God with whom Israel since ancestral time has been related as to a divine parent (Exod. 3:6, 15; 4:22–23). Job's doubt and their theology alike betray an as yet insufficient appreciation of what it means for human experience to be the image of such a God.

(7) Finally, there is the sharpness of the retort aimed at the wife as a preface to his almost intolerably ambiguous confession: "As one of the foolish women *(nebalot)* would speak, so you speak." The severity of the retort lies in the meaning of the word "fool" *(nabal)*. Robert Gordis comments that the

54

word "refers not to intellectual weakness but to moral obtuseness and blindness to religious truth." S. R. Driver defines the word, more expansively, as meaning "Moral and religious insensibility, a rooted incapacity to discern moral and religious relations, leading to an intolerant repudiation in practice of the claims which they impose" (*Commentary on Deuteronomy*, p. 256). The usage in Psalm 14:1 provides perhaps the closest parallel to the present context. To do what his wife and the rift in his own interior consciousness suggest would be unthinkable, and Job reacts from it in horror. It is Job's awareness of such a possibility already welling up within himself, and his horror of choosing it, which gives such force to his outburst. Poor wife! She is not the first nor the last to be scolded and condemned for her misunderstood—or subconsciously understood but intolerable—helpfulness to God and to her human companion.

Once again, then, the husband-wife dialogue gives access to the essence of things, and what it discloses is an inner turmoil which will be longer resolving itself than the turmoil occasioned by the snake in the garden—longer in coming to a decision, but quite different in outcome. Meanwhile, it needs to be said again: We must set aside one of the stereotypical themes in modern commentary tradition concerning the Book of Job. That theme concerns the supposed contrast between the "patient, faithful" Job of chapters 1—2 and the "impatient, doubting" Job of chapters 3—31, a contrast amounting to such a religious and theological incompatibility as to require the hypothesis of divergent authorship. Such an analysis arises from a failure to attend with sensitivity to the way in which Job's character unfolds as the narrative proceeds. The contrast is viewed in terms of incompatibility because such an analysis abstracts narrative moments from their narrative setting, examines them in their abstracted isolation from one another, and then compares them as logically alternative static views on how Job responds to affliction. But life, in contrast to logic, is immersed in time, where one expects to see variation and change over time in an individual's response to experience. Such a change we have begun to detect in the narrative contrast between Job's first and second responses. Through the second response, there is the deepest connection between the prologue and the dialogues in this respect.

55

Job 2:11–13
Narrative Conclusion:
Introducing Job's Friends and
Alluding to His Growing Pain

Formally, as we have seen (see section On the Structure of the Prologue), 2:11–13 *(A')* forms a narrative inclusion with 1:1–5 *(A)*, surrounding the heavenly and earthly dialogues of sections *B, C, B', C'*. (In the epilogue, two scenes correspond to the scenes *A* and *A'* of the prologue; but the order is reversed, for 42:7–9 balances 2:11–13 and 42:10–17 balances 1:1–5. Thus, formally, the whole narrative comes round to its beginning. As we shall see, however, the content, or meaning, has undergone a transformation.) The inclusionary character of *A* and *A'* in the prologue itself is reinforced by a number of additional features. For example, as Gordis observes, the personal and place names in 2:11 are all drawn from the Pentateuch, which gives them a ring of antiquity to Israelite ears. These names thus balance the "long ago and far away" effect of the names Uz and Job. Again, the stylized enumerations of *A* and *A'* (3 friends, 7 days and nights; cf. the 7,000 sheep and 3,000 camels, 7 sons and 3 daughters, 500 yoke of oxen and 500 she-asses) draw the two passages together in the back of the reader's awareness. However, this juxtaposition of the two passages serves only to heighten the painful contrast: In 1:4 the children of Job used to assemble to feast the good fortune of one of them; whereas, as a result of the events that have transpired out of the assembly of the children of God, the friends of Job assemble to condole with and to comfort the exceedingly ill fortune of one of their number. Finally, whereas formerly Job was known for both his character and his prosperity to be the greatest *(gadol)* of all the people of the East, now three of these Easterners see that his suffering *(ke'eb)* is very great *(gadal me'od)*.

56   The three friends come for a dual purpose. They come, first, to condole, that is, to be in sorrow with him. The Hebrew verb *nud* in such a context refers to a bodily motion of shaking, moving to and fro, nodding the head. Theirs is a condolence so deeply felt as to be inarticulate, expressible only through those bodily movements by which one undergoes sympathetically the embodied sufferings of another. (The word *ke'eb* in v. 13 encompasses both mental and physical anguish.) In their own way, like a spouse, friends are bone of one another's bone, flesh of one another's flesh; so the first act is one of identification.

The second purpose of the visit, while grounded in the first, and while having its validity only in such a prior grounding, is somewhat different. They come to identify, but not only to identify. They come to comfort *(nhm)* Job. The precise meaning of this verb has been variously derived and defined. Space does not permit a discussion of the variety of proposals. Our own close study of this word leaves us convinced of the soundness of E. A. Speiser's analysis *(Genesis)*, according to which the root *nhm* describes a "change of mind." For future purposes, we may note here that the Hebrew word for "mind" is *leb/ lebab*, a word which, more inclusively, names the inner self in respect to one's affections and emotions, understandings and attitudes, intentions and volitions (cf., e.g., the commentary on 11:12, 13 and on 12:3). Such is the inner reality in Job that the friends seek to change. Occurring in the middle/reflexive voice, the verb means "to repent," that is, to change the way one feels, thinks, and intends concerning *('al)* some state of affairs. Occurring in the active voice, the verb means something which no English verb quite captures. It refers to the action (usually the action of speaking, at times expressed as the action of "speaking to the heart" or *lēb*) by which one hopes to bring about a change in or hopes to encourage another to effect a change in how that other feels, thinks, and intends concerning a given state of affairs. Close study of the few passages using the expression "speak to the heart" will illuminate what the friends are after (Gen. 34:3; 50:21; Judg. 19:3; Ruth 2:13; I Sam. 1:13; II Sam. 19:7; II Chron. 30:22; 32:6; Isa. 40:2; Hos. 2:16). The friends hope to enter deeply with Job into his condition and then to help him come out of it in a manner which enables him to go on with his life in a spirit other than that of perpetual bereavement (cf. Jacob in Gen. 37:35 and Rachel in Jer. 31:15).

The friends are presented as undertaking their dual purpose in exemplary fashion. Formally, one observes that verse 11 introduces this final scene of the prologue, while the scene itself is bracketed within the two balancing statements:

57

(a) when they <u>saw</u> him from afar, <u>they did not recognize him;</u>
(a') for they <u>saw</u> that his <u>suffering was great.</u>

The end of (a') makes explicit what is implicit in the ending of (a): Job's suffering has rendered him all but unrecognizable (cf. Isa. 52:14). Many have had this experience, of visiting a familiar friend or family member and of being shocked at the altered appearance. It is not just the physical features that have altered, but something deeper. It is as though the calamity or the suffering has claimed the other in an experience alien to us. The other is no longer fully or even primarily in our familiar world, but inhabits a realm whose terrain is strange and foreign to us. We sense a chasm across which we cannot or will not venture and from which we draw back in self-protective fear onto the safe ground of our familiar world. Or we attempt to cross the chasm somehow through sympathetic, perhaps symbolic, identification, hoping to draw the other back with us into the familiar world.

Between statements (a) and (a'), and arising out of the depth of the impression his suffering makes on them, comes the description of the friends' response: They say not a word, but weep, tear their robes, sprinkle dust upon their heads as an expression of their being appalled (see below), and sit silently with Job upon the ground. (If, as commentators suggest, an oriental ash-heap was a huge refuse-mound, we may imagine them sitting with him amid the ashes.) Job's first response was twofold, comprising conventional symbolic action and conventional speech; his second response was initially silent and his action was ambiguous. In their silence the friends resemble the latter rather than the former Job. That silence suggests the depth of their condolence and of their primal mode of attempted comfort.

One small item is problematical: the reference to the action of sprinkling dust upon their heads "heavenward" (RSV, following the Hebrew). Such an act is not only difficult to interpret but grammatically awkward. By a slight emendation of the text (*hšmym*, vocalized *hašmem*, instead of *hšmymh*; see Tur-Sinai), we may gain a reading "... sprinkled dust on their heads, appalled." The friends' attitude toward Job, then, is like that portrayed in Ezekiel 3:15 and Ezra 9:3, where one is portrayed (without the dust) as being *appalled* over the fate announced over others (Ezekiel) or the judgment implicitly invoked on

58

others by their actions (Ezra). One may also compare Job 18:20 and commentary thereon. To such a reading of Job 2:12*b*, Robert Gordis objects that "putting dust on one's head is the act of the mourner, and not of his comforters." He fails to appreciate that in performing such an act the friends are not acting as comforters but as condolers and that their use of dust in such a way symbolizes their sympathetic identification with Job as fellow mourners.

In *C'* (2:7*b*–10) we argued for a positive construal of the role of Job's wife, wherein she acted as a genuine and true friend and partner. As will become apparent, we view the friends also as serving Job better than he knew even if otherwise than as they intended. In *C'* the wife articulated Job's incipient feelings, thoughts, and intentions when as yet his established views and attitudes would not allow him to do so. In the dialogues, it should become clear, the friends serve an analogous function, though this time on the other side of the same issue. When, in time, Job becomes quite vocal in his newly-born suspicions, doubts, and fears, their thankless task is to articulate comprehensively and relentlessly the settled views and attitudes which once constituted the whole of his religious and moral sensibility, and which still are the reason for his excruciating spiritual agony. We must not overlook the fact that the intensity and the durational stubbornness of Job's questions grow out of his own settled views, and have their force against the background of those views. (Despair generally, it may be observed, feeds upon the very hopes out of whose ruin it arises.) Apart from a sensibility formed into and by such views, Job's anguish would be logically and psychodynamically inexplicable. The importance of the friends' persistence in their views lies in the consideration that, whereas a logical proof need be demonstrated only once to be cogent, psychotherapeutically such issues as this book deals with are resolved—to the extent and in the manner in which they may ever be said to be resolved—only through prolonged and much-reiterated confrontation and engagement. The friends serve as the dramatic and dialectical means by which Job's own settled views come to articulation alongside the new tones which his sufferings have given to his voice. Were Job to have to undergo this dialectic solely within his own mind and heart, who knows whether he might not disintegrate under such pressures? But with part of himself represented by his friends, he gains a certain freedom to give

59

himself over to another part of himself. This means, however, that merely to side with Job against his friends is to side with one half of Job against his other half. Since it is the half which shares the point of view of the friends which produces his vehement complaint, merely to oppose the friends is to have no basis in oneself for sympathy with Job's complaint. Such a half-identification with him leaves little promise of our participation, eventually, in the whole-hearted resolution later in the book, signaled in Job's own use of the root *nḥm*, "repent" (42:6).

Meanwhile the friends sit where Job sits, and they share his silence; and the small pebble inside him continues to roll down the slope, gathering momentum and loosening other hitherto settled landmarks and structures of feeling and attitude and disposition. His integrity *(tumma)* is in doubt. The dramatic point to which the prologue brings the issue, giving a final additional inkling of this gathering momentum, may lie in a generally overlooked grammatical feature in the last clause. Whereas in 1:2 and in 1:19 the theme of "greatness" was indicated by the adjective *gadol,* in 2:13 the theme is indicated by a shift to the verb *gadal* which, ingressive in meaning, properly signifies the process of "growing, becoming great." The shift to the verb here may indicate the friends' "seeing" that Job's agony is not abating, even under the comfort of their condoling presence, but is deepening in silent intensity with each passing day. Such a reading of the last clause of the prologue gives a further inkling of the beginning in the prologue of that interior process to which Job finally gives utterance in chapter 3.

PART TWO

Dialogue: First Cycle
JOB 3—14

Job 3
Job's Opening Soliloquy:
"To Have Been or not to Have Been"

In words addressed to no one but himself, and thereby in words which deepen his solitariness, Job speaks. First he utters a curse against the day of his birth and the night of his conception. Taking up and reversing the language of creation in Genesis 1, this curse thrusts the world and its Creator, as well as Job's own past and future life, away from him. Then, from within the confinement of such a self-imposed excommunication and solitariness, he reaches out toward life and the world and God through a series of questions which blindly grope for the meaning of his experience. The curse and the questions attest the existential contraction and expansion, and thereby the dividedness, of his vital energies. It is these energies which drive and draw him through the dialogues, in alternations of despair and hope.

*   *   *

Immediately after the second calamity Job engaged in two wordless, ambiguous actions. So he remained silent for seven days, not having sinned with his lips, but apparently displaying signs of ever-deepening agony. Now he opens his mouth and curses the day of his birth (in Hebrew, simply "his day")—that day through which, as through an umbilical cord, one receives all the goodness of creation and of its creator, that day the remembrance and celebration of which renews one's participation in the positive powers of the world order and its divine orderer, that day through which, as he now perceives it, he was given entry into bitterness of soul and a sense of the enmity of God. Implicit in the celebration of one's birth is a natural response to life experienced as good, a response

61

having the character of what we may call "creatural piety."
Job's experience finally elicits an altogether different sort of
response. Yet the implicitly dialogical character of that response is intimated by the Hebrew of verse 2: "And Job *answered* and said."

The soliloquy may be analyzed according to the following
structure:

> A *curse* leveled at
>   the day of his birth (vv. 3*a*, 4–5)
>   the night of his conception (vv. 3*b*, 6–10)
> A series of questions with corresponding statements:
>   Why not die at birth? (vv. 11–12)
>   then, one would be like kings (vv. 13–15)
>   Why not an untimely abortion? (v. 16)
>   then, one would be like the slave (vv. 17–19)
>   Why life to such as I? (vv. 20–23)
>   for now, look what comes (vv. 24–26)

Job Curses the Day of His Birth (3:3a, 4–5)

The day on which Job was born was the day on which he first
saw light (vv. 16*b*, 20*a*). Job curses that day with language
which directly reverses the primal creative word and the narrated action in Genesis 1:3–5. God had said "let there be light";
in stark contrast Job says (translating literally) "that day—let
there be darkness." After each creative act God saw what was
created; Job says "may God above not seek it." Each created
thing God saw, God approved as good; Job says "nor light beam
(with approval) upon it" (cf. 10:3 and commentary). This day is
such a sort of evil that it can be "redeemed" (v. 5, for RSV
"claim;" the Hebrew is *ga'al*) only if gloom and deep darkness
obscure it from view and from memory. In Genesis 1, God
separated the light from the darkness; here they are to remain
confused. The verb "redeem" often refers to kinship actions
undertaken to keep alive the name and memory of the childless
dead. The usual meaning here is ironically reversed. The day of
the unfortunate birth of Job is to be redeemed by actions which
obscure it from memory. The clouds which are to settle on such
a day should enshroud it in a manner analogous to the mood of
a day given to bitter mourning. This mourning stands in contrast to the day which attends days of birth (Jer. 20:15) and days
of creation in general (Job 38:7).

Job Curses the Night of His Conception (3:3*b*, 6–10)

The curse moves from Job's birth to the more radical time of beginnings—his conception. The imagery graphically portrays the moment of conception, though in negating terms. The night itself is to be barren (v. 7: *galmud*, a term elsewhere applied to barren women), in that no joyful cry is to be heard in it (v. 7). This cry of sexual ecstasy structurally balances verse 10, where the woman's womb opens to receive the beginning of life. Since that night was not barren in the past, when Job was conceived, let it be barren henceforth. Let it become barren, not only by the power of Job's curse, but by the power of those (v. 8) who curse the day of an enemy's birth and thereby strike at the root of the enemy's existential power, those who lay a curse on the day in which an enemy and his wife seek conception—those who are skilled to arouse and to invoke the negative efficacy of the dragon of the chaotic deep, Leviathan. That night is not even to give birth to morning stars, nor to see the dawn (v. 9). The night of Job's conception is to be without "issue," temporally or generatively, in contrast to the pre-creation darkness of Genesis 1 and the generativity intimated in the sequence "And there was evening, and there was morning" (Gen. 1:5). Such a curse comes upon this night because its generativeness, in the case of Job, issued in trouble (v. 10).

First Question, with Corresponding Statement (3:11–12, 13–15)

The first word from Job (vv. 3–10) was one of rejection, of pushing away a life whose experienced meaning was now all too vividly clear and unwelcome. The second word (vv. 11–26) takes the form of a series of questions, which seek to draw toward Job a meaning which would be welcome but will not come. Verses 11–12 open with a salvo of three different Hebrew interrogatives which in English become a reiterated "Why?" These three interrogatives trace the early life-sequence, from womb to knees to breast. Had Job died at this point, immediately at birth, he would have found rest *(nuaḥ)* with the royally prosperous and fortunate (vv. 13–15) as ones enjoying the light of life with none of its darkness. Formally, one may note the manner in which the threefold reference to royal possessors is interwoven with the threefold reference to their royal possessions: kings and counselors, restorations; princes, gold and silver.

Second Question, with Corresponding Statement (3:16, 17–19)

The curse in verses 3–10 had moved from the day of Job's birth to the more radical time of the night of his conception. In the series of questions, the move from verses 11–12 to verse 16 is similar: from death at birth to the more radical pre-natal death. Had he been aborted and quickly buried, he would still be well off. In a culture where life seems to have been understood to begin with conception, an aborted fetus might normally be supposed to compare unfavorably to a full-term baby (as, perhaps, "knowing" or "seeing" only darkness with no following light). But there where the dead are (the "there" in vv. 17–19 is repeated three times in Hebrew), all human comparisons are leveled: weary or wicked, prisoner or task-master, slave or master (again, three sets of comparison), it makes no difference. "There" (i.e., Sheol as in 1:21), small and great alike find a place of rest (for the second time, *nuaḥ*).

One may note that whereas in verses 13–15 Job compares himself to the prosperous (kings, etc.), in verses 17–19 he implicitly compares himself to the ill-fortuned (weary, etc.). Is there a suggestion in the shift in imagery that human life which is allowed to come to full term (to "die in a ripe old age" as in 29:18) is a form of royal good fortune? And that a life which suffers such calamity as Job's is a form of existential abortion, conjuring up experiential images of weariness, prison, and slavery? When human life, however, takes on the aspect of a wearisome slavery, what is the other side of the coin? Is it not that divinity takes on the character of master (v. 19), and taskmaster (v. 18) and even wickedness (v. 17)? For the last word in verse 19, "Master" (Hebrew *'adonay*), serves also in the Old Testament to refer to God as Lord. Under the influence of the positive experience of God in the Exodus and otherwise, it may be supposed that the Israelite use of the term "lord" for God emphasized the positive connotations of that term. As the synonyms in verses 17–18 indicate, however, for Job the implied divine Lord now begins to resemble the Babylonian divine taskmasters who created humankind for the purposes of slave labor on their earthly estates. From such a divine-human relation, death would be a setting-free and a liberation (v. 19*b*).

Third Question, with Corresponding Statement (3:20–23, 24–26)

Normally one would suppose that the greatest treasure—as the pre-condition for all other treasures—is life itself and the light which accompanies it. As we shall see (e.g., at 12:22), "light" connotes in part human consciousness. For Job, light is a bitter gift which leads him only to long for a greater treasure: the "royal fortune" of death (vv. 21–22). Like the aborted and hidden fetus, Job knows death to be hidden treasure.

Job's questions began in verse 11 with himself, "I." His line of questioning leads him gradually to the divine other, who, however, is not yet addressed as "Thou," for this is a soliloquy. In 2:10 Job's questions are so incipient, so tentative, as to mask themselves behind the form of rhetorical questions. Now they come out openly: The straightforwardly affirmative "gave" of 1:21 and the ambiguous "receive" of 2:10 become the unambiguous "*Why* is light *given* (v. 20) to one whose way is hid? (The negative connotation of this third "hid" thematically reverses the positive connotations of the two earlier "hiddens" in vv. 16, 21.) God's firmament or "hedge" in creation had held back the powers of chaos and destruction; but now the orders and structures of creation have themselves converged on Job like God's confining hedge (v. 23). That is, the orders and structures of creation had formerly had a positive, sustaining and protective character. Now Job experiences these very same orders negatively, converging on him like a confining hedge or straitjacket. Just so, for example, the very nervous system which had once made possible one's experience of sensuous delight in the world, now can become the basis for extreme suffering of bodily pains. Why? The reader, who through the prologue was given access to the proceedings in the divine council, has at least a partial answer; but Job, who has not enjoyed that access, is left in the dark.

Job's third question (vv. 20–23) is followed by a statement (vv. 24–26) which, this time, is not hypothetical but actual. Whereas the supposed conditions in verses 13–15 and 17–19 would be greatly desired, Job's actual condition in 24–26 is intolerably miserable. This passage, which concludes the soliloquy by focusing on Job's present condition, achieves unusual rhetorical density by the way in which it draws together and integrates a number of reiterated terms. The motif of rest (*nuaḥ,* sounded in vv. 13, 17) appears a third time in verse 26. This time it also serves as the third and climactic member of a threefold series of negative synonyms: no ease, no quiet, no rest. The motif of trouble which sounded in verse 10 (*'amal*) and verse 17 (*rogez*) appears a third time as the very last word in verse 26. The unit itself is built out of three couplets, each of which contains the existentially loaded "comes," a verb which dramatizes the human destination of the action whose divine origin is alluded to in the verb "given" in verse 20. Altogether, and with a force which the oral reader may try to capture, the passage ends on the contracting focus of the miserable present: Sighing comes, groanings are poured out; the dreaded comes, the feared befalls; no ease, no quiet, no rest, but comes—trouble.

Further Reflections on the Soliloquy as a Whole

We have noted a number of particular features common to verses 4–10 and Genesis 1. A further large-scale contrast remains to be considered. First, there is the overall movement of the two passages: In Genesis 1 the divine speech begins with "let there be light" and ends on the motif of rest (*šabbat* or sabbath) for the divine artesan (Gen. 2:1–3; and cf. Exod. 20:11 with its reference to the divine *nuaḥ* or rest); here, Job's soliloquy begins with "let there be darkness" and ends "I have no rest." What is the significance of this negative parallel, this contrast to cosmic creation in the curse of Job 3?

In addressing this question, it will be helpful to begin with Michael Fishbane's observation that in Akkadian literature "cosmologies were often used as a preface to a magical incantation and its resulting praxis." By this means, he states,

> the magician-priest wants to insure that this specific act, which was established by the creator-god *ab origine,* as part of his Cosmic Ordering, will participate in the power and efficacy of that primordial event. Conversely, it is to insure the working of the noted forces present in the archetypal power-order event at the appointed hour for the indicated purpose" (VT 21:155).

One may suggest a related use of cosmological tradition in the Old Testament, for example in Psalms 104 and 148, where the very act of praise is not only a bare response to the creative event but in some sense a participation in it. (This observation will become relevant again at Job 38:7, in a context where the divine speech from the whirlwind reverses Job's reversal in chapter 3 of creation language.) Another related use in the Old Testament lies in the central of the three words of priestly blessing in Numbers 6:24–26, where the utterance "Yahweh make his face to shine upon you" participates in the primordial event in which God says "let there be light." What Fishbane speaks of in regard to the cosmos may be applied also to the celebration of the micro-cosmic event of one's birthday: To celebrate one's birthday is implicitly to invoke the powers active in that originative day that they may be present and active for one's present and future well-being. As Fishbane goes on to suggest, Job's soliloquy has just the opposite aim. He calls 3:1–13 "nothing less than a counter-cosmic incantation" (V.T., p. 153). The intention is to reject and to push away a cosmos and a total order which, once experienced as supportive and nourishing (e.g., v. 12), is now experienced only negatively, as a confining and imprisoning and baffling obstruction and hedge (v. 23).

One may wonder whether it is not futile to curse a day that is past (Pope). Yet God blessed the seventh day—an action presumably not futile. (The blessing there comes at the end of the day, paralleling the preceding day-closing acts of seeing each day and pronouncing it good in retrospect.) Moreover, modern psychological insight and ordinary experience attest how the attitudes and feelings, the affections and intentions, with which one relates to one's past and future have everything to do with one's general present condition. The past offers itself as a source of determinate vital energies; and wholeness or integrity presupposes in part the willingness and the capacity to accept and to appropriate this past into oneself. Again, the future offers itself as a relatively indeterminate field of possibilities; and integrity presupposes in part the willingness and capacity to accept and commit oneself to the future in its uncertainty and risk. Job, however, is sorry that he was born; he curses that day, and thereby places all his past under an interdiction. No longer is it to bless him with its memories genetic, cultural, and spiritual. Job also seeks death (v. 21) as preferable to that future signaled in his present condition. Accusing God of having hedged him in so that his way is hid (v. 23), Job cuts himself off from past and future by a curse which hedges him into the solitary confinement of his present misery. In one sense and at one level, Job seems to have lost his integrity. Is he in fact blameworthy? Perhaps it is better to say that Job has lost one

67

sort of integrity—the sort that consists in unquestioning (and relatively reflexive, quasi-conscious or dreaming) trust in a God who had given knees to receive him and breasts for him to suck. That integrity has been shattered. The question which remains is whether a new integrity may arise within his new-found solitariness, an integrity which is able and willing to embrace a terribly broken past and to move into a future whose uncertainty is now more starkly appreciated.

Job's first action, in cursing his day, if taken by itself may suggest a negative answer to the question just posed. In such a manner to cut himself off from the cosmos and its creator is to place himself in an isolation within which he will surely die.

Job's second linguistic action counter-balances the first, by reversing the direction of his existential energies. If the first action contracts Job's being and seals it behind the wall of a curse, the second action expands his being in the outreach of a quest for meaning: Why? Why? Why? This probing desire takes Job beyond the walls of his confinement in a blind groping for the meanings now hidden from him, if indeed they exist at all. This desire and quest for meaning is a digging for hidden treasures as intense as the digging for the non-meaning of death (v. 21). Indeed it is this quest for meaning which now constitutes his basic existential energy, within which the energy of the quest for death arises as a particular moment and a momentary theme. The very vital energy of Job's quest for meaning gives the lie to his quest for death.

We should not, however, interpret the sequence of curse followed by question to mean that the question displaces or supersedes the curse. Rather (in part by the way in which quest for death and quest for meaning are literarily interwoven), we should suppose that with the end of the soliloquy both the explicit negation in the curse and the affirmation implicit in the question are established as polar energies making up Job's divided soul. Therein they mirror, as a mode of the image of God, the manner in which the divine presence has polarized itself in the figures of Yahweh and the Satan.

On Soliloquy and Consciousness

68   Several times in the above comments we have characterized Job's words in chapter 3 as a soliloquy. It is significant that he breaks his long silence, not in direct prayer to God, nor in direct address to his friends, but in the mode of soliloquy, a

mode of speech in which the solitary self is both speaker and first listener. Other listeners do not so much hear as overhear. (To overhear a soliloquy is not the same as hearing a direct address. For if soliloquy arises out of the solitariness of the speaker, by virtue of being *over*heard it enters into the over-hearer's own "non-addressed" solitariness—whether, in this instance, the overhearer be one of Job's three friends or the reader of this chapter—giving rise to a sort of soliloquy there, where one converses with oneself on the import for Job and for oneself of what has been overheard.)

This dramatic effect may be said to resemble the effect of another classic soliloquy on the relative merits of death and life in view of the burdens of the latter:

> . . . who would fardels bear,
> To grunt and sweat under a weary life,
> But that the dread of something after death,
> The undiscovered country, from whose bourn
> No traveller returns, puzzles the will,
> And makes us rather bear those ills we have,
> Than fly to others that we know not of?
> Thus conscience does make cowards of us all, . . .
> (William Shakespeare, Hamlet, III, i, 76–83).

Recent interpretation has tended to take the word "conscience" here in its earlier meaning, "that of which we are conscious," or "meditative reflection." (Engleberg, *The Unknown Distance* pp. 14–15). Hamlet and Job unite across the centuries in an act of solitary consciousness, an act in which consciousness takes on a peculiarly complex and existentially fateful character. A brief rehearsal of some aspects of consciousness will help to indicate the significance of such an act.

There is that state of consciousness in which we are aware, without much critical reflection, of what fills our attention—for example, if we lie in a lawn chair under a warm sun and the pleasant sound of bees and children's laughter moves in and out of our hearing. Or, we are at work and are performing, one after another, the tasks that are routine or that we had planned for the day. In such instances, where our attention is fixed on what is positively present, our consciousness in some degree still slumbers or sleep-walks. To use Job's imagery in verse 12, we are comfortable on the knees and at the breast of life and experience. Suddenly we become aware of something of a different order: We become aware of something by its absence. Sud-

69

denly, for example, we become aware that the children we are tending have not been heard for some time; or that a fellow worker is not present beside us; or (in the case of a baby) that we have not been fed. The awareness comes as a sudden start into awareness, a vivid sense of what is *not* the case, what is *not* present. We are, often, more conscious of a family member's worth and particular character in that person's absence than when all goes routinely in the home.

Thus, consciousness can attend to what *is* present; or it can attend to what *has been* present to experience but now is not. The latter instance attests to a consciousness more intense and vivid than in the former case. There is another state of consciousness distinct from both the above states which involve positive and negative modes of perception. This state Job will display at a number of points, and indeed displays briefly in the present chapter. This state is one of imaginative outreach. Of it Whitehead writes,

> It [consciousness] finally rises to the peak of free imagination, in which the conceptual novelties search through a universe in which they are not datively exemplified (Alfred North Whitehead, p. 245).

That is to say, the "conceptual novelties," the entertained notions or images, are novel in that they do not correspond to any actual present "data" as positively perceived. But moreover, they are novel in that they have *never been* a datum or "given" present for positive perception. They are present if at all only to the imagination.

Shakespeare's Hamlet concludes his soliloquy with the decision to go on living. For his "conscience," his meditative reflection on that of which he is conscious, has contrasted "those ills we have" with "others that we know not of." Hamlet's imaginative outreach here confronts he knows not what. Job at this point succeeds in imagining a death which he prefers to life. It is a death which, in a bizarre twist, resembles the climax of the creation story insofar as it offers rest. But it is not a rest given *by* God (cf. Exod. 20:8–11; Deut. 25:19; Ps. 95:11; Matt. 11:25–30; and Heb. 4:1–10); it is a rest *from* God the divine *Adonay* and task-master (3:19).

The *fact* of Job's imaginative outreach, as an act of solitary and thoroughly awakened consciousness, is perhaps more significant than its *content* and *tendency*. For now, it signals his awakening from the "dogmatic slumbers" in which he had formerly lived in creatural piety. Before too long his imaginative outreach will begin to move in other directions (9:33–35; 14:13–17; 16:18–22) until it reaches a climax in 19:23–27.

Meanwhile, we may now perhaps appreciate how the form of Job's first speech is appropriate to his condition. At a point where he is overwhelmingly aware of a creatural existence which has been taken away from him, in its intense contrast with the misery which he does experience, and where he so vividly imagines that "undiscovered country" which no one has ever returned to report on—at this point he speaks in soliloquy. Yet, by a deep paradox, it may be that such a state of consciousness and such a solitariness is the condition for a new mode of dialogue, as of "deep unto deep," a new mode of participation in the presence of the Solitary One.

Job 4—5
Eliphaz's First Response: "Remember the Consolation You Have Given Others"

Eliphaz responds to Job diffidently and tentatively, seeking to offer to him the encouraging advice he formerly had offered others in times of their misfortune. The advice derives from two sources: experience and observation, as remembered in the community, and divine revelation as received in a private nocturnal communication. Correspondlingly, the advice serves to reassure Job of the stability of the moral order and to remind Job of human finitude and its incapacity for ultimate wisdom. Let Job take these words to heart, and he will find that they do him good.

* * *

Eliphaz's reply to Job is aptly diffident and tentative at the outset (4:2), breaking in as it does after a soliloquy and not a direct address to him. He begins with a reminder of how Job used to counsel others (vv. 3–4) and then attempts to give Job the same kind of counsel. That this first response of Eliphaz, in chapters 4—5, is not leveled at Job in accusation, but is prof-

71

fered in encouragement, seems to be indicated by the diffi-
dence of verse 2, the background in verses 3–4, and the emphasis in verses 6–7 on the eventual well-being of the pious, the
blameless, the innocent, and the upright—three of which terms
reiterate the terms in which the narrator described Job in 1:1*b*.
The argument of the two chapters may be analyzed into the
following sections:

Reassurance of a Reliable Moral Order (4:6–11)

A Contrasting Perspective on the Human Condition (4:12—5:7)

Divine Pedagogy within a Reliable Moral Order (5:8–27)

The first section seems to be set off, not by formal indicators but
by its content, as an initial consideration of the eventual fate of
the upright (vv. 6–7) and the wicked (vv. 8–11). The second
section is set off by its shift in perspective: it reports a divine or
revelatory word (vv. 12–16), in contrast to the human experiential perspectives at the base of the counsel in the first and third
sections (cf. 4:8 "I have seen" with 5:27 "this we have searched
out"). Also, the second section sets forth a rather different assessment of the human situation than that presented in the first
and third. Section three is set off by the "inclusion" of "seek"
and "unsearchable" at the beginning (5:8–9) and "this we have
searched out" at the end (5:27).

One notes that Eliphaz's rehearsal of understandings common to himself and to Job is not primarily speculative in its aim,
but practical. As has Job in the past, he seeks to strengthen,
uphold, make firm the pious one whom calamity has robbed of
strength, energy, and the will to go on. This theme of moral and
existential energy—the need of it and the source of it—will
recur often hereafter in the book. The tension between Job and
his friends arises, in part, in the different sources of their dialogical energies: The friends derive their energies from their established systems of meaning, whereas Job derives his gradually
increasing energies from his tortured desire to know the truth
at whatever cost to such systems and even, possibly, at the cost
of meaning itself.

Reassurance of a Reliable Moral Order (4:6–11)

Eliphaz's first word of comfort touches on Job's self-knowledge.
Echoing the terms of 1:1*b* and 1:8, Eliphaz encourages Job to
draw hope and energy from the fact of his piety, integrity,

innocence, and uprightness. For it is with such persons as it is with the wicked (vv. 8–11): there is an organic relation between moral action and religious disposition, and their consequences. That moral relation may be viewed as something built into the structure of the created world, analogous to the organic relation immanent in the processes of plowing, sowing, and reaping (v. 8). Ultimately, this relation between action/disposition and consequences is expressive of the will of a transcendent God (v. 9). Human bullies and predators—portrayed in the biblically conventional figure of the ravaging and predatory lion—will surely come to grief, their plots against the innocent thwarted (vv. 10–11).

A Contrasting Perspective on the Human Condition (4:12—5:11)

Eliphaz now turns from conventional wisdom arising from observation and experience of the moral order (v. 7, "think now;" v. 8, "as I have seen") to a privileged perspective granted in an auditory revelation. The introduction to this perspective (vv. 12–16) powerfully conveys a sense of the numinous, of the Holy. In 4:6–11 and 5:8–27 humankind is classified under two moral categories: righteous and wicked. In 4:12—5:7, humankind (here named as "mortal," Hebrew *'enoš*) is viewed under the categories of wisdom and folly (4:21; 5:2–3) and in such a way as to encompass all of humankind under folly and to suggest that wisdom is humanly unattainable. Even the heavenly servants of God (v. 18) are untrustworthy because of their proneness to err. How much less may God expect from those much more lowly and frail creatures, of the earth earthy (of "clay" and "dust," v. 19), and transient as a moth. In this image of humankind, we hear once more a theme and a question which runs through *Job*. What Eliphaz, of course, does not know is that in imputing to humankind the qualities of inevitable untrustworthiness and inevitable error, he (or his "revelation") is speaking on one side of the issue already joined in the heavenly meeting between Yahweh and the Satan. In that meeting, we recall, it was the Satan who called Job's moral and religious status in question, and it was Yahweh who was willing to risk the test in hope of Job's vindication. From the perspective of the prologue, then, we may appreciate two things: (1) The "inspiration" of Eliphaz derives, not from God, but from the Satan. (Cf. closely the sources of the prophetic messages of Zedekiah and Micaiah,

73

in I Kings 22:5-28.) (2) Insofar as Eliphaz claims to speak by heavenly inspiration, we see here one of the many instances in Job where the author ironically subverts a speaker's intended meaning. For, of course, in the present instance the question of 4:17, offered rhetorically (and so echoing the question in 1:9), actually functions as a genuine question. If in Genesis 15:1-6 Abraham could be accounted righteous before God in view of his faithful response, so also Job now stands before the question of his response in the face of his circumstances. No doubt Yahweh sees in Job a creature of dust and clay, a transient mortal; but what God looks for in just such a creature is piety freely given (the *hinnam* of 1:9). The fact that God even looks for such piety makes the question of 4:17 open and genuine.

In 5:1-7 Eliphaz continues to speak in the vein of 4:17-21. Dying without wisdom, humankind cannot even turn to the hosts of heaven for help—those who, in any case, are untrustworthy and error-prone (4:18). But if wisdom is not to be attained, yet human folly reaches its peak when one is vexed *(ka'as)* and impassioned *(qin'a)* over "The slings and arrows of outrageous fortune" (Hamlet) (5:2). Such a reaction does no good, but only stirs up more trouble. For—and here Eliphaz departs from the analysis in the first section (see 4:8)—affliction and trouble do not spring up from the immanent laws and explicable orders of creation epitomized by the dust and the ground (the *'adama*). They spring up, rather, from that creature of dust called *'adam* (5:7), in whom moral and religious behavior inexplicably does not follow organic laws. As sparks fly upward in contradiction to all that naturally falls, and seem to go where they will, so "It is man *('adam)* who gives birth to evil *('amal)*," as Robert Gordis translates 5:7. This freedom within the human heart, along with human corporeal frailty (4:17-21), renders wisdom impossible and trouble inescapable.

Divine Pedagogy Within a Reliable Moral Order (5:8-27)

Eliphaz now draws back from the sombre and pessimistic vision of the second section (4:12—5:7) to reaffirm the moral integrity of God and therein the hope (5:16a) of humankind. However inaccessible God's ways may be to finite penetration (5:9), this much may be gathered from experience and observation (see 5:27): The fault lies not in God. Recurring to the organic processes of planting and growth as a figure for the moral life (5:10; cf. 4:8), Eliphaz restates the two sides of the divinely instituted moral order, wherein the innocent needy are delivered and the wicked oppressors reap the results of their "wisdom" (5:11–16; cf. 4:6–11).

Whereas in the second section trouble and affliction are innate in the human condition, in both the first and the third sections trouble takes on a twofold significance: It enacts God's judgment for sin and it embodies a divine pedagogy to train up the responsive to a life of piety and virtue which will display the sort of organic quality exemplified in field and beast (5:23), issuing not in trouble (5:7) but in prosperity and happiness (5:24–26).

Further Reflections on Eliphaz's Words as a Whole

We have observed that in the first and third sections on the one hand, and the second section on the other, Eliphaz has offered two contrasting perspectives on existence. In the opening and closing sections he sets forth a view of life as governed by organic and reliable laws of moral cause and effect, paralleling and of a piece with laws observable in the vegetable and the animal world. In the middle section, he reports a revelatory word according to which human existence, without respect for categories of persons, is troublous and opaque to understanding. How can one entertain such diverse views at one and the same time? Such a question, however, is perhaps overly preoccupied with logic. The fact is that persons often do entertain logically incompatible views, which arise from the multifarious character of human experience.

In the heat and under the pressure of debate, such as Job and his friends soon fall into, the tendency is to move toward one or another single perspective, to affirm and to entrench oneself in it and to ignore or reject the other view and the experiences on which it rests. In commenting on the closing verses of the prologue, we have suggested that the friends have the thankless task of articulating one side of Job's views while he explores the other side. Now we are able to identify the beginnings of this division. From 4:3–4 we are enabled to gather that, in former times, the "consolations" of chapters 4—5 have been heard from Job's own lips. Both sections one/three and two manifest diverse forms of creatural piety: the second opens, for example, with explicit reference to the "Maker" (4:17) and to humankind as dust and clay (images which echo the creatural consciousness articulated in Genesis 2); and the prominence

75

given to natural organic analogues of the moral life imparts to sections one and three the same flavor of piety. Under the pressures of experience this creatural piety can tend decisively in one of these two directions. In the face of experiences to which the moral calculus of sections one and three is simply inadequate, all human experience is included under the categories of finitude, ignorance, and the mystery of evil. In its conventional form this latter view in section two attributes the mystery of evil to the mystery of human freedom.

In the dialogues which follow, we shall see the friends move toward one/three solely while Job moves toward two. In the process, the common-sense validity of the views in one/three is thrown in question by the rigid way in which the friends expound and insist on them. For his part, Job will reverse the analysis of that mystery and that fault which renders wisdom unattainable; for he will locate that mystery and that fault in a God whose arbitrary freedom from moral considerations confounds human attempts at understanding and meaningful action. (It has been suggested that such a skeptical view was sufficiently widespread in late pre-exilic and exilic times to call for the hope-filled counter-statements of such prophets as Zephaniah and Deutero-Isaiah.) Yet, though these two views—or, more deeply, these two existential sensibilities—are at loggerheads in the debates of Job and his friends, the two sensibilities in fact presuppose one another. For the sensibility articulated in section two arises as the sensibility of sections one/three becomes skeptical of itself; and in its doctrinaire form the sensibility of sections one/three entrenches itself out of a nagging awareness of the possibility of the truth of that of two. The dialogues seesaw between these two positions, only infrequently and inadvertently betraying clues to a third possibility awaiting articulation or at least intimation.

Job 6—7
Job Moves from Soliloquy to Dialogue with the Friends and with God

76

Job's experience of misfortune has left a bitter taste in his soul, for his experience directly contradicts what he has always believed. Insofar as Eliphaz's words of intended comfort only reiterate his former belief, the contradiction between belief and experience is only intensified and gives to the intended comfort as well a bitter taste. Thus cut off from the past and its wisdom, Job has no appetite or strength to go on and he longs to die. Human existence has been reduced to mere slavery, and divine providence has taken on the character of harsh overlordship. The Israelite vision of humankind as royal image of God (Psalm 8) is parodied to provide a picture of slave humanity as favorite target of the bullying divine overlord.

* * *

Job's response to the words of Eliphaz comes in two movements, each of which itself displays two sub-movements. The first movement is organized around the theme of *taste,* and the second around the theme of *slavery/overlordship:*

The Taste of Job's Experience (6:2–7)

The Taste of Eliphaz's Words (6:8–30)

Human Existence as Slavery (7:1–6)

Divine Overlordship as Harshly Overdone (7:7–21)

The first movement at the beginning (6:2–7) has almost the character of a soliloquy on Job's own present experience, continuing the appetitive imagery of 3:20, 24 before turning in verses 8–30 to address Eliphaz and the other friends. The second movement likewise resumes the imagery of 3:17–19 in quasi-soliloquy fashion, before Job turns in verses 7–21 to address God (the verb "remember" in 7:7 is second person singular, in contrast to the second person plural verbs in 6:24–29). It is as though Job's suffering has driven him so deeply into himself that even in his response to others his solitary consciousness persists. As we shall see, throughout chapters 3—31 Job will move between these two dimensions of his being, the social and the solitary. In this respect, the dialogues may be viewed as a dialogue between Job's social and his solitary self. In chapters 6—7, the first part of each movement explores further themes that he has entertained in his first words in chapter 3; while the second part of each movement evaluates the appropriateness of the manner in which his friends and God, respectively, are related to his condition so explored.

77

The Taste of Job's Experience (6:2–7)

Eliphaz has cautioned Job against the folly of speaking in "vexation" (5:2); but who knows the weight of that vexation (6:2–3)? In 3:20 Job has spoken of himself as "bitter in soul." (The aptness of the appetitive term "bitter" with "soul" is vivified by the fact that *nepeš* means not only "breath, life, soul," but also "throat, appetite, desire.") Here, "bitter in soul" refers to the concrete character of Job's life as experienced or tasted, much in the manner of the lines of Gerard Manley Hopkins: "I am heartburn; I am gall; God's most deep decree / Bitter would have me taste—and the taste was me." Job now elaborates this imagery (vv. 4–7): God has deprived him of proper experiential "food," and so, like ox and ass, his bellowing and his braying should be understandable. God has apportioned him such unpalatable experiences that he cannot stomach them. His *nepe š* (v. 7)—not only his "appetite" (RSV) but his very soul or being as appetitive—rejects them with visceral loathing. One may note that the imagery of food-eating-satisfaction (as figural for human experience), and also the image of the wild ass, will recur often, the latter image coming to final and decisive use in chapter 39.

The Taste of Eliphaz's Words (6:8–30)

These verses may be considered as still part of Job's quasi-soliloquy, insofar as they continue the theme of 3:11–19, 21–22. Yet they also address themes which Eliphaz has put forth, and so they show Job beginning to turn more directly toward him and what he has said. In 4:3–4 Eliphaz recalled how Job had often strengthened other sufferers by his words; and in 4:6 and 5:16 (as well as, implicitly, in 5:26) Eliphaz held out hope for Job. He responds that his appetite and his hope is for one thing—to die (vv. 8–10).

For how can he go on? He has no strength to go on. Verses 11–13 give a sensitive articulation of the close relation between existential energy and one's sense of the future. The first couplet (v. 11) portrays patience (which, in Hebrew, means "waiting") as a "strong virtue." Waiting is not a passive virtue nor a state of inertia; it is an activity which enacts moral strength. The Hebrew idiom translated "I should be patient" (RSV) means, literally, "to extend or stretch out or lengthen one's *nepeš*." The idiom names that inner activity in which, tempted by the unpalatability of one's experience to give up the ghost, one takes responsibility for one's own appetitive outreach toward the future and one goes on, for the sake of a worthwhile end. Job has lost sight of any end toward which to extend his life, any end the prospect of which would give energy for such an outreach. And this is because (v. 12) unlike the impassiveness of stones and bronze which enables them to endure, human existence is a matter of vital and sentient flesh (cf. 1:5), that flesh by means of which the *nepeš* embodies itself in organic relations with other selves and with the animal, vegetable, and material orders of creation. These organic relations are worked out in terms of food, shelter, possessions, and bodily well-being, all carrying an overtone of value and meaning which is at once quite this-worldly and at the same time spiritual. So that human strength is a function, in part, of the well-being of these organic and embodied relations, human strength is not the impassive strength of stones and bronze but the vital and vulnerable strength of flesh. Job cannot imagine any embodied future worth hoping for. Moreover, insofar as human strength is a function also of such "help" and such "success" as comes from God (v. 13), that too is quite gone from Job. Thorkild Jacobsen writes of the rise of the experience of the personal God in the ancient Near East at the point where the individual has a sudden, perhaps unexpected, surge of uncanny good fortune enabling that individual to succeed. He writes, ". . . one might almost say that the god was a personification of the power for personal success in that individual (*The Treasures of Darkness*, p. 155). Such a description would have fit the Job of 1:1–5 admirably. In that case, so far as Job can now make out, he has been deserted by his personal God, from whom there is no reason to hope for further success.

Job now turns directly toward his friends (6:14–30), and addresses them with a claim which, he says, they do not honor: "A sick man should have loyalty (*ḥesed*) from his friend, / Though he forsake fear of the Almighty" (v. 14, following generally Pope's trans.). Though God may desert one (v. 13), one should be able to count on friends—even if circumstances lead one to lose faith in God. But the friends' loyalty has been as short lived as a freshet (v. 15), and as disappointing (v. 20); like the caravans in the southern deserts who looked and hoped for water but were disappointed, Job's disappointment in his friends is measured by the degree of his former confidence in them.

That help need not have been such as materially to change

79

his condition by rescuing him bodily from it (vv. 22–23). He would be content to be helped simply to understand his condition. In verses 25–26, Job picks up the word "(re)proof," which Eliphaz has used in 5:17, and repeats it three times as he pleads "teach me . . . make me understand" (v. 24). Why should he accept the others' words at face value, when they discount his words as so much wind? (We follow Pope who translates v. 26: "You think to reprove me with words, but count as wind my words of despair.") Such discounting of another is as unjust, and as unfeeling, as bartering over one's friend. The theme of fatherlessness here aptly articulates Job's sense of the loss of God as divine parent. With the word "friend" in verse 27, Job concludes the complaint begun with the same word in verse 14. If the friends doubt his words (v. 26*b*; cf. 6:2–3), let them look again, closely, at *his* experience, and not just to human experience generally (5:27 and 4:7–8). To look closely at him and to continue to talk as they do will be to wrong him (v. 29*a*). He calls on *them* to turn from *their* way, for his righteous cause (*sedeq*, RSV "vindication") is at stake (v. 29*b*). For his part, he knows that his words carry the truth (v. 30*a*). On the other hand, his palate is capable of enough discrimination to know that they are speaking nonsense (translating v. 30*b* with Pope: "Can my palate not discriminate words?"). This last verse, following after verses 4–7, suggests that Eliphaz's words are experienced as only adding to the bitterness of soul to which Job's recent experience has subjected him.

Human Existence as Slavery (7:1–6)

The taste of his own experience now leads Job to explore the universal human condition as one in which the general human lot, in which Job shares, is one of misery (*'amal*, v. 3*b*). Whereas Eliphaz in 5:1–7 attributed the human lot of "trouble" (*'amal*) to human sinfulness (5:6–7), Job attributes it to other causes. For he now sees human life as lived out under conditions of slavery and hard service. The way in which the miserable slave conditions of human life in 7:1–6 are followed in 7:7–21 by an accusation against God for rough treatment, tends to confirm the suspicion that in 3:17–19 the terms "wicked, taskmaster, master" veil (at that point perhaps even from Job) a reference to God. (The word *ṣaba'* which is translated "hard service" in 7:1, usually—about 480 times—refers in the Bible to military service. Only in Job 7:1; 14:14; and Isaiah 40:2—and in the much later Daniel 10:1—does this word refer to slave service. That

Job and Deutero-Isaiah share this extremely rare usage of the word suggests the appropriateness of an exegesis which compares the plight of Job in his sufferings and Israel in exile, and which explores the thematics of each book generally in the light of the thematics of the other.)

Divine Overlordship as Harshly Overdone (7:7–21)

In Chapter 3 Job did not speak directly of God until verse 23, and even then in the third person. This time, having resumed in 7:1–6 the theme of 3:17–19, Job continues with words addressed directly to God. Having begun to characterize the lot of the slave in terms of the unbearable experience of time—time both as intolerably slow and as unbearably swift in its passage (7:2–6)—Job addresses this time-awareness directly to God in verses 7–10. In 6:2–3 Job justified his "rash" words by appeal to the heavy burden of his calamity; here he justifies the bitterness and anguish of his words (7:11) by appeal to the shortness of his life (7:7–10). If he is to be heard at all, he must be heard now.

In 5:1–7 Eliphaz had attributed human troubles to human sinfulness. To this, Job objects to God: "Am I the Sea, or the Sea-Dragon . . . ?" (v. 12, RSV "a sea monster). Granted that he is a sinner like all humans (see 7:20–21), is he such a threat to cosmic order, on the scale of the primordial figure of chaos and destruction, the Sea and its Dragon? Must God hedge him in, so to speak, with a special guard (v. 12; cf. 1:10; 3:23; and 38:9–11)? Recurring briefly (vv. 13–14) to the imagery of 7:2–4, Job resolves again on the preferability of death over life. He would choose strangling—the Hebrew idiom is, literally, "my *nepeš* chooses strangling"—and death rather than his bones. His "bones" represent here his embodied existence, as part of the phrase "flesh and bones" (cf. 2:5 and Gen. 2:23). The mention of bones alone here, without flesh, refers more specifically, however, to his sense that his body is bereft of all that makes embodied existence worthwhile (see comment on 6:12 and on 19:20).

The meditation on the low slave-estate of humankind under the relentless and ever-present attention of God now leads Job to an ironic reversal of the vision of humanity presented in Psalm 8. The way in which this Psalm is echoed and parodied in 7:17–18 is so important for the interpretation of some later passages and of the book overall that it merits extended presentation.

Though Israel continued to use the older Mesopotamian

81

metaphor of lord/slave to characterize the relation between God and humankind, the more recent metaphor of parent-child was also prominent (e.g., significantly, Exod. 4:22–23). As part of the imagery of the rise of personal religion in which context (according to Thorkild Jacobsen) Israelite religion arose and received its basic stamp, this parent-child imagery over the centuries worked to soften the harsher features of the older master-slave and monarch-subject imagery. One outcome of such a shift may be identified in the high view of humankind in Genesis 1:27 and in the closely related Psalm 8. In this psalm, the psalmist begins with an overpowering evocation of the sense of the majesty of the cosmos and of the even greater majesty of its creator—all in contrast (at the outset) with the frail mortality (*'enoš*, Ps. 8:4a; RSV "man") of the human, the earthling (*ben 'adam*, "child of earth," Ps. 8:4b; RSV "son of man"). Yet this mortal earthling (whom Eliphaz had also described in some of the same terms in 4:17–19), as an earthling is at the same time called to a high vocation and status, as one made "little less than God" (i.e., in the divine image and likeness) and crowned with royal splendor. Thus crowned with something of the very glory and honor of the creator who is above the heavens (8:1b), mortal earthlings are given royal dominion over all creation. In view of other references in Job to the thematics here presented, it is worth noting the realm over which royal humanity is to reign: (1) land animals, domestic (8:7a) and wild (8:7b); (2) air and sea creatures (domestic? wild?) as well as the enigmatic "whatever passes along the paths of the sea" (8:8). Given that fish have already been alluded to in verse 8a, one suspects an allusion in verse 8b to the "great sea monsters" of Genesis 1:21, the same figure as referred to in Job 7:12. What this suggests is that humankind as royal is not given creation as a playpen full of pets pre-tested for safety; the other creatures are not given to humankind as a tamed menagerie. They are to become royal subjects as humankind encounters them in their natural state: wilderness and the watery deep (two biblical images, of course, of chaos and the unordered).

Job's experience now moves him to a savage critique of the vision of humankind which Psalm 8 sets forth. Having elaborated a view of the master-slave relation untempered by parent-child sensibilities (7:1–3), from that point of view he now stands Psalm 8 on its head. Beginning, like the psalm, with the question "What is mortal (man, RSV) . . . ? and the child of

82

earth . . . ?" he asks, why should such a creature be the object of so much divine attention? In the psalm that question is answered by the vision of humankind as God's vice-regent on earth. Job sees things differently: To be a human being is to be subject to God's daily visitation and moment-by-moment testing and trial (v. 18), at whatever cost of suffering. For Job, the end of such an existence is to lie in the dust (v. 21, *'āpār;* RSV "earth"), a destiny which disillusions the fond dream of Psalm 8.

Understandably it does not occur to Job that the experience which he is so agonizingly undergoing may fall within the vocation of mortal earthlings to live as the image of God. As the dialogues continue, however, and even as Job's articulated doubts and accusations mount in intensity and descend to ever darker depths, gradually one may observe in some of his imagery, in some of his sudden reaches of imagination, and in the general form which his existential energy takes, the emergence of what we may call a transformed royal consciousness. By the end of Job's last words, in 31:35–37, this emergent consciousness has in effect reestablished the vision of Psalm 8, though on new bases. Meanwhile, it may be suggested that such a royal consciousness cannot emerge so long as humankind is hedged about securely in the manner of Job 1:10. It can emerge only when the earthling who is created to bear the divine royal image is thrust, or is allowed to move, into realms of experience beyond guaranteed structure and into freedom. Until then, though an heir, one remains a child, and this is no better than a slave, though one is owner of the estate. For the heir is under guardians and trustees until the date set by the divine parent (Gal. 4:1–2).

Job 8
Bildad's First Response:
"Trust the Tradition of the Ancestors"

Continuing in the irenical spirit of Eliphaz, Bildad urges Job to maintain his confidence in God's justness. The life span of an individual or generation is too short for the acquisition of adequate views based on personal experience. Therefore one must rely on the accumulated wisdom of past generations. This wisdom may be summed up in the familiar parable of the two plants, with whom the fate of the wicked and the destiny of the upright may be compared. Job will yet rejoice; for his end will be greater than his beginning.

* * *

Bildad's first response to Job is offered in a remarkably irenical spirit. To be sure, his first word is rather tart (v. 2), picking up Job's image of 6:26*b* and giving it back to him. It need not, however, be taken as suggesting that he has been "driven into a fury" (Gordis) by Job; rather, it shows one concerned to correct a friend who is talking nonsense. Following his opening reference to Job's words in verse 2, Bildad's own response may be analyzed as follows:

> Reassurance of a Reliable Moral Order (8:3–7)
>
> Appeal to Tradition (8:8–10)
>
> A Parable of Two Plants (8:11–19)
>
> Application of the Tradition to Job (8:20–22)

As did Eliphaz, Bildad throughout assumes Job's innocence, and attempts to reinforce the doctrines which Eliphaz had advanced in the first and third sections of the latter's response. Thus we see that, while Job in chapters 6—7 has picked up and inverted the second section of Eliphaz's counsel, Bildad picks up and reinforces sections one and three.

Reassurance of a Reliable Moral Order (8:3–7)

Bildad opens with a rhetorical question designed to elicit Job's agreement on something which is common knowledge: God does not pervert justice *(mišpaṭ)* or the right *(ṣedeq)*. The way he picks up Job's word *ṣedeq* of 6:29 ("righteous cause;" RSV "vindication") shows that he has heard in Job's words an implicit accusation as to God's injustice. That accusation, it should be noted, did not come directly and explicitly, either in chapter 3 or in chapters 6—7, but only lay under the surface of Job's words. Bildad's rhetorical question is meant to settle the implicit question before it comes out into the open.

Following the rhetorical question in verse 3, Bildad offers one possible explanation in verses 5–7 of Job's calamity. The "if-then" utterance in verses 4–6 is not offered as a genuine conditional statement, as though Job's purity and uprightness might be in doubt. Rather, as in verse 3 so in verses 4–6, the

84

statements all assume a positive answer and intend to reassure Job. The outcome in such a reassurance is that Job will receive a rightful (*ṣedeq,* as in v. 3*b*) habitation (v. 6*c*). In terms which strongly remind one of Deutero-Isaiah's vision of the "former" and the "latter" things (e.g., Isa. 43:18–21), Bildad assures Job that his former condition (*re'šit*) will be insignificant in comparison with the outcome (*'aḥarit,* "latter days") of his present experience.

Appeal to Tradition (8:8–10)

In 5:27 Eliphaz had urged Job to hear and to know for himself what Eliphaz and others have "searched out" (the Hebrew verb *ḥaqar;* cf. the noun form of this verb in 5:9*a,* "unsearchable"). Job in chapters 6—7 has appealed from this general observation and "lore" to his own immediate experience in view of the transience of his own and of general human life (7:1–10). Bildad now agrees with Job—human life is too short lived for any one person or generation, including his own, to acquire genuine insight. So he appeals to the accumulation of generations of investigation and lore, "what the fathers have found," the *ḥeqer* of the ages. In 6:24 Job had appealed for sound teaching; Bildad now points Job to the teaching which comes from the depths of the past (v. 10, "words out of their understanding" or "words out of their hearts").

A Parable of Two Plants (8:11–19)

This passage, which has puzzled many commentators in part, has been clarified by Robert Gordis, who identifies a parable in two parts, describing the wicked (vv. 12–15) and the blameless (vv. 16–19) in terms of two kinds of plant. Other biblical passages turning on two kinds of plant (e.g., Ps. 1 and Jer. 17:5–8) indicate that Bildad here is drawing on a well-known figure to reiterate a well-known teaching.

   Bildad opens his parable with another rhetorical question (v. 11), which turns on the analogy between the moral life and the organic processes of the vegetable world (cf. Eliphaz in 4:8 and 5:23–26). On the one hand, the godless may flourish momentarily; yet their hope and their confidence will crumble and vanish. His house (sic) "does not stand, does not endure" (v. 15). The other sort of person, though destroyed from one's place so that it denies one saying "I have never seen you," does in fact have hope. That hope has been obscured by translations of verse 19 which presuppose that verses 16–19 continue the description of the godless. When these four verses are taken as a description of the righteous, verse 19 may be translated as follows:

> Behold, this is the joy of his way;
> that from the dust *('apar)* later *('aḥer)* he will sprout.

We may notice how this second plant has a happy outcome later, like Job in verse 7; for "later" *('aḥer)* echoes the "latter" *('aḥarit)* in that verse.

Application of the Tradition to Job (8:20–22)

The positive bearing of the parable on Job's case has already been signaled by the way in which "later" in verse 19b echoes "latter" in verse 7b. Similarly the theme of "joy" in verse 19a is continued in verse 21. This latter verse also, however, contrasts with verse 2, through the common reference to Job's mouth. Whereas he now is speaking nonsense in his despair (see 6:26), soon his joy will fill his mouth with an altogether different kind of sound. Job has lamented that under God's harsh treatment "I shall be gone" (7:8, *'enenni*) and "I shall not be" (7:21, *'enenni*). Bildad adopts Job's last word for his own last word: "will be no more" (8:22, *'enennu*), but shifts the pronoun reference from second-person to third, to reassure Job that it is only the wicked who will come to such an end. For, as is clear from Bildad's use of the terms "upright" (v. 6) and "blameless" *(tam,* v. 20), he still views Job in the same terms in which the latter was introduced in 1:1.

Reflection on Tradition, Experience, and Rhetorical Questions

The unfeeling supposition in Bildad's words of 8:4 grates on the ear of the reader. Yet his response on the whole comes as a remarkably positive and conciliatory word, offering the wisdom of the community. The appeal to what the ancestors have found is an appeal to sensibilities which have arisen through many centuries of experience assessed, interpreted, defined, and taught in story, parable, and precept, until fresh experience itself has come, not only to be interpreted but itself to be *shaped,* by the "lore," the *ḥeqer,* which has been accumulated and handed along. This lore and teaching may in part, then, be a social construct; but it is a construct arising over generations of living, a tradition which (as a Japanese friend once put it) has the character of "long time common sense." As such it is a hedge within which life has meaning.

At what point does the tradition cease to grow, and become instead a fixed lens through which all experience must from now on be viewed and had? At what point does the vital dialogue between the transmitted construct and fresh experience become a monologue of the former? Granted the transience of a given generation or individual, has the latter no right, and no responsibility, to honor the spirit of the traditioning process by continuing the dialectic between tradition and experience? How does one most deeply honor the ancestors? By simply embracing the results of their search, the *ḥeqer* which they have found out? Or by entering like them into the search itself?

Bildad's rhetorical question in verse 3 is intended to appeal to the consensual results of ancestral experience, by inviting Job to respond in accordance with Job's own sensibilities as shaped by that consensus. Such always is the assumption implicit in rhetorical questions—they appeal beyond the momentary consciousness of the hearer to the deeply ingrained sensibilities of the hearer, sensibilities which structure themselves into and around communal convictions articulated in stock figures and parables. But, we may remind ourselves, the Book of Job was probably written at a time when generations of Israelite "long time common sense," since at least the Exodus, and articulated through the ancestral stories, was called in question through the insistent particularities of national and individual experience, in the events of the fall of the nation, the destruction of the temple in Jerusalem, the dethronement of the monarchy, and the entry into what Deutero-Isaiah called the "hard service" of exile.

In such a context, Bildad's rhetorical questions—asked straightforwardly from the platform of the traditional view— are heard differently by one for whom raw experience has begun to de-construct the old structures of experience. The invitation contained in the question becomes, for such a person, a question not to reaffirm and embrace tried-and-true views, but to entertain and explore other possible answers to what has become a genuine and agonizing question. Against the background of 6:29, and chapter 7 as a whole, and with an eye to the burden of Job's words in chapters 9—10, we may suppose that in Job's ears the questions of 8:3 rang unrhetorically:

87

> "Does God pervert Justice?
> Or does the Almighty pervert the right?"

Insofar as Bildad's words are offered in one fashion, and are to be taken in another, he may be said at this point to have contributed unwittingly, and ironically, to the subversion of his own intentions and views. Yet in so doing he serves Job well. For just as the wife's question in 2:9 fulfills the thankless task of exegeting and drawing out the feelings and views already buried within Job, so Bildad's question in 8:3 moves beyond the charge implicit in chapter 7 and moves Job to formulate the charge of divine injustice explicitly in chapter 9. It remains only to remind ourselves again that the vehemence of Job's charge in chapter 9, and the vehemence there of his disagreement with the friends, demonstrates how deeply he shares with them the ingrained sensibility and the communal conviction that God ought to deal fairly and justly with humankind.

Job 9—10
Job Responds to Bildad by Seeking Common Ground with God in the Sensibilities of Law-Court and Workshop

Job is well aware that, for all that may be implied in the metaphors of personal religion, God is not simply like humankind. If God were, Job and God could argue on the common ground of shared sensibilities, such sensibilities as are exemplified, for example, in human law courts and their concern for justice and in artisans' workshops and the appreciation and valuation of human artifacts. Job's questions deny these sensibilities to God; yet these same questions, by the way they are hurled at God, seem to have the aim and hope of finding such sensibilities after all. These questions, unknown to himself, are Job's response to the divine questions addressed to him in and through his experience, questions whose divine aim and hope is to draw Job on to a new common ground with God.

88

* * *

As we have just seen, it is Bildad who first raises explicitly the question of God's justice (8:3); though by the way in which he raises it, one sees that he is in no doubt as to the answer: God does not pervert justice. The answer is not so clear to Job, and he now takes up the rhetorical question to explore its dark underside. While his response in these two chapters takes its topic from Bildad, his language shows that he is responding at the same time to Eliphaz. In chapters 6—7, Job had addressed first the friends (6:14–30) and then God (7:7–21) directly. Now Job confines his direct address to the friends. But matters are dialogically not quite so simple as that. For in 10:2–22 we find Job telling his friends what he would say (10:2; not "will say") to God, if he could meet God under the conditions described in 9:32–35. This means that we are to hear 10:2–22 as directed first to the friends, and yet at the same time to God. Why this "indirection" in chapter 10? Job's accusations against God in this chapter are so radical that, it may be, Job cannot bring himself—yet—to make them directly.

The accusations against God in these two chapters come in the terms of *justice* and of *creative purpose,* in terms of the sensibilities of the *law court* and those of the *artisan's workshop.* One suspects that underneath the accusations as such Job is making a plea to God in a search for common ground. It is as though, in hurling at God (indirectly through the friends) the images proper to law court and workshop, Job is attempting to touch in God such sensibilities as might correspond to human concerns for justice and creative purpose. We may analyze Job's words as follows:

God and the Concern for Justice (9:2–31)

Job's Wish for a Common Ground with God (9:32–35)

God and the Concern for Creative Purpose (10:1–22)

The relation between the two concerns is instructive: The questions in chapter 9 lead to the more radical questions in chapter 10; the sensibilities of the law court are grounded in the primal sensibilities of the workshop. If we may leap forward for a moment to the divine speeches in chapters 38—41, this relation between the concerns for justice and for creative purpose may help us to interpret a puzzling feature of the divine speeches: They seem to say so little about justice, and a great deal about creativity. In the light of the movement in chapters 9—10 from justice to the deeper problem of the character of creative purpose, it may be that in chapters 38—41 the deeper problem is dealt with and thereby the more immediate problem is answered implicitly. With this brief anticipatory comment, we may now turn to look more closely at the chapters at hand.

God and the Concern for Justice (9:2–31)

Job opens with an almost exact quotation of Eliphaz's words in 4:17a, as he says "Truly I know that it is so (or, as we may translate, "Truly I know that you are right"): 'How can a mortal be just before God?' " The irony of Job's affirmation is clear from the way in which he proceeds to turn the tables on this assertion in the verses following. The irony is intensified by Job's use of a term which, in legal settings, has the force of solemn oath. For he begins with the word "truly," Hebrew 'omnam, an adverbial form of the more familiar 'amen.

The irony in Job's quotation of and agreement with Eliphaz is disclosed in the reasons Job gives for the impossibility of being just before God. Eliphaz had explained the impossibility as due to human error and sinfulness (5:6–7, as interpreted above), human frailty (4:19b–20) and human lack of wisdom (4:21). Job agrees with Eliphaz that these are the proper terms of comparison between humankind and God. But within these terms he shows the problem in each case to lie with God. God's strength (e.g., 9:4, 19) is such as simply to overwhelm Job; and God's wisdom (e.g., 9:4) is nothing more than the amoral skill to get one's way, even to the point of turning the innocent one's case into a conviction of guilt (9:15–16, 30–31).

In 4:17b Eliphaz had referred to God as divine Maker ('oseh). In 5:9–16 he had elaborated on the theme, using a hymnic form common in the Psalter, the description of God's creative or redemptive acts by the use of Hebrew participial clauses, clauses which usually are translated into English as relative clauses. (The laudatory clauses which should be so translated begin, respectively, "who does ['oseh]" in v. 9, "he gives" [v. 10], "he sends" [v. 10], "he frustrates" [v. 12], "he takes" [v. 13].) Job seizes on this traditional laudatory form and inverts it, expressing through it his newfound suspicions as to the character of the divine wisdom and the ends of the divine strength: they are not creative and ordering, but destructive and bewildering (9:5–10). By saving Eliphaz's couplet (5:9) until the last in his series of relative clauses (9:10), Job gives it a new and negative meaning: The "unsearchability" (RSV "beyond understanding" in v. 10a translates 'en heqer, the negative of the term found at 4:27 and 8:8) is not, now, a positive mystery, but a negative and baffling enigma. It is noteworthy that Job's catalogue of Hebrew participial (English relative) clauses numbers seven, as if to imply that God's acts are completely baffling. As described here, those acts all have to do with the created order. Verses 5–10, then, raise in a general way the theme of the divine Creator, and so prepare for 10:3–13 where that theme is applied to Job's particular situation. Included as it is within a chapter which otherwise is given to the issue of justice, the negative portrayal of creation in 9:5–10 (as we have noted above) identifies the prior concern in which the concern for justice is embedded.

The imagery of chapter 9 is predominantly that of the law court, from the technical terms "contend" and "answer" in verse 3 to the imagined situation in verses 32–35. These last verses are especially interesting, as envisaging a setting in which God would not be allowed to employ brute strength or to engage in conniving tricks suggested by an amoral wisdom. In such a setting Job might find himself on some kind of common ground, in which he would be able to speak as he outlines in 10:2–22. We will return to 9:32–35 below; but first it will be helpful to consider the content of Job's supposed words to God in such a setting.

God and the Concern for Creative Purpose (10:1–22)

Job prefaces his hypothetical address to God with a reference to the bitterness of his soul, echoing his words in 7:11 and, before that, 3:20. As we shall see, he concludes this address in 10:21–22 with imagery which echoes 3:4–5. As these verbal connections between chapters 3 and 10 indicate, Job now returns to the theme of the divine creativity and to the question of the purpose of that creativity in a life such as his.

In Genesis 1, God had been portrayed as (1) creating or making, then (2) inspecting (seeing) what was made, then (3) pronouncing it good and, implicitly, (4) sustaining it in the course of further creative actions until the whole was pronounced very good. In Job 3:3–4 Job has already inverted this language, with the desire that (1) his birthday be darkness, (2) God not inspect it by seeking it, (3) God not beam (the divine approval) upon it, and with the desire that (4) his own life might have ended at birth or sooner instead of continuing until the day of trouble. In the present chapter Job picks up this language at verse 3, as he asks: "Does it seem *good* to you to oppress, / to

91

despise the work of your hands, and *beam* upon the designs of the wicked(italics added)?" Surely God should beam with approval upon the divine handiwork (such as Job), not oppress and despise it; just as God should despise the designs and actions of what is not God's handiwork—the wicked. The logic implicit in Job's question is as follows: If there is any analogy, any common ground, between human and divine artisanship, then a God who can beam with approval upon the designs of the wicked is of a piece with a God who can oppress and despise a divine handiwork which earlier had been pronounced good, a handiwork which in Job's own case his own conscience also tells him is good (10:7a). Then it becomes incomprehensible how God in any intelligible sense can be thought of as an artisan.

Job now describes in elaborate detail the painstaking craft with which God had fashioned him. One notes particularly the repeated reference to the divine artisan's *hands* (v. 3b, 7b, 8a), to the details of conception and gestation (vv. 10–11), and to Job's birth and providential sustention (v. 12), all seemingly enactments of divine steadfast love *(ḥesed)* and care. Apparently all this served a hidden divine purpose (v. 13) whose moral and spiritual character makes no sense. Job has seen potters at work. They take clay (v. 9a) and fashion it carefully, with hands so sensitive, strong, and value-discerning that the hands know when to throw the clay back into the raw pile (cf. Jer. 18:1–4) or when they have a good pot emerging under their touch. It is almost as though the potters appeal to their hands as well as to their eyes for a verdict on their work. Job's appeal to God's hands and to God's eyes (v. 4) is an appeal to the sensibilities of an artisan: How can creative hands destroy what those very hands worthily created? In such a case, what sense does it make to shape something from clay, only to turn it to dust again (v. 9)? Continuing the questions asked at the end of chapter 3, Job says, if that was the hidden purpose why was Job born at all (v. 10)? Why not go directly from womb to grave (vv. 18–19)?

In chapter 3 Job had wished only that he had never been born. But in 7:19, and now more strongly in 10:20, Job begins to shift toward a desire for life. If God will only ease up on him momentarily, he will be able to "brighten up" a bit (the verb here, whose translation is adopted from RSV footnote, is the same as that in 9:27 which RSV translates "be of good cheer"). The Hebrew verb means "to smile, to gleam," and as such continues to play on the light-darkness thematics which were set in motion in chapter 3.

These light-darkness thematics are now amplified in verses 21–22, in a passage whose exquisite poetry has, unaccountably, escaped scholars and translators for the most part, leading often to emendations and deletions. The contrast in verses 20–22 is between a life in which Job might "gleam" (v. 20*b*) and death's journey to a place of no return characterized by unrelieved darkness. Using a number of terms introduced in 3:4–5 and adding to them a number of synonyms, Job describes that place as

> a land of darkness and death-shadow,
> a land of gloom like blackness,
> of death-shadow and no orders,
> where you beam like blackness (author's translation).

In Genesis the primal created light had come from God, who elsewhere and often in the tradition is characterized in terms of uncreated and divine light. On the fourth day of creation (Gen. 1:14–19) God had created the heavenly bodies, the sun, moon, and stars, to rule the day and the night (cf. Job 9:8–9). In neighboring cultures the patterns and orders and constellations of the stars, as construed in terms of the zodiac and other astrological systems, had aided humankind to explain and make sense out of life. In Israel such planetary and explanatory systems were thoroughly subjected to the implications of Israel's monotheistic faith: heavenly bodies were given by God to organize the days and the years in terms of meaningful times and seasons. It might be said that in such a world even the darkness with its fearful connotations contained within it—in the presence of the constellations—a witness to the ordering rule of God. But Job now speaks of a land—the land of Sheol—where the darkness is unrelieved by any ordering and ruling presence of stars. (Such a use of the Hebrew word *sedarim* finds its parallel in a similar use of the Babylonian verb *sadarum*, in the systematic astrological treatise relating to the divinity Ishtar who has to do with the planets and the stars.) But not only is that "place" or land of Sheol devoid of such delegated signs of order and meaning; it is devoid (as for example Ps. 88 also laments) of the presence of God. For the word translated as "light" (RSV) is in fact a verb which may be taken as either a third person

93

feminine or a second person masculine singular. The verb is that one which occurred first at 3:4c and which has just occurred again at 10:3 with the meaning "to beam (approval)." Structurally, the occurrence at 10:3 and 10:22 serves to signal the opening and the close of the issue that Job would chiefly wish to raise with God: the issue of the purpose and point of divine creativity.

The last line in chapter 10, as here translated, may be taken to signal God's absence from Sheol. This would presuppose, however, the conventional association of God's presence only with light. In view of 10:13 however (where Job suspects, to adapt a well-known hymn line, that "Behind a smiling providence / He hides a frowning face"), the truth of 10:22b is open to another meaning: God may indeed be present in Sheol to beam divine approval, and that presence, like that which it approves, then has the character of darkness. When Job next speaks, in chapter 12, he picks up the thematics of hiddenness (10:13) and of light-darkness and makes just such a charge (see comments on 12:22).

Job's Wish for a Common Ground with God (9:32–35)

Our comment on this passage is based on the adoption of the Revised Standard Version footnote to verse 33a: "Would that there were an umpire between us, / who might lay his hand upon us both." This wish comes directly after Job's vivid awareness of the deep difference between God and a mere human. Were Job and his adversary both humans they could go to trial together, where disputes could be settled neither by brute strength nor by mere cunning, but by commonly agreed upon criteria and values. For one function of human courts is to neutralize inequalities of the sort that lead to injustice and to allow disputants to settle a case on common ground. Were God human, courts (as a sort of umpire or arbiter) already exist in which their dispute could be heard. But God is not human (v. 32).

Job now engages in a momentary act of imaginative outreach, of the sort which we have briefly described in Chapter 3, "On Soliloquy and Consciousness." He imaginatively searches through the universe for something which he does not believe to exist—something on the analogy of a human arbitrator—some figure who would arbitrate between Job and God. Such a figure, if it existed, would provide the common ground on which Job and God could come to some kind of agreement. Failing such a figure, there remain just the two incommensurate grounds for proceeding—Job's grounds, that is, his human understanding of justice, and God's grounds, that is, the purposes and dealings with Job so hidden in the divine heart (10:13) as to be inscrutable and unsearchable or, as the Hebrew word *ḥeqer* literally can mean, unfathomable (9:10).

What is called in question by 9:32–33 and by Job's experience generally is the Israelite version of that Mesopotamian mythos which viewed divine-human relations in terms of the parent-child metaphor. Israel had radicalized this metaphor in the view of humanity (earthlings) as God's image. Of course the danger with this Mesopotamian metaphor, and all the more with its Israelite radicalization, lay in the temptation to interpret that metaphor anthropocentrically. Such a temptation and such a tendency would mean that God would be understood and held to account according to human categories of understanding and valuation. Humankind would become the measure of all things, even of God. Job's susceptibility to this temptation is betrayed in 9:32, in his wish that God were human; but his experience keeps him honest in the recognition that God is not human. Does this mean that there is no common ground? Is it possible that the image itself is that common ground? We will return to this question.

Meanwhile, let us reflect on the intent of Job's questions thrown out indirectly to God in chapters 9 and 10. What is the purpose of these questions? Is it not to draw God onto Job's ground, as defined by his sensibilities concerning justice and creative purpose? Or, to put this another way, are his questions not designed to probe God's conscience and heart for evidence that God in some sense shares these sensibilities? So Job through his questions searches for common ground.

All the while, another search is going on. For we must not forget the prologue and its questions which arise in heaven concerning Job. Such a reminder of the prologue comes in at least two places in chapter 9: at verse 17, where the "without cause" (*ḥinnam*) echoes the "for naught" of 1:9 and, more pointedly, the "without cause" of 2:4 (both phrases also translating *ḥinnam*); also, at 9:20–22, where the threefold "blameless" (*tam*) echoes the repeated occurrence of the terms "blameless" and "integrity" of the prologue. In this fashion the very words which appear on Job's lips in chapter 9, as part of his questions to God, appear earlier on God's lips as part of the divine discussion and questions concerning Job. From the point of view of narrative technique, we are reminded here of the function of the question which the wife directs to Job in 2:9, "Do you still hold fast your integrity?" (See commentary on this verse.) There, it is as though the "horizontal" question of wife to husband at the same time is the vehicle for the "vertical" question of God to Job. Somewhat similarly here in chapters 9—10, Job's questions to God take up not only some of the terms, but some of the very energy of God's questions to him.

For, deeper than Job's search for common ground with God is the divine search for a common ground with humankind, alias Job. It is not a search for a ground which either is or is not already there; it is a search, an outreach of the divine creative imagination, for that which is nowhere (yet) "datively exemplified," nowhere yet in existence as an actual datum, but which may perhaps come into existence. Job's questions are his response to and participation in these divine questions and this divine search, this creative purpose. Insofar as there is such a participation, something of the existential nature and dynamics of the image of God begins to emerge more clearly: The common ground between God and humankind is found in those questions which arise between them, questions which both constitute and sustain the covenant relation between them, a relation which itself may be marked by the severest testing and doubt in the name of loyalty.

Such an appreciation of the significance of Job's questions involves a shift away from the merely anthropocentric tendencies of the metaphor of humankind as divine image. For it establishes God as the measure of all things; and therefore it gives to the divine image the character of a teleological or eschatological human self-understanding.

God's call to Job comes in and through Job's questions. But only as Job's questions—framed as they are in narrow retributionist terms—continue to lead nowhere, will the merely human basis on which they arise slowly be eroded, until Job is inwardly (though perhaps unconsciously) prepared for a new vision. Job's formation as a blameless and upright person came through his response to divine creative energies working through settled natural and social structures of life and meaning. Some of those social structures of meaning included traditions of reward and punishment, of moral cause and effect. Now, Job's transformation comes through his questioning re-

96

sponse to divine creative energies working through the very questions he asks.

In Psalm 8, human royal rule on earth received encouragement from the stars, those ordered and ordering lights which govern the night and thereby give assurance that even in the dark God's creative and ordering rule is present. In the Sheol to which Job sees himself going (10:21–22)—indeed, in that Sheol in which his soul has already begun to find itself as in a dark night—neither the stars nor God shine. Job is left to rule in solitary isolation, illumined only by his own conscience and sense of integrity.

Job sees none of this. So far as he can see, experience suggests only a malevolent purpose hidden deep within God and within his own past life (10:13). It is to this latter suspicion as to what is hidden within God that Zophar responds.

Job 11
Zophar's First Response:
On the Hidden Depths of Divine Wisdom

Zophar charges Job with forgetting the difference between the limited wisdom accessible to humans and the infinite depth and hiddenness of divine wisdom. Then, forgetting that he himself is limited by that difference, he proceeds to tell Job what God would say if God were to speak: It would have to do with Job's exceeding guilt. Having accused Job of empty-headed stupidity, Zophar concludes with the attempt to lure him to repentance by portraying its outcome as a reversal of Job's fortunes.

* * *

The Stupidity of Job's Superficial Self-understanding
(11:2–12)

Eliphaz had responded to Job's initial soliloquy with words diffident and courteous (4:2). By the time Zophar speaks, the mood is changing rapidly (11:2–3). Zophar rebukes Job (vv. 4–5) for his presumption in asserting his innocence and for asserting as the corollary of this innocence that God's initial display of creative purpose and providential care has only masked a deeper and destructive intent (10:13). In thus speaking of God's hidden

97

intent, we recall, Job had picked up Eliphaz's words of 5:9 and had inverted their meaning in 9:5–10, applying the words to himself in 10:13. Zophar now comes to the defense of Eliphaz's original affirmation of God's "unsearchable" ways, as he develops the theme of the hidden depths of divine wisdom (11:6–9).

Verse 6 (as the RSV note indicates) is difficult to interpret or to translate with assurance. We are inclined to follow Gordis, who construes the Hebrew word behind "manifold" (RSV) as the defectively spelled word for "wonders, difficult things." So construed, the text may be translated as containing a synonymous couplet: "that he would tell you the hidden things of wisdom, / indeed, the surpassing wonders of understanding." Like so many, Zophar seeks to confound Job's interpretation of experience by hiding its meaning behind a veil of unfathomability and then seeks to excuse himself from such a limitation as he produces his own unambiguous interpretation: What is hidden from human view is only the extent of Job's sin, which is even greater than God's treatment of Job suggests (v. 6c). Forgetting that the figure destroys his own confident interpretation, Zophar then waxes eloquent in elaboration of the depth-imagery. (The "deep things" of God in 11:7 are the *ḥeqer* which we have encountered in 9:10 and earlier.) The transcendent infinity of God contrasts with the finite character of the world in its fourfold dimensionality: height, depth, length, breadth (vv. 8–9). In the face of this contrast, humankind is left powerless (What can you do?) and ignorant (What can you know?). It is not God's moral obtuseness and bullying strength (so Job in 9:4), but God's infinitude and human sinful finitude that leaves one such as Job helpless and perplexed. It is for such reasons that one cannot hinder God (11:10; cf. 9:12), when he acts as he has done to Job. (The same Hebrew verb underlies "passes by" in 9:11 and "passes through" in 11:10.)

Zophar now employs a rhetorical device which Martin Buber identifies as a standard item in the prophetic repertory: Confrontation of the wicked in terms which hold out no hope or possibility of change, in a last effort to break through the hard crust of moral resistance and spiritual obtuseness and to touch and activate in the wicked some last remaining power of positive response (*The Prophetic Faith*, pp. 104–05). One thinks for example of Jeremiah 13:23, which resembles Job 11:12 in the manner in which it draws an analogy between genetic givenness and the impossibility of moral change. Zophar says to Job, stingingly,

> The inane man will get sense
> when a wild ass is born tame.
> (This adopts the translation posed by Marvin Pope.)

Job had compared himself to a wild ass in 6:5, in a manner calculated to evoke pity. Zophar unfeelingly turns the figure back on Job, with an effective play on words and sounds. In the first line, "inane man" translates a Hebrew idiom which literally means an empty or hollow person: and "get sense" translates Hebrew *yillabeb*, which literally means "to acquire a *lebab*, a heart." This verb *yillabeb* in the first line is balanced in the second line by the verb *yiwwaled*, "is born"; and the sound similarity between them reinforces the portrayal of the unlikeliness of moral regeneration.

For all the apparent unlikeliness of such a change, Zophar's following words show that he offered the pithy figure of verse 12 in hope of stinging Job into turning. After all, verses 11–12 describe the worthless and the inane in the third person; but now Zophar turns to address Job directly in verses 13–19.

Repentance and Obduracy and Their Outcomes (11:13–20)

In verses 13–19 Zophar resorts to Bildad's reasoning as set out in 8:4–7, and presents his own version of the "if/then" argument. But Bildad's "if" clauses assumed Job's innocence and attributed sin only to Job's children. In contrast, and in keeping with his words in 11:6, 11–12, Zophar assumes Job's need to repent of both wrong attitudes (v. 13) and wrong actions (v. 14). He attempts to sweeten the lure to repentance with a variety of images which render concrete the comparatively general and abstract outcomes which Bildad had asserted in 8:6*b*–7. Noteworthily, he picks up a number of items from earlier words of Job and turns them around: Job will lift up his face without blemish (v. 15*a;* cf. 9:27); he will be secure and not fear (v. 15*b;* cf. 3:25); he will forget his misery (v. 16*a, 'amal;* cf. 3:10, 20 and often) and remember it as waters that have passed away (v. 16*b;* cf. 6:15; his life will be brighter than the noonday, v. 17*a;* cf. 10:20*b* RSVn); and the darkness to which he sees himself going without hope of return (10:21–22) will be like morning (v. 17*b*). The last line in 11:17 is a particularly vivid reversal of Job's last line in 10:22.

In 3:26 (as we noted in commentary there), Job piles up terms expressive of his troubled life as devoid of rest; and in 6:11–13 Job lamented the absence of the sort of hope that would give one strength to go on. Zophar draws these two themes together, portraying the repentant life as one to which hope is restored along with rest (vv. 18–20). The imagery of lying down in hope contrasts with Job's language in 7:4–6.

The wicked, of course (v. 20), have no such prospect, for their hope expires with their breath (as we would translate v. 20c). Like Bildad, Zophar ends thus with a reference to the wicked. While he does not distinguish explicitly between the wicked and Job, in the manner of Bildad (8:22 "you" vs. "the wicked"), Zophar does still have the residual good grace to make this reference to the wicked in the third person plural, thus shifting it rhetorically away from the second person singular references to Job in the preceding verses.

Further Reflections on Zophar's Response

Two items in Zophar's words call for special comment. (1) Zophar's graphic elaboration of the image of hidden depths in the divine mystery sets the stage for Job's words in chapter 12. Moreover, his very terms will much later be taken up at the denouement: When Yahweh says to Job, "who is this that *hides* counsel . . . ?" (42:3, italics added), the italicized verb is cognate with Zophar's noun in 11:6a which RSV translates as "secrets". Also, when in 42:3 Job responds that he has uttered "things too wonderful for me," he uses a cognate of the word in 11:6b which we have translated as "surpassing wonders." This observation should once again caution us against too quick a repudiation of the words of the friends just because we know how the story comes out. In some sense Zophar is proven right: There is a hidden wisdom, to which Job is not (yet) privy (cf. I Cor. 2:7). The irony, of course, lies in the fact that when Yahweh finally does speak according to Zophar's desire (11:5), nothing is said of Job's guilt (11:6c).

(2) Zophar's analogy in verse 10 is telling. It has its significance both within the specific thread of "wild ass" references throughout Job beginning in 6:5 and ending in 39:5–8, and within the wider thematics of animal imagery so prominent in the whole book. Zophar's analogy turns on the assumption that the only good ass is a domesticated one. Such an assumption is native to a mind and a sensibility for which the wilderness (or

"outlaw" country) is synonymous with chaos in its unstructured and life-threatening aspect. We may remind ourselves that the Hebrew term *tohu* ("without form" in Gen. 1:2) often is used in the Old Testament to characterize the wilderness. That Job shares Zophar's sensibility on this matter is illustrated by his own depiction of wilderness in 12:24–25.

Job 12—14
Job's Response to Zophar
Concluding the First Cycle

Zophar has attempted to convince Job of the mystery of God's hidden wisdom. Job accepts the language of hiddenness but turns it back on the friends. He asserts that beneath the appearance of a God of justice and order whose purposes may be symbolized by light, lies hidden the reality of a God who delights in confounding order, a God whose purpose is only to bring to light the deep secret of reality as deadly darkness. In view of such a situation, the doctrines of conventional religion are but a coverup. He will have no part in such a lie, but will dare to confront God without the pseudo-comfort of such illusions. So Job comes to perhaps his darkest moment. Yet he wonders if such an illusionless stance may not after all be his salvation. He briefly entertains the hypothetical possibility of a life-restoring reconciliation with God beyond the grave. This outreach of his imagination fades, and he concludes on a note of pain and mourning.

*　*　*

The unusual length of Job's response to Zophar may be connected with the fact that it concludes the first cycle of the dialogue. The pebble of suspicion, of which we gained an inkling in 2:8–13, and which came to utterance first in chapter 3, has now reached the proportions of an avalanche. Such a rhetorical connection between chapter 3 and this long response is signaled, for example, by the recurrence of some key terms of the earlier chapter. The word "trouble" which occurred in 3:17 and as the last word in 3:26, recurs (for the last time) in 14:1. Also, the word "deep darkness," which Job introduced in 3:5 and then used twice in his intense evocation of the character of

101

Sheol in 10:21–22, recurs in 12:22 where Job levels his gravest charge against the God of creation. On the other hand, in this same response Job engages in an act of imaginative outreach (14:14–17) which contrasts sharply with his first such act in 3:11–19 (see commentary under the heading "On Soliloquy and Consciousness"). In chapter 3 Job had longed never to have been born, rather than to have had to face a life now viewed in terms of slave labor. In 14:14–17 Job imagines a universe in which death (as slave service, *ṣaba'*, 14:14) would be marked by patient waiting for renewal. This very ambivalence in the response of chapters 12—14, between gravest accusation and most radical outreach of hope, also befits this response as a conclusion to the first cycle.

For convenience in discussing this very complex response, we will proceed according to the following outline:

> The So-called Wisdom of Tradition (12:2–12)
>
> The So-called Hidden Wisdom of God (12:13–25)
>
> God's View of Tradition's Theodicy (13:1–12)
>
> Job's Strange Hope for Salvation (13:13–19)
>
> The Courage of Absolute Vulnerability (13:20—14:6)
>
> Shall One Who Dies Live Again? (14:7–22)

The So-called Wisdom of Tradition (12:2–12)

In 9:2 Job had opened his response to Bildad with an ironic affirmation of Eliphaz's words in 4:17, using the asseverative word *'omnam*, "truly" or "indeed." Likewise here, using the same asseverative word, Job mockingly affirms Zophar's claim to superior wisdom. (RSV "no doubt" translates *'omnam*.) Then, against 11:12–13, Job claims as much understanding (*lebab*, "mind, heart") as they (12:3). What he cannot understand, however, is that one who calls upon God for an answer can be held in derision by friends (v. 4; cf. 6:14 as interpreted). He can only conclude that those who are at ease (v. 5), having no basis in their own experience, fail to sympathize with misfortune and construe it as judgment for those who have gone astray (v. 5). They fail to note, however, that the wicked often escape unscathed (v. 6), showing that life does not yield to a neat moral interpretation.

Zophar has claimed that God's infinite wisdom transcends the cosmos in its fourfold regionality: high *heavens*, depths of

Sheol, wide *earth,* and broad *sea* (11:8–9). Now (12:7–10) Job asserts that this "wisdom" is well within the knowledge of the lowly creatures of these four regions: the beasts of the *field,* the birds of the *sky,* complainers of the *underworld,* and the fish of the *sea.* The third region here is inhabited by those who complain *(śiaḥ),* a term which occurs frequently on Job's own lips (7:11, 13; 9:27; 10:1; 21:4; 23:2) as it does on the lips of the psalmist in Psalm 55:2, 17; 77:3. By the use of this term of complaint for the inhabitants of the underworld, Job characterizes common creaturely knowledge (v. 9) as knowledge of that divine action which leads to complaint against the one from whom there is no escape (v. 10). Zophar's so-called wisdom is as insipid and distasteful as is the experience which gives rise to complaint (v. 11; cf. 6:4–7 and commentary). Job concludes his introductory response (v. 12) with the same ironic affirmation as he began, mockingly "celebrating" human wisdom and understanding *(ḥokma, tebuna).*

The So-called Hidden Wisdom of God (12:13–25)

Job's tone of mocking irony continues, as he turns to "celebrate" the divine wisdom, might, counsel (or purpose/design, as in 10:3), and understanding *(ḥokma, gebura, 'eṣa, tebuna).* Zophar has lauded the depth, hiddenness, and mystery of God's wisdom (11:6, 8). Job now catalogues those characteristic phenomena in which God's "wisdom" is disclosed. With the exception of verse 22, every line in verses 14–25 reverses what conventional wisdom would claim to be a manifestation or revelation of the benign wisdom of God in human affairs. One example of this reversal may suffice to characterize Job's thrust: Earlier (at 7:17–18) Job had taken Psalm 8 and stood it upon its head. Now he takes a verse from Psalm 107, verse 40, and re-contextualizes it in 12:21a and 12:24b. In Psalm 107 the couplet "he pours contempt upon princes / and makes them wander in trackless wastes *(tohu)*" serves the theme in verses 39–42 of affirming the wise intervention of God to deliver the poor and needy from their oppressors. The passage and the whole psalm, as a celebration of God's justice and mercy, concludes, "Whoever is wise, let him give heed to these things." Job would have us give heed to those same things, but by his manner of cataloging them in 12:14–25 he places a different construction upon them. For in these verses God is portrayed not as overthrowing oppression in deliverance, but as frustrating all

103

human effort at ordering existence meaningfully. Eliphaz had said of the *wicked* that "they meet with darkness in the day-time, / and grope at noon day as in the night" (5:14). Job accuses God of dealing with *everyone* that way, even the chiefs of the people (12:24–25). All of human life is plunged into *tohu* (v. 24*b* "waste") and darkness (v. 25*a*), terms echoing the formless dark of Genesis 1:2.

This, certainly, is where God has thrown Job (cf. 10:21–22 and commentary). This is the depth and the hidden mystery, Job charges, in which God's "wisdom" resides and is to be found. In the midst of his specific examples of divine wisdom, Job inserts a general and a primal accusation, which (as a culmination of his own reversal of creation language in 3:4–5) reverses the conventional understanding of the divine intent in saying "let there be light" (Gen. 1:3). For he characterizes God as a malevolent creator who

> unveils the depths from darkness
> and brings forth to light deep darkness *(salmawet).*
> (12:22, author's translation).

In the beginning, there was only a darkness which obscured all things. Why did God create light (Gen. 1:3)? To dispel the darkness and to make a space-time world in which life might emerge and dwell (cf. Isa. 45:18–19)? No, says Job—God created light so that the deep character of the primordial reality might come to light. And that reality has the character of deathly darkness *(salmawet).* The psalmist, likening God to a shepherd (Ps. 23), had affirmed that the valley of deathly darkness was but a trial through and even in the midst of which God would be present to lead safely. Job uses related imagery to portray God as leading astray into darkness and formless waste (12:24–25) in order to disclose the depth of existence as—deathly darkness. In the words of Robert Frost's sonnet "Design," God's purpose in this (as is intimated already in 10:13) is seen as a "design of darkness to appall."

In chapter 3 Job had asked why *light* is given to one born to *see* (to experience and to be conscious of) trouble. In this context, light is not simply life, but more specifically life as sentient, appetitive, capable of discrimination and taste, and above all perhaps, as conscious. Earlier ("On Soliloquy and Consciousness"), we suggested that the rise of consciousness goes hand in hand with the rise of the sense or awareness of contrast. Considered in such terms, 12:22 may be seen to bring to a

climax the questions in 3:20 and context. Job charges God with
not being content with *ṣalmawet* as a deep, hidden mystery,
slumbering (unknown perhaps even to itself) under the mantle
of darkness and the unconscious. The sole and ultimate purpose
of creation, culminating in creatural consciousness, seems for
Job to be that in a creatural consciousness such as Job's the
primordial reality behind creation may become manifest and
revealed. The cruelty of the revelation lies in the deeply and
bitterly felt contrast between all the meaning that humankind
invests in the image of "light," all that the biblical tradition had
thought to imply in portraying God's primal creative act as
commanding "let there be light," and on the other hand all that
is implied in the anguished awareness that, deeper than that
light, deathly darkness is primordial and the final word.

In 3:11–23, Job's existential questions have become for him
the form of covenant loyalty (see commentary, "Further Reflections on the Soliloquy as a Whole," on "Job's second linguistic
action"). That these questions, and the ones which have followed
in the dialogue so far, have a covenantal character, is suggested
by the way in which, repeatedly, they have led Job to turn
toward God in complaint and accusation. In 12:13–25 Job seems
no longer to wait upon God for answers, but to formulate his own
answers unilaterally. Therein he appears to be on the point of
breaking covenant. Yet even after chapter 12 he continues to
question God, and twice he takes an oath before God (27:1–6,
chap. 31). These later actions indicate that verses 13–25 do not
rupture the covenant, but in fact are a most extreme form of the
questions he still is asking. In the commentary on Zophar's
response, at 11:12, reference was made to Martin Buber's identification of a prophetic rhetorical device: The prophet pro-
claims certain doom, in hopes of touching the residual power of
human response buried under hardness of heart and unheeding.
In 12:13–25, it would appear that Job's accusation has much the
same character and point: In covenant fidelity he challenges
God to respond. When the divine response finally does come, the
specific terms with which it opens (in 38:2 and following) will be
seen to pick up the thematics of 12:22.

God's View of Tradition's Theodicy (13:1–12)

Job's words now recur to what he has said in the beginning:
Compare 13:1–2 with 12:1–3, and 13:3 with 12:4*b* (which is
here translated "one who calls upon God that he may answer
me"). From a focus upon the general experience of humankind,

Job turns back to his friends and takes up their doctrines, giving another twist to the thematics of "what is hidden and what is revealed." In their defense of God in purely retributive terms, they are in fact engaging in a coverup. Will it be good for them when God searches (*ḥaqar*, as in 11:7, "deep things") them out? Here Job engages in a strange witness to the God whom he has just accused of malevolent creative intent. It is as though the God of 12:13–25, however dark in intent, is at least intent upon disclosure of the true state of things. And such a God, who creates in order to reveal—even though what is revealed is deep darkness—will have no truck with a dishonesty which seeks to cover up the deep truth of things, even if that coverup puts a pretty face on reality. The charge that the friends are worthless physicians (13:4) resembles Jeremiah's charge against priest and prophet who heal the people's wound only superficially, saying " 'Peace, Peace,' when there is no peace" (Jer. 6:14; 8:11).

How strange a witness! It is as though Job and God are deeply at one in Job's mind, concerning the unflinching commitment to truth however unpalatable that truth may be. Does Job realize the implication of his words here? Surely if God were *merely* intent on deathly darkness, such a God would have no concern for truth, and indeed would delight in the endless confusion of humankind concerning what is true. Such a God would not call either Job or his friends to account for their mistaken views. In chapters 9—10, Job had sought common ground with God on concerns of morality and creative purpose, and he had failed to find it. Now, briefly, he affirms such a ground—if not at the point of morality and creative purpose, then at least at the point of the concern for truth. In such a strange way, Job witnesses to the covenant still alive between him and God; and he levels a devastating critique against religion and its custodians in their attempts to absolve God of implication in the pain and darkness of the world.

Job's Strange Hope for Salvation (13:13–19)

In verse 11, Job holds up before the friends the prospect of the dread majesty of God, before which their "proverbs of ashes" and "defenses of clay" will not avail. We may note here a telling use of Eliphaz's imagery in 4:19–21. There, Eliphaz had spoken of human existence as clay and dust, devoid of wisdom. These terms are picked up in 13:11, to dismiss the friends' counsel as so much human unwisdom. What is offered, on the one hand, as a coverup (or theodicy) of God, is now seen also to be a cover and a defense for frail, finite human "ashes and clay." Job scornfully forsakes all such attempts to shelter from the truth. He will speak the truth even if it costs him his life (vv. 13–14). To be sure, he has no hope, since God is bent on slaying him; nevertheless he will argue his ways to God's face. The word *'okiaḥ* is not happily translated by "defend" in verse 15*b*. It is the verbal form of the word which in 9:33, as a noun, is translated "umpire." There Job had longed for an umpire, a referee or adjudicator, to equalize the discrepancy between the dread power of God and fearful Job (9:34). By now Job is willing to argue his own case. Again Job gives strange witness to the God whom he experiences as his enemy. For inexplicably he discovers within himself a conviction or a suspicion that such a willingness to appear nakedly before God might give salvation, in a world devoid of any hope of salvation. Does "salvation" in verse 16 refer to some outcome? Or does it refer to the inner integrity which he will enjoy, in contrast to the inauthentic situation of his whitewashing friends? The answer is not clear. Nevertheless the reader once again notes an alliance with the hidden God. Deep is answering to deep; and the answer which is beginning to sound in Job's depths signals the resolution of the question asked in 1:9: Will Job fear God *(ḥinnam)*—freely and for nothing?

The Courage of Absolute Vulnerability (13:20–14:6)

In verse 17 Job still addresses his friends, calling on them to watch as he proceeds to take his case to God. His case has been laid out (v. 18), and he now calls on God, "Who is he that contends with me? For now I will be silent and die." Now he is ready to hear God's answer and to die at God's hands (see v. 15*a*).

The courage which Job had manifested in verses 13–16 now shows itself in his direct address to God. It is not that he is devoid of fear; for he is still filled with terrifying dread (v. 21). Moreover, having characterized his friends as ashes and clay (13:12), he portrays himself as a driven leaf and dry chaff (13:25), a rotten thing and a moth-eaten garment (13:28), a withering flower and a fleeting shadow (14:2). Yet there is a difference between him and his friends. Their need to cover up bespeaks a fear which cannot face what it fears; his direct address to God,

107

in the face of his dread and his overwhelming awareness of his own finitude, bespeaks a courage which arises from the core of his vulnerability. Stripped of all vestiges of the hedge and devoid of any hope, he fears God freely.

Shall One Who Dies Live Again? (14:7–22)

A short while ago Job said "I have no hope" (13:15), and went on then to dwell on the ephemeral character (14:1–2) and the temporal limits (14:5) of human life. In view of those limits he now returns to the theme of hope and explores it in a sustained exercise of imagination. What are the phenomena which might give grounds for hope?

His imagination fixes first upon the tree (14:7–9). Picking up the imagery which Bildad had offered in 8:18–19 (see translation above, and commentary), he finds momentary encouragement in the way a tree, cut down, will sprout again. The latter verb, "sprout," translates Hebrew *yaḥlip* which will recur in noun form in a few verses (and which, in a suggestively analogous context, occurs in Isa. 40:31 with the meaning "renew"). Meanwhile we note in verse 8 the use of the word "dust" (RSV "ground"), which signals the close association Job feels between such a tree and himself as destined to dust (7:21; 10:9). And we note how Job describes the turning point for the dead tree: At the scent of water it will bud and put forth branches.

The suggestiveness of the tree, however, wanes as Job attempts to apply it to human experience (v. 10): Where is the human analogue to the newly budded tree? His imagination searches for such a datum and finds it nowhere in experience. In his despair he rejects the tree for another natural phenomenon, water. Lakes and rivers vanish and do not reappear; and so it is with humankind. The terms in which Job describes human destiny should be noted carefully: Three times he characterizes death as a sleep from which one does not arise, awake, nor from which one is aroused *('ur)*. This threefold description elaborates the brief "Where is he?" of verse 10. Within the cosmos as presently ordered ("till the heavens are no more"), nature is cruelly ambiguous: Some of its processes (like the tree) strike the analogical imagination with solicitations of hope; some of its processes offer analogies which only reinforce despair. Nature is no sure help.

The hope which has been aroused in Job by the tree will not yet die and like the tree sends out its shoots in search of

108

"water" by which to sustain and revive itself. If nature (including human experience) will offer no sure evidence, his imagination will search in another direction, toward a God whose ways may, after all, not yet be fully manifest in the phenomena of nature. In a manner familiar to artists and path-breaking scientists, Job turns his back on what is known and explores a novel possibility purely in its own terms, purely in terms of its hypothetical inner logic, before asking after its plausibility: "If a man die, shall he live again?" (v. 14). Job then offers an imaginative model of the conditions which might be supposed to characterize a post-mortem hope: Sheol would be a place of hiding and concealment, until God's wrath was over (v. 13); then, at an appointed time (cf. Hab. 2:3 with its reference to "appointed time"), God would remember Job—as God had remembered Rachel in her barrenness (Gen. 30:22) and Israel in its oppression (Exod. 2:24). If such were to be the case, time spent in Sheol would take on the character, not of hopeless finality, but of a period of hard service (*saba*'; cf. 7:1 and Isa. 40:2n) during which Job would wait. The latter verb "wait" is the same as the verb translated "hope" in 13:15 and is synonymous with the noun in 14:7. (Cf. also 6:11–13, where in contrast to 14:13–17 Job had despaired of any end worth waiting for and therefore had despaired of any strength to wait or be patient.) God's remembrance of Job would effect Job's "release" or, more precisely, his "renewal"—the noun *halipa* in verse 14c is from the same root as the verb translated "sprout again" in verse 7b. This rhetorical connection between verses 7 and 14 suggests a further association between the reference to the "scent of water" in verse 9 and verse 15 "thou wouldest call, and I would answer thee." In, for example, Hosea 2:21–22; 6:3; 14:5–7 and in Isaiah 45:8; 55:10–11, God's redemptive and world-renewing word is likened to rain which waters and revives the dry ground. So here, Job, creature of dust, after he has returned to dust, will answer when God calls; and his answer and his renewal would be one and the same thing. All this, however, would turn on whether the divine artisan still longed for the work of the divine hands (14:15b; cf. 10:3–13). This would also suppose a God who so cared for humankind that, far from being a "watcher of men" to take account of human sins (7:20; also 7:12), like an understanding parent would take note of every step of the human child, but quietly overlook those steps in which the child went astray. Thus in verse 17 we see yet one more varia-

109

tion of the continuing theme of the revealed and the hidden.

But, Job concludes, such a vision does not correspond to how things really are. The imaginative model disintegrates at the point at which one of its elements confronts present experience. For everything in Job's present awareness goes to suggest that God will *not* be forgiving, that God is watching over his steps to attack and to destroy him. Indeed, God's actual treatment of him (in contrast to what Job imagines in vv. 16–17) calls to mind another analogy from nature: the relentless erosion of rock by water (vv. 18–22). The torrents wash away the soil (or dust—*'apar*) of the earth (v. 19*b*), and God destroys the hope of mortal *('enoš)* humankind. In verses 7–9 it was the scent of water which gave hope to the tree and renewal; in verses 13–15 it was the sound of God's voice which would enable hoping and waiting for renewal; in verse 19 God destroys human hope the way water washes away dust; and in this latter instance the "change" that is effected is not a renewal but a passing and a being sent away (v. 20). The last couplet in this chapter poignantly draws together the two dimensions of Job which were mentioned in 2:4–6 and repeatedly thereafter: his flesh (RSV "body") and his soul (RSV "himself"): "His own flesh gives him pain, / and his soul mourns over him." Job's body, on its way back to the dry dust of death, pains him; and his soul, his appetitive *nepeš* which lives by a "water" appropriate to it, also withers in mourning. Thus the imagery of hope with which he had begun in 14:7–9 seems also to have withered in his imagination.

Further Reflection on the Imaginative Outreach in 14:14–17

It is noteworthy that Job's brief but incandescent vision of a positive outcome to his sufferings arises in the very context of his darkest suspicions concerning the depth and the ultimate significance of those sufferings. It is noteworthy also that, under such conditions, the vision reaches clearly beyond classical Israelite convictions concerning a purely historical or "this-worldly" restoration of the community or the individual, to possibilities which may be described as proto-apocalyptic in scope and character. As we have noted in our Introduction, F. M. Cross suggests that "Job belongs in the main line of the evolution of Israel's religion." He goes on to write,

110

> It is intriguing that Job's importance was not forgotten in apocalyptic circles. At Qumrân it alone outside of the Pen-

tateuch survived in the Paleo-Hebrew script, and there is evidence that it was always so distinguished and received de facto-canonization as early as the Pentateuch, in advance of the prophetic canon (p. 345).

If we reflect on the themes and the images of chapters 12—14 in light of Cross's comments, we may discern a number of nascent elements of what will become characteristic features in later apocalypticism. Among such elements are the following:

(1) There is in these chapters (as throughout Job) a stubborn concern with the *cosmic* scope and significance of human suffering and divine action.

(2) This cosmic, one may say spatial (12:7–8), concern is matched by a *temporal* sense, in which existence is divided into what has gone before as suffering and what will follow after as redemption (14:13; cf. 24:1, as well as 8:7 with its anticipatory use of the terms "former" and "latter").

(3) The point of temporal division is established as a divinely *appointed decree* (14:13; cf. Dan. 2:21), and one assumes toward this set time an attitude and a posture of patient waiting under conditions of hard service (14:14; cf. Hab. 2:2–4; 3:17–19; Isa. 40:31).

(4) The intervening time is lived out under the conditions of the current cosmic order, conditions so *stringent* as to offer no hope, in themselves, of anything beyond (14:12, "till the heavens are no more"), yet conditions which, viewed from the perspective of hope, have the character of a divine wrath from which the faithful are sheltered (14:13).

(5) The new age is inaugurated in a fashion which may include individual resurrection.

(6) This resurrection is reminiscent of original cosmic creation, insofar as it arises as a divine longing for the work of the divine hands; moreover, it is like the original creation in that it arises through the initiative of divine speech followed by human response (14:15).

In none of these elements, of course, are the apocalyptic themes and images present in any full-blown way. It is more a matter of a nascent tendency. In several respects, however, Job 14:14 contains elements in close connection to Second Isaiah. Some of these elements have already been noted in passing. They may be summarized as follows:

(1) Job 14:13 shares with Isaiah 40:2 the unusual use of *ṣaba'* to mean "time of hard service" under the mysterious rule of

God. (The other such uses are Job 7:1 and, significantly, Dan. 10:1).

(2) This time of hard service will come to an end as an effective and final resolution of the problem of human sin (Job 14:16; Isa. 40:2).

(3) Such an end is to be waited for patiently; and the outcome is such a change (*ḥalipa*, Job 14:14) as already to renew (*ḥalap*) the strength of those who so wait (Isa. 40:31).

(4) Outside of such hope, despair is imaged as driven leaf and dry chaff and as withered flower (Job 13:25; 14:2; Isa. 40: 6–7); inside of such hope, vegetative imagery serves as the vehicle for the envisagement of new life (Job 14:7–9; Isa. 40—55 in many places).

(5) Meanwhile the Servant of Yahweh (for so Job is termed in both the prologue and the epilogue) has no light, but walks in darkness (the dialogues as a whole; and in this context 12:25*a*, with which cf. Isa. 50:10).

(6) All of this occurs under the aegis of God whose mysterious working is seen not only in the forming of light and the making of *weal*, (*šalom*) but also in the creating of darkness and woe (Isa. 45:7, with which cf. Job 12:22).

The preceding observations have been offered in an attempt to place Job 14:14–17 and its immediate context within the wider context of the history of Israel's religion, following the lead indicated in the remarks of F. M. Cross quoted above. Even if these observations are plausible, however, as they stand they remain on the level of historical analysis. One may go further to venture a theological interpretation, in response to this question: What is the ontological and theological status and significance of imaginative outreach as instanced in Job 14:14–17? Since Freud one common view has it that such outreach represents the fatal triumph of human wishing over the willingness to face reality. Yet such outreach may not be merely an escapist reaction to the intolerable pressures of this-worldly experience. Granted that such conditions threaten human experience with meaninglessness, Job is not willing to flee into cheap or flimsy meanings at the expense of existential honesty (13:1–12). Yet out of the core of his unflinching honesty and naked vulnerability (13:13—14:6) comes the brief vision of 14:14–17. May it not come as an imaginative budding of this blasted human tree, in response to a hidden call and a hidden divine presence (14:15)? This much is clear: From this speech on, Job argues with ever-

112

renewing strength; and though his brief vision is immediately negated in 14:18–25, yet it is difficult to resist the suspicion that the energy derived from its brief presence in his imagination continues to work hiddenly in him as one source of that strength. For we shall see the vision of 14:14–17 flare up again several chapters later.

PART THREE

Dialogue: Second Cycle

JOB 15—21

Job 15
Eliphaz's Second Response to Job Challenging His Implied Standpoint

Eliphaz initiates the second round of the dialogues with words which largely reiterate what he said in his first response, but less sympathetically. Charging Job with subversion of religion, he goes on to accuse Job of preposterous claims implicit in the latter's words in chapters 12—14. These claims amount to saying that Job has listened in on the secret counsels of God and was present at creation. Eliphaz concludes with a vigorous portrayal of the fate of the wicked.

* * *

Eliphaz, having heard all of the ensuing exchange against the background of his own first words (chapters 4—5), now presses his views again, in part reiterating them with increased force and in part drawing on his friends' words for support. We may outline this response to Job as follows:

> Eliphaz's View of Job's "Wise" Words (15:2–6)
>
> A Challenge to Job's Standpoint (15:7–10)
>
> Reassertion of Eliphaz's Revelatory Word (15:11–16)
>
> The Fate of the Wicked (15:17–35)

Eliphaz's View of Job's "Wise" Words (15:2–6)

Job has claimed a wisdom which counters and overturns the wisdom of his friends. Eliphaz characterizes Job's speech as so much hot air (vv. 2–3) and as the utterance of a sinful person (vv. 5–6). Cruelly he takes up Job's words of 9:20a and twists them into a fourfold refrain (mouth:tongue:mouth:lips). In the midst of this elaborate characterization, he charges Job with subvert-

115

ing religion (v. 4). Here he responds defensively to Job's charge in 13:4–12 that the friends' religion is a cover-up for God and for humankind in face of the terrible truth of existence. In his view, such a vision as Job has set forth in chapter 12 will bring an end to piety and religious utterance directed to the divine. (The word which RSV translates as "meditation" in v. 4*b* is *śiaḥ*, which at 12:8 we have translated and commented on as "complaint.") What Eliphaz fails to appreciate is that the very Job who set forth the stark vision of chapter 12 has gone on, in the same breath, to demonstrate his piety in his own desperate complaint to God in 13:20—14:22, a complaint the very extremity of which is integrally related to the exalted if brief vision of 14:14–17.

A Challenge to Job's Standpoint (15:7–10)

In 12:22 Job has claimed to be privy, not merely to a wisdom manifest in creation, but to secrets which lie prior to creation and which constitute the mystery of God's abysmal purpose. Echoing (as we shall see) the opening lines of the apostrophe to wisdom in Proverbs 8:22–31, he challenges the implicit claim that Job stood with God prior to creation—he who was born a mere man (*'adam*). The rhetorical assurance of verse 7 seems thoroughly warranted; but the phraseology of verse 8 signals to the reader that what Eliphaz is denying is not so quickly to be ruled out. For "listening in the council of God" is a claim common to a number of the prophets (e.g., I Kings 22:19–23; Jer. 23:18, 21–22; Isa. 40:1–8), and prophets like Hosea and Isaiah contrasted their prophetic message as true wisdom against the so-called wisdom of others. Against Job's claim to such privy wisdom Eliphaz counters the friends' more plausible if (or because) more modest creatural claim to a wisdom based on long-standing tradition (vv. 9–10, and vv. 17–19). In verses 7–10 one is reminded of those several instances recounted in the prophetic books where priest, prophet or other member of the establishment confronts and rebukes a prophet's "pretensions" in speaking against communal consensus.

Reassertion of Eliphaz's Revelatory Word (15:11–16)

116

In his first response, Eliphaz had moved from an opening statement of traditional wisdom (4:7–11) to the report of a revelatory word (4:12—5:7) and then back to a further statement of traditional lore (5:8–27). This pattern is repeated in the present chapter, as the two references to traditional wisdom (vv. 9–10,

17–19) are interrupted by a passage which reasserts the content and the form of 4:17–19. (The three-stage argument in 15:14–16 exactly reproduces the argument in 4:17–19 with slight shifts in nuance.) In the fact that Eliphaz's argument employs the same pattern in the second as in the first response, we have a formal indication that the dialogue is bogging down in increasingly intransigent positions.

Bildad had allowed for the likelihood that Job is "pure" (8:6, *zak;* on the verse, see commentary), to which Job had retorted that even if he were purified by cleansing (the verb *zakak*) his hands in lye, God would plunge him in filth (9:30–31). Now Eliphaz asserts the inherent impossibility that mere mortal (*'enoš*) should be "clean" (the related verb *zaka*), when even the holy ones in heaven are not clean. Again, Eliphaz introduces the note of divine trust (v. 15*a*), to reiterate that God can trust no one. Thereby he inadvertently recalls the reader to the fact that the trial launched in the prologue comes as an act of trust in Job on Yahweh's part.

In another respect verses 14–16 resume a theme introduced since chapters 4—5. For 4:17 had opened with the question, "Can mortal be righteous before God?" Job had picked up the word "mortal" and the question form in 7:17, but had recast the question in terms of Psalm 8: "What is mortal . . .?" Eliphaz now uses Job's recast form, "What is mortal . . .?" The references to "his holy ones" and "the heavens" in verse 15 are reminiscent in part of the reference to "thy heavens" in Psalm 8:3. (As we shall see, when Bildad in 25:4–6 re-uses Eliphaz's twice-repeated argument, Bildad's formulation even more strikingly echoes that psalm.) By this means, the issue of the status of humankind in the universe and before God is kept before the reader. For Eliphaz, the issue is resolved in an emphasis on human iniquity, more abrupt and intense this time than in 4:19—5:7.

One further item in this passage remains for comment. The "word" of 15:11 is not simply the friends' doctrine generally; it is, specifically, the "word" referred to in 4:12. This is indicated not only by the common content and form of 15:14–16 and 4:17–19, but by the synonymity of 4:12*a* and 15:11*b*. The first line (4:12) reads, "Now a word was brought to me stealthily," effectively characterizing the covert and esoteric mode of reception of the revelation. In 15:11*b* the word translated "deals gently" (RSV) should be taken to describe how the word has come to Eliphaz: covertly and as a whisper ("the covert word that is with you"). Given the content of this word—that mortals are frail, ignorant, and sinful, it is striking that Eliphaz should now (v. 11a) characterize such a word as "the *consolations (tanḥumot)* of God." We have seen that Job in chapter 14 used a number of terms which crop up again in Isaiah 40. Here again, Eliphaz's characterization of his revelatory word as "consolations" draws on the same root *(nḥm)* as opens the revelatory scene in Isaiah 40:1: "Comfort, comfort my people" (with the verb *nḥm*). On Eliphaz's behalf, it may be noted that in certain contexts the reminder of one's frailty, ignorance, and sinfulness may come as a distinct means of comfort in the form of acceptance of the way things are. It is just that in the present instance such comfort is out of Job's context.

The Fate of the Wicked (15:17–35)

In his first response Eliphaz had followed the sombre "consolations" of 4:12—5:7 with an encouraging appeal to Job to commit himself to a God who would restore him (5:8–27), an appeal which only in passing alluded to God's dealings with the wicked (5:13–14). This time, he follows his reminder of God's revelatory word by dwelling exclusively on the fate of the wicked. Ignorant as he is of the imagery of the stretching forth of the hand in 1:11–12 and 2:3b–6, Eliphaz diagnoses Job's plight as the result of his having stretched forth his hand against God (15:25a). He elaborates the military image in verse 26 in a way that triggers Job's counter charge with the same imagery in 16:7–17. Then Eliphaz portrays the result of such rebellion against the divine (in vv. 28–35, translating v. 28 "he will live in desolate cities . . . ," a common prophetic image for divine judgment).

In part Eliphaz concludes his portrayal of the fate of the wicked by elaborating Bildad's picture of the doomed plant, in 15:29–34 (cf. 8:11–15). In part he recurs to one of his images in 4:8. In the latter passage the imagery of reproduction (plow, sow, reap) was offered as a reassurance from nature of the trustworthiness of the cause-effect character of the moral order. In 15:35 the same point, by means of the closely related imagery of human reproduction (conceive, prepare, bring forth), is directed at Job as a warning.

Further Reflection on Religion and Its Subversions

We have commented on Eliphaz's charge that Job's talk subverts religion as "meditative address to god;" and we observed that Job's continuing address to God, in which *śiaḥ* as meditation takes on the character of *śiaḥ* as complaint, gives the lie to that charge. The matter, however, is not quite so simple. The fact is that Job's words both disavow and confirm what Eliphaz accuses him of doing; they do this by deconstructing religion at one level to reestablish it at another. In discounting the words of his friends while claiming to have penetrated to the real truth of things (e.g., at 12:22), Job indeed limits wisdom to himself (15:8). Thereby he subverts the fear of God as conventionally understood and practiced.

One clue to the presuppositions underlying Eliphaz's thinking is given us in his word "teaches" in verse 5. The verb *'allep*, "to teach," occurs only in Job 15:5; 33:33; and 35:11 (all, we may note, on the mouths of those who attempt, misguidedly, to help Job.) The cognate adjective *'allup* means "tame, docile, friendly," and the cognate noun (occurring 7 times in the O.T., including Ps. 8:8) is *'elep*, "cattle." For Eliphaz, to teach is to tame and render docile; and one basic function of religion is to tame the wild and wayward spirit to fruitful and profitable (15:3) modes of life. That is why moral stupidity can be compared to the behavior and spirit of a wild ass (11:12), a creature in some contrast to the tame cattle. Eliphaz accuses Job of being "tamed" by sin, of conforming to the teachings of sin (cf. Jer. 13:23: "you . . . who are accustomed [literally, 'taught' or 'schooled'] to do evil"). As 39:5–18 shows us through its celebration of wild animal existence, Job is indeed being taught, not by his iniquity, but by that which seeks something other than a taming unto docility. Job is being taught a freedom for creativity.

One may go so far as to suggest that it is Job's heavensent vocation to subvert conventional religion as a sufficient and final basis for human self-understanding in the world and before God, a religion which has become content to "pay / Meet adoration to [its] household gods" (Tennyson, "Ulysses"). Such subversion, however, is to open the way for a piety and a covenanted address to God freshly conceived.

Further Reflection on the Standpoint of True Wisdom

In 15:7–10 Eliphaz has challenged Job with claiming too much for himself. It is as though he is not a mere human caught in the sequence of time (much younger even than the elders from whom human wisdom comes as tradition), let alone that first creative moment before the hills were brought forth. Does

Job think he was in the council of God, and present at creation?

We have already pointed to the prophetic tradition, with its several references to prophets privy to the divine council, as an implicit subversion of Eliphaz's attempted denigration of Job. Two other passages are particularly relevant to our appreciation of the issues raised in 15:7–10 and in Job generally. They are Proverbs 8:22–31 and Isaiah 40 and 53.

Proverbs 8:22–31 is echoed in Job 15:7–8 in a number of ways. Before we identify and interpret these echoes, a brief consideration of the passage in Proverbs is in order. Wisdom uses birth imagery to portray her origins as the beginning and the means of Yahweh's creative rule in and over the cosmos. (RSV "created me" in v. 22a, "I was set up" in v. 23a, and "I was brought forth" in v. 24a all should be understood in birth terms and may be translated "begot me," "I emanated," and "I came to birth.") Specifically, this wisdom was "brought forth before the hills." This cooperative wisdom worked beside Yahweh as a master-artisan, working with delight and playful joy. That play-in-work comes to a climax (as it does in Gen. 1:26–31) in the statement that creative wisdom delighted in, or better *with,* the children of earth. If Proverbs 8:31 may be taken as another way of sounding the theme of humankind in the divine image, then we may envisage human vocation as follows: The call of wisdom to humanity in Proverbs is a call to conform oneself to the divine creative activity which, present before the hills were brought forth, continues to go on through the continuing works and play of wisdom, including the wisdom displayed in those who respond to wisdom's play. This implies that human self-understanding is incomplete when it is solely creatural self-understanding and that it becomes complete only when the creature becomes a co-creating creature. A further implication is that in so responding to the play of that wisdom which was at work already before the hills were brought forth, in some sense the responding creature is not solely fixed in time somewhere after the sixth day, let alone merely after a long chain of human tradition. In some sense those who enter into the play of creative wisdom find themselves re-positioned with her prior to the creative process, in the pre-creation dark of Genesis 1:2. Or perhaps (with Job's present situation in mind) we may say that those who find themselves in the dark-

120

ness of unmerited suffering, in that fact may find themselves re-positioned for creativity.

Isaiah 40 and 53. In the commentary on chapter 14 we identified a number of terms and motifs common to that chapter and to Deutero-Isaiah, in part to Isaiah 40. That Isaiah 40 and 53 together offer an appropriate hermeneutical point of reference for 15:7–8 is suggested by the following considerations: In Isaiah 40:12–14 Yahweh asserts the solitariness of God in the creation of the cosmos—a solitariness acting creatively in justice *(mišpaṭ)*, knowledge *(da'at)*, and understanding. Yet in this prophetic tradition above all others, the language of cosmic creation is used also in speaking of Yahweh's redemption of Israel. And in 40:1–11 the prophet of this message of redemption is portrayed as privy to the proceedings (or at least to the results of the proceedings) of the divine council. Moreover, whereas the cosmos was created solely by Yahweh acting with justice and knowledge, the servant is shown to participate in the work of redemption, in terms which characterize that redemptive work as of a piece with creation. For the servant who has the task of bringing forth redemptive justice (42:1, 3, 4, *mišpaṭ*) carries that task through by a knowledge (53:11, *da'at*) which is the praxis of his sufferings and thereby his participation in the work and play of redemptive wisdom.

In this interpretation, both of the above passages imply a human status and activity commensurate with human participation in the divine creative/redemptive activity. Eliphaz's questions in 15:7–10 may be taken as challenging Job's claim to a special kind of "gnosis" or hidden wisdom. If Job makes a claim to gnosis, it is unlike the Gnosticism which attempts to rule the world or escape from it through lofty spiritual illumination. The gnosis of Job, like the "knowledge" of the servant in Isaiah 53:11, arises through participation in the travail of the world, and only therein and thereby as a participation in the creative/redemptive activity of God. To be in such a place is, paradoxically, to exist in the world as a creature and yet to respond to the play of God's wisdom in a manner which makes one's standpoint in the world analogous to that of wisdom "at the first," in the pre-creation dark. Once again, then, a rhetorical question from one of the friends is seen to serve other meanings than those intended by the speaker. Those meanings will be further advanced in chapters 38—41.

Job 16—17
Job Responds to Eliphaz II:
On Comfort, Witness, and the Energy of Hope

Job charges that, instead of comforting him, the friends are joining their words in conspiracy against him. He re-presents his situation to them, in hope that they may become true witnesses to the fact that it is not he who assaults God, but God who is assaulting him. Then, despairing of them and of God, he reaches out blindly and nakedly in an imaginative affirmation of the existence of a true witness, somewhere, to his situation. As if to appeal to another kind of witness on his own behalf, a witness internal to himself, he presents himself as, on the one hand, wasting and waning physically, yet on the other hand growing in inner energy and staying power. Stripped of his past and of his future, he yet discovers within himself hopes and desires in the light of which he no longer wishes to die. Nor will he affirm death and the grave as the progenitor of his future.

* * *

Since chapter 3, each of Job's responses has begun with words directed to the friends and has ended with words directed to God (6:7–21; 10:2–22; 13:20—14:22). In this response to Eliphaz's second speech he directs only a brief word to God, in the midst of words to and concerning the friends, and before he concludes with what may be a soliloquy (17:11–16).

Comfort Expected and Not Given (16:2–6)

Job's opening words echo a number of themes in the past part of the prologue, 2:11–13. There the three friends had made an appointment to come together and to condole (*nud,* shake the head) and to comfort him. Job accuses them (v. 4) of joining words together (in a conspiracy) against him and of shaking their heads against him in accusation and enmity (cf. Ps. 22:7). Were the roles reversed, he asserts, he would strengthen them (cf. 4:3–4) and the solace (*nid,* condolence) of his lips would assuage. Whereas in such circumstances his words might assuage their pain, in the present instance his speaking does not

122

assuage his own. (V. 6*a ke'eb* echoes the same word which RSV translates "suffering" at the end of 2:13.) In fact, whether he speaks or whether he remains silent, Job's suffering remains constant.

What is the significance of Job's remark in 16:6? Is it merely a wry passing observation? Or are we hereby shown a Job who, no longer tied to the past by a debt of gratitude or to the future by a debt of hope, is free in the present? In 13:13-19 Job prepared to speak as one who had nothing to gain or to lose by speaking; that is the case again in 16:6. This means that we are listening to one who acts *hinnam*—freely (see 1:9 and commentary). Where there is nothing to gain either way, what is the significance of speaking rather than keeping silence? Is it that the silence would break off the relationship, while the speaking keeps Job turned outward, to the friends and to God?

Appeal to the Friends to Witness His Case (16:7-17)

Not only should they have comforted him, but the friends should have performed another communal task: They should have served as witnesses to the crime against him and sought redress on his behalf. (The theme of witness is introduced in v. 8 and is resumed in 16.18-22.) In 15:25-27 Eliphaz had portrayed the wicked under the figure of one mounting a military assault on God. Job picks up this figure and elaborates it (16: 7-17), but reverses it to portray God in such an assault on him. Job's strategy here is noteworthy. In the friends' capacity as a witness to Job's experience, the image under which they have come to *perceive* Job is the image of military assault. In 16:7-17 he attempts to re-present the experience before their eyes, as he is undergoing it, in the hope that this time they will become witnesses to the experience for *what it really is.* By choosing Eliphaz's image, Job stays as close as possible to Eliphaz's perceptual experience. By expanding the details of the imagery and by conforming it to the themes and the tones of the lament of the innocent (cf. e.g., 16:10 with Ps. 22:7, 13; 16:13 with Ps. 22:14), Job seeks to draw the friends into the experience in such a way that they will perceive the aggression to be in the other direction. In chapter 19 Job will continue this theme of the communal witness, under the figure of the *go'el,* the kin redeemer. Meanwhile, his present appeal to them gains no result, as he concludes that "thou hast closed their minds to under-

123

standing" (17:4). (This last word translates *śekel,* from a root the basic meaning of which seems to be "to look at, give attention to, ponder.") He turns from them in another act of imaginative outreach.

A True Witness Imaginatively Found (16:18—17:5)

"O earth, cover not my blood, and let my cry find no resting place." The very fact of Job's violent death will surely continue to cry out like the blood of Abel—until it is covered over and hidden from view and forgotten. The tone of this outcry gives voice to the horror that engulfs the soul when the truth of one's life becomes confined within its own privacy, closed off from public view by misrepresentation and falsehood. Since Freud, the modern age has become adept at a hermeneutics of suspicion and self-suspicion—as though the deepest dynamic of the soul were one of deception. Is there, however, a deeper need and desire of the soul than that of deception, a need for truth? Does this need for truth in part take the form of a need to be known (at whatever cost) for what one is (Psalm 139)? Is not the denial and frustration of this need a form of hell—that enforced isolation from which there is no escape except perhaps by deliverance? Already in 13:13–18 Job has voiced such a need for the truth of his life to be known; now he reiterates the need in a terrible cry.

To know that one is known in congruence with one's self-knowledge, and to know that one knows oneself in congruence with how one is known—these are complementary aspects of what is meant by a good conscience. Job's appeal to the friends to become true witnesses is his appeal for their confirmation of his conscience. Failing to find this confirmation from them, he turns to the earth—to the ongoing local scene which, by keeping his innocent blood in view, will do after he is gone (16:22) what his words have attempted to do in 16:7–17.

Yet, earth does cover blood by the natural processes of the passage of time and the passing of witnesses who care, or by the opaqueness of earth's witnesses (17:4). In the absence of any earthly witnesses, now or in the future, Job turns elsewhere in hope. Perhaps in heaven he may find a witness (v. 19). Meanwhile, he returns to his present situation: He is scorned by his friends *(rea');* his eye pours out tears to God, that God would maintain the right of a man against the deity and that of a man with his neighbor *(rea')* (vv. 20–21). In these four lines, Job identifies his problem as twofold: *vis-à-vis* God, and *vis-à-vis* his friends; and though in the face of his friends' scorn he cries out to God, he is not heard. For God does not "maintain his right" (the verb so translated is *yokiaḥ*, and is cognate with the noun *mokiaḥ*, translated "umpire" in 9:33).

Who, then, is the heavenly witness to which Job appeals in verse 19? Such a question is misguided, and specific answers blunt the significance of Job's affirmation. The point is precisely that, in the face of a universe whose earthly and heavenly figures—friends and God—are all against him, Job imaginatively reaches out into the dark and desperately affirms the reality of a witness whose identity is completely unknown to him. It is here as it is in Esther 4:14, that desperate affirmation in the midst of a tale which does not once mention God: Faith manifests itself not in allegiance to a figure known to be there, but in a naked and blind affirmation of what is unknown, yet which must be there if one's own truth ultimately matters.

Verse one of chapter 17 may signal a reaction of exhaustion from the effort of the imaginative outreach of the preceding verses (cf. 19:27c and commentary there). Or it may be that this verse should be taken as a continuation of the preceding lines, to read, "For when a few years have come / I shall go the way whence I shall not return, / my spirit broken, my days extinct, / the grave ready for me." From this prospect Job then turns back to his friends who, rather than bearing him true witness, mock him. Then (v. 3) he returns to address God in the spirit of 16:19–21. The language of 17:3 is striking in its employment of terms which are found together elsewhere only in three proverbs. In Proverbs 11:15; 17:18; 22:26, the verbs "pledge" and "give surety" occur in cautionary sayings to warn against the entanglement of rash pledges. Apparently the wise and prudent person will secure oneself against loss by avoiding such entanglements, whereas those who enter into such agreements will smart for it (Prov. 11:15). Job's use of this language in 17:3 indicates his suspicion that the friends are withholding true witness from him out of prudence: They fear that to implicate themselves on Job's side will place them in jeopardy. So he appeals to God to become implicated on his behalf. This will mean, surely, that God will not let the friends triumph against him (v. 4). The financial figure of verse 3 is then extended to verse 5: Not only have the friends refused to risk themselves in surety for him; they are informing against him in hopes of gain

125

at his expense. If God will become surety for him, however, their plans will be turned back on their own head (v. 5*b*). Structurally, then, we see that the friends act (v. 5*a*) out of the blindness imposed on them by God (v. 4*a*); the result of their actions (v. 5*b*) comes likewise from God (v. 4*b*).

The Strange Presence of the Energy of Hope (17:6–16)

Now Job turns to consider his own condition again. His life force has waned (v. 7*a; cf.* Gen. 27:1; Deut. 34:7), and his body has wasted away (v. 7*b*). Those who behold his condition make him a byword of godlessness (vv. 6, 8). In view of what Job has said about such people in verses 4–5, we must suppose his description of them as "upright" and "innocent" (v. 8) to be heavily ironic. For in the next breath he reappropriates such categories for himself, as he utters an affirmation which reverses the tenor of verse 7. If his friends look upon him as waning in his life force and wasting away, they had better look again. Not only does he hold to his way, but he actually increases in strength. This marks an important change in Job. In 6:11–13 he had confessed to a complete loss of existential energy and patience, as the result of the loss of any sense of an end to hope for. In 16:5 he expressed his disappointment at not receiving strength from the words of his friends. Where now does his increasing strength come from, a strength which enables him to challenge his friends with renewed vigor (17:10)?

The strength does not come as a resource from his past life, for his days are past (v. 11*a*). Nor does it come from any future which he had formerly projected for himself (v. 11*a*). It comes, rather, from a strange place, a "no-place," the utopia which he has briefly explored from time to time in the outreach of his imagination. Such is the implication when we repunctuate the text with a period at the end of verse 11*a*, and read the next lines as follows: "The desires of my heart / make night into day: / "Light is near (they say) in the face of darkness." At a time when the very light of God is as darkness (10:22*b*), or when God's light serves only to disclose the deep mystery as deep darkness (12:22), a new light has begun to shine within the dark night of his soul, a light which shines in the form of the desires of his heart. This light now leads Job to reassess his earlier expressions of desire and hope for death (e.g., 3:21; 6: 8–9; 7:16; 10:18–22). In the light of this strange spark of energy he disavows his earlier longing.

To continue to long for death (vv. 13–14) would be to be-

126

tray the hope that still lives, or lives anew, in him (v. 15). The imagery of verses 13–14 is most interesting. Death and its environ are portrayed in the images of home, couch, and parents. It is as though the pit and the worm, through what they do to the one dead and buried, become the progenitors of that one's nothingness. To die and to become nothing is to be an offspring of pit and worm. The images here for father and mother are obviously sexually suggestive, though with an eye to, for example, Isaiah 51:1–2, oddly reversed. Job will not affirm pit and worm as his parents. To do so would be to deny that hope (v. 15) which somehow, obscurely, lodges and stirs within him as a seed for new life.

It is not that this hope takes on any distinct or clear content. Might it portend his deliverance from an imminent death? Or will this hope go down to Sheol with him, there to wait with him until the set time when God will call (14:13–16)? At this point the question has no such answers. More importantly, the question functions in Job as an existential energy which testifies to the secret strength of the covenant between him and God. The operation of this energy in Job, as of a light in darkness, is a manifestation of the efficacy of his imaginative perceptions, and thereby is one sort of claim for their truth. (The analysis of 17:11–16 offered here rests on the study of Jay Southwick, *Encounter* 45.)

Job 18
Bildad's Second Response to Job:
The Place of the Wicked in a Moral Universe

Job has voiced his horror at the prospect of the total obliteration of his righteous life and unjust death from the face of the earth. Bildad retorts that Job's counter claim amounts to a requirement that the whole earth be moved out of its place to make room for such a one as he. Such is not the tolerance of the moral order, which instead must expel the wicked and destroy all trace of the place they once occupied.

* * *

127

For some time now the speakers have been introducing their responses with derogatory retorts against their predecessor's words. Bildad follows suit by the use of a telling image:

"How long will you set word snares?" (v. 2a, following the translation of Marvin Pope). Proverbs 1:10–19 offers a portrait of the enticing sinner who, attempting to ensnare others, falls into one's own trap. Bildad accuses Job of indeed "joining words together" (see 16:4) to ensnare the friends in subversive talk (15:4). As the proverbial sinner, however, Job will only bring about his own downfall; for in the end he will fall into his own net (18:7–10). Before we explore Bildad's use of this imagery, however, verse 3 merits a brief comment.

The Comparative Status of Humans and Beasts (18:3)

Bildad's question in verse 3 picks up once again the human-animal comparison which runs like a thread through Job, and which comes to a climax in the divine speeches (see, e.g., 5: 22–23; 6:5; 11:12; 12:7–9). The frequency of this comparison is intriguing. Genesis one and two, in diverse ways, emphasize both a close relationship and a distinct difference between human and animal species. The two species alone are created on the climactic sixth day (Gen. 1); and at first it appears that they might be fit helpers (Gen. 2). Yet the animals apparently do not share in the divine image (Gen. 1); and after trial, the animals, being found not to provide fit (or parity) help, are subordinated through naming (Gen. 2). The comparative status of humans and animals is of course reiterated in Psalm 8. Against such a thematic background, the frequent resort to animal imagery in Job appears to serve the book's reexamination of the status and place of humankind in the created order.

The Place of the Wicked (18:4–21)

Now Bildad comes to the main part of his response. He takes up Job's words (earth, place) and Job's concern in 16:18 and attempts to invert them. The opening words (v. 4, earth, place) and the closing words (v. 21, dwellings, place) frame and define the point of the intervening imagery.

Job has appealed to the earth to preserve his blood in visible evidence of his innocent place in the scheme of things. In Bildad's view, it is impossible for Job's blood to remain in evidence without threatening the very stability of the earth itself. Evil such as Job's so contaminates and destabilizes the created order that, like the sin of Achan, it must be purged from the cosmos (cf. Josh. 7:15 with Job 18:14–19). Bildad portrays that purging through a powerful threefold repetition of a sustained figure of expulsion.

128

(1) The wicked person is driven out of house and home as the light therein is extinguished. Thereby the person is driven into darkness, falls into one's own traps, and is brought into the realm of death where one's limbs are consumed. In this imagery, one's home is (as our idiom would put it) one's "place" in the universe. As in Ecclesiastes 12:1–8, the language of tent and home is a figure for embodied existence; and the expulsion therefrom is a figure for death. Earlier in Job, "light" carries also the connotations of consciousness (see commentary on 3:20 and on 12:22; and cf. Prov. 20:27). So in 18:5–6, the extinction of the light in the tent bespeaks the extinction of human life and consciousness. It may be that Bildad's figure is inspired partly by Job's words in 17:7.

(2) The extended figure of verses 5–13 is then recapitulated in verse 14, traversing in two terse lines the final journey from tent to "the king of terrors." Now Bildad turns to consider the place which the wicked person had formerly occupied. Not only the wicked individual is obliterated, but also the former habitation (v. 15) and all offspring who might carry forward the family name (v. 16). Not only is the consciousness of the wicked extinguished, but all memory of such a one is extinguished from the consciousness of others (v. 17).

(3) The incomprehensible horror of such a fate is evoked by the primal language with which, for a third time, that fate is set forth: "He is thrust from light into darkness, / and driven out of the world." This is the ultimate banishment, of which the exile from the garden and the exile of Cain are but parables.

Bildad reiterates the theme of verses 15–17 in verse 19 and then finally presents the reaction of others to such a spectacle: At such a fate people everywhere will be appalled and filled with horror (v. 20). What is it that gives rise to the horror? Is it not the incomprehensible reference of the repeated "such" (Hebrew underlying RSV "these" and "this") in verse 21? For these demonstratives point to what once was—what once occupied a place—but now has vanished without a trace. In a strange way, the horror at this point touches the horror in Job's outcry in 16:18.

**Further Reflection on the Mystery of Place
and Its Obliteration**   129

It has been suggested above that the "light" of 18:5–6 betokens also the inner light of human consciousness. We recall Milton's words in *Paradise Lost,* "The mind is its own place. . . ." It is not just that to be part of the created order is to *occupy* a place. More radically, to be a part of that order is to *be* a place, a specific locus of awareness and intelligence, of desire and intention. When people are aware of one another, they are aware of more than a locus occupied by a corporeal biped of a certain size and shape. They are aware of a locus of subjective consciousness and proper identity, from which may emanate words and emotions and to which one may direct words and intentions. The recognition of subjective consciousness as a "place" may come only retrospectively, after the death of another. Nothing materially has changed. The body is where it was. But something has vanished. In Gertrude Stein's words, humanly and vitally speaking, "there is no [longer any] there there."

It may well be the case, as Bildad supposes in his rhetorical question of verse 4, that morally the earth has no place for those human places which have become wicked. The ecology of the moral realm may be thought to require that such places must be extinguished for the sake of the survival of the world as a whole. So at least Bildad supposes. To that degree, his sustained retort to Job's cry in 16:18 may be held to lack any sympathy with the pathos of that cry. But the very way in which Bildad portrays the reaction of others to the fate of the wicked (vv. 20–21) suggests that Bildad's own moralism here is somewhat qualified by a residual sympathy with Job's plight. One recalls a newsreel from World War II, which showed what outraged Italian mobs did with the lifeless body of their erstwhile Il Duce Mussolini, dragging it through the streets, hanging it heels-up against the wall, than pelting it with stones and spitting at it. In viewing the scene, one was drawn into the moral energy of the action; yet, more deeply, one felt a pathos of horror that any human being, no matter in what moral state, could be so driven out of the world.

Insofar as verses 20–21 come from Bildad's lips, they show him, if only unwittingly, not completely devoid of sympathy with Job. Such a sympathy is also implicit in his concern to create the horrifying imagery in verses 5–19, imagery which (in the manner of a Jonathan Edwards) seeks to move the intransigent sinner to a more tenable place in the world and before God. It is easy for readers, in sympathy with Job, to be out of sympathy with the moral concern of Bildad. The specific conclusions to which that concern leads him may indeed lie beyond the reach of any readerly sympathy attuned to Job's cries. The question remains, however, whether the Book of Job can be read adequately apart from a deep appreciation for and, in part, an identification with the moral sensibility of the friends. With an ambiguity that resists logical resolution, their specific moral vision embodies a loyal if refracted articulation of a primal intuition that things must somehow hang together morally. Their failure may lie in the supposition that the moral dynamic at the heart of things must work only to expel that which is evil; it may lie in the incapacity to imagine a universe in which moral concern may somehow bind together all the elements of the created order, though some of those elements are evil in character. Such a universe, and such a moral concern, will be seen to emerge in the divine speeches.

Job 19
Job's Response to Bildad II: A Sense of Kinship Beyond a Sense of Total Abandonment

Job has come to the point of feeling totally abandoned by friends, relatives, servants, family, and God—anyone who might perform the customary office of the kin redeemer. In the midst of such abandonment he clings loyally to his own body, only to find that even it is deserting him, to leave him a bony figure of death. In such extremity his imagination once again turns away from the actual situation and searchingly affirms the existence, somewhere, of a kin redeemer who, sometime, will arise on his behalf. Who this redeemer is, he does not know. Momentarily, he is convinced that once this redeemer has acted on his behalf, he will be restored to embodied life and that God and he will be at one, for God will no longer be estranged from him.

* * *

Job's response to Bildad in this chapter is shorter than any of his other utterances since chapter 3. Yet it achieves peculiar density through the way in which it draws persistent themes into a renewed statement of his plight and his hope. Moreover,

131

the history of religious appropriation and interpretation of verses 25–27, and the more recent history of scholarly reassessment of this passage, calls for special consideration. In view of the complex character of the following analysis, a rather full outline of our procedure is given at the outset.

Opening Retort (19:2–4)

A Futile Call for Help (19:5–22)

Imaginative Envisagement of a Kin Redeemer (19:23–27)

On the Difference Between Older and Recent Interpretation of 19:25–27

On Evidence for Job's Multi-level Participation in Existence

Two Thematic Vectors Relevant to 19:25–27

Translation of 19:25–27 and Exegetical Comments

Another Warning to the Friends (19:28–29)

A General Reflection on Hermeneutical Appropriation of 19: 25–27

Opening Retort (19:2–4)

Job hyperbolically accuses the friends of wrongly accusing him "these ten times" (v. 3). The hyperbole is perhaps understandable when we consider that, though the Satan was allowed to touch only Job's bones and flesh and was enjoined from touching Job's life (*nepeš*, 2:5–6), the friends by means of their words have had the effect of breaking him in pieces (or, as the verb suggests, of pulverizing him and reducing him to dust) and of tormenting his innermost self (*nepeš*, v. 2a; RSV "me"). Contrary to the child's taunt, sticks and stones hurt only bones, but names cut much deeper.

Job is willing to grant that he may have erred. Even if he has, he asserts, "my error remains with me only overnight" (v. 4b; the verb translated "remains" in RSV means "to lodge, spend the night," indicating a transient "overnight" condition as in Ps. 30:5). In contrast to such a relatively minor problem, the friends blow up Job's sin out of all proportion: "If indeed you magnify against me / and reprove me with my humiliating condition" (v. 5). The friends look at Job, see his condition, interpret it in retributive terms, inflate it, and press it against him accusingly as a massive weight of evidence for his moral condition. Instead of doing this, they should gather from his

132

condition that God has attacked him unjustly (vv. 6–7), and they should pity him for this. In 18:8–10 Bildad had used the image of the net for God's judgment on the wicked. In 19:6 Job accuses God of wickedly entrapping the innocent in a net (cf. Prov. 1:11).

A Futile Call for Help (19:5–22)

This section is marked off by verses 5–6 at the beginning and verses 21–22 at the end: Both the friends and God are Job's adversaries, when in fact he ought to have been able to appeal to them for help. In verses 7–20 this theme is set out in two dimensions:

(1) Job's "hey Rube!" call for help ought to have evoked a divine response on his behalf. Instead, God and the hosts of heaven have turned completely against him (vv. 7–12). They attack him from all sides to wall him in, to pull up his hope like a tree (note Job's recurrence to the imagery of 14:7), and to strip from him his royal glory. It is significant that Job equates royal glory with conventional evidences of it—power, riches, status, and the good life (cf. chap. 29). It does not yet occur to him (though later, in 31:35–37, his words will intimate otherwise) that another kind of royalty may become visible only in and through such circumstances as he now is in.

(2) Not only are God and the hosts of heaven arrayed against Job, but all human acquaintance, even the most intimate, is turned against him. When he calls for help against violence (v. 7), anyone who might be expected to come as a kinsman redeemer, whether divine (vv. 8–12) or human (vv. 13–22), has become estranged from him. (Verses 13, 15, 17, where RSV translates "estranged, . . . stranger, . . . repulsive," all contain some form of the root *zrh* which will reappear in v. 27 as "another.")

Job's solitary plight comes to vivid expression in verse 20, just before he makes a last futile plea for his friends' pity. The verse has been variously translated and interpreted. The following linguistic observations underlie the translation and interpretation here offered: (1) In verse 20*a*, the noun *'aṣmi* (RSV "my bones") can refer to Job's own self, as it does in other biblical contexts, to give "I cleave to my skin and my flesh." (2) The verb "cleave" may refer not simply to the physical act of clinging but to the moral act of cleaving loyally, as in Genesis 2:24 and Ruth 1:14. This existential and moral (rather than

133

merely physical) overtone is perhaps supported by the fact that the present passage shares with the passages in Genesis and Ruth the same Hebrew preposition ("cleave *to*"), in contrast to the different preposition in the expression in Psalm 102:5. (3) In verse 20*b* the sentence "I have escaped *by* the skin of my teeth" is enigmatic. If (as in Gen. 32:11) the Hebrew preposition is translated "with," indicating what one has been able to take or bring with one, the sentence and the couplet yield a vivid and contextually forceful figure: "I cleave loyally to my skin and my flesh, / and I have escaped with the skin of my teeth." Deserted by the wider community (human and divine), he seeks solace and companionship in his embodied self, in a covenant loyalty which seeks at least to keep soul and body—or bones and flesh—together. Even in this he fails. In his attempt to come through with soul and body intact (to "save his skin," as the English idiom has it), all he is able to save is the skin of his teeth—that is to say, nothing. In saying this, Job speaks as though he is already a shriven skeleton, a totally denuded and naked self. This means that he is in that state to which the Satan would have him driven (2:5)—the state of naked and totally unsupported consciousness. In 18:5–14, Bildad's extended figure has been taken as portraying the departure of the wicked from embodied existence. As the climax to 19:17–19, Job's ghastly figure in 19:20 may be taken as his appropriation of Bildad's portrayal (triggered perhaps by 18:13). In this reappropriation, of course, Job shifts the moral perspective to show how his loyal cleaving stands in contrast to the desertion of him by all others.

Imaginative Envisagement of a Kin Redeemer (19:23–27)

It is from within this existential situation, imaged both in terms of "walled-up" confinement and isolation (v. 8) and in terms of absolute disembodied nakedness (v. 20), that Job undertakes perhaps the most celebrated (but in modern biblical studies now controverted) of his imaginative outreaches. It is, of course, not the fact of such an outreach which is controverted but its content. In this commentary, one important clue to the content of verses 25–27 is found in the way these latter verses reverse the imagery which has been employed already in verses 5–22. What Job imaginatively envisions in verses 23–27 is a kin redeemer. Such a figure he has not found though he has searched everywhere in his *actual* world, as described in verses 5–22.

134

Briefly, imaginally, he becomes convinced that such a redeemer exists, or will exist. Moreover, what he imagines in
verses 23–27 is the restoration (one might say the reinvestiture)
of a vital state of which (by v. 20) he has been as good as
divested.

The thematic connections between verses 5–22 and verses
23–27 are manifold, but two themes are particularly significant:
(1) In verses 5–22 Job had sought and despaired of finding help
from acquaintance or kin. For everyone is estranged *(zar)* from
him. Yet in verses 25–27 Job affirms the existence of his kin
redeemer, his *go'el,* with the result that he will see God and not
as a stranger *(zar,* v. 27; RSV "another"). This thematic reversal
by means of the word "stranger" parallels another word reversal
at the heart of the second theme. (2) Job's community has shrunk
to such a narrow and indeed non-existent circle, that even his
loyal attempt to cleave to his own skin and flesh fails (v. 20; cf.
16:8 and 17:7). The fate of his flesh serves only as the mark of his
deadly plight (v. 22). But then the negative tenor of the references to his flesh in verses 20 and 22 is reversed when that word
reappears in verse 26, "then from my flesh I shall see God."

In verses 23–24 Job resumes the concern which he had
uttered in 16:18, this time exploring another possibility for an
earthly memorial to his complaint. (On the graphic imagery
here, cf. Isa. 30:8–11 and Jer. 17:1.) But then, as he did in
16:19–21, he shifts his focus from earth to heaven (vv. 25–27) in
an affirmation which—even in the light of more recent scholarly commentary—it is difficult to hear any more without ba-
roque choral overtones.

On the Difference Between Older and Recent
Interpretation of 19:25–27

The above allusion to Handel and the *Messiah* indicates the
hermeneutical problem which besets our attempts to hear this
text with the full range and reach of its imaginative reference
but without violating its boundness to historical and literary
contexts. The problem is nicely posed by Robert Gordis, who
notes, "The older Jewish and Christian exegetes saw in this
verse and the following an affirmation of faith in bodily resurrection. This view has been rightly surrendered by modern
scholars" *(Job,* p. 204). In the same vein, and by way of giving
partial grounds for the modern view, he writes, "Virtually the
only element of consensus among moderns, as against older

135

exegetes, is that the passage does *not* refer to resurrection after death, in view of Job's clear-cut rejection of the doctrine in 14:7–23" (*Job*, p. 528). (In his commentary on the passage, Marvin Pope writes to the same effect, noting of the supposed affirmation of immortality or resurrection that "Chrysostom quite correctly refuted this interpretation with the citation of xiv 12ff [p. 135].") Nevertheless, Gordis affirms, the passage "is of crucial importance, marking the crescendo of faith to which Job attains" (*Job*, p. 204). Elsewhere, Gordis discusses what he calls "Job's three levels of faith" manifest at 9:33 (an arbiter), 16:25 (a witness), and 19:25 (a redeemer). Peculiarly, he does not include in this vector of faith the imaginative outreach in 14:13–17.

It is our contention that the so-called modern consensus is mistaken and that the ancient view is substantially correct. Before we examine chapter 19 more closely, it will be helpful to reconsider the supposed negative bearing of chapter 14 on the ancient view.

Those who follow Chrysostom in supposing that the negative outcome of chapter 14 as a whole rules out the possibility of another imaginative envisagement of resurrection in chapter 19, err in their construal of the character of the progression in the Joban dialogues. Implicit in their exegetical logic is the assumption that in the dialogues one possibility after another is raised, exploded, and left irrecoverably in the wake of a linear inquiry whose only truth lies at the very end of its process. The Book of Job simply does not work that way. For, in fact, again and again views which at one point seem to have been irrecoverably negated are rehabilitated within enlarged or transformed perspectives. If indeed the Joban dialogues are to be read in strict linear fashion, why does Job keep turning to *any* kind of hopeful affirmations after so many reiterated portrayals of hopelessness?

To take a specific theme as a case in point: Gordis has finely shown how, in spite of his vehement denial of God's justice conceived solely in retributive terms, Job's "growing attack upon God's violence in the present is accompanied by a new and deepening conviction of God's ultimate justice" (*Job*, p. 526). Thereby, he writes,

136

> Job is affirming his faith that behind the God of violence, so tragically manifest in the world, stands the God of righteous-

ness and love—and they are not two but one! Thus, Job's attack
upon conventional religion is actually the expression of deepest
trust (Gordis, p. 527).

In his comments on 19:28–29 Gordis makes similar comments
on the apparent logical and psychological contradictions in
Job's views.

If in the midst of despair Job can turn however briefly to
hope, and if in the midst of his deep suspicion of God's injustice
he can keep returning to affirm God's ultimate justice, then
there is no reason why he cannot return in chapter 19 to an
envisagement of resurrection earlier entertained but meanwhile abandoned. But the flaw in the linear logic of Chrysostom
and his modern followers is exposed already within the progression of chapter 14 itself. In that chapter, everyone agrees,
verses 13–17 set forth an envisagement of postmortem revival.
Yet, by linear logic that should not be possible. For immediately
prior to these verses, Job in verses 7–12 had denied the possibility of a death followed by rising, awaking, and being aroused
(*'ur*) from sleep. If, so soon after the negative conclusion of
verses 7–12, Job in verses 13–17 could imagine resurrection in
such poignant (if hypothetical) detail, there should be no difficulty in a resurrectionist reading of 19:25–27 if the details of the
latter passage are seen to point in that direction. Indeed, we
shall see that some of the details in the latter passage carry
forward some of the themes of chapter 14. (Such a literary
connection between the two chapters is signaled already in the
resonance between the two images in 14:7 and 19:10*b*.)

Job's Multi-level Participation in Existence

Reference has been made above to the apparent logical
and psychological contradictions in Job's views. These apparent
contradictions may be taken as symptomatic of Job's participation in existence at two levels simultaneously. On the one hand,
he still participates in the conventional frame of reference of his
friends and hence protests the unjustified violence done to him,
taking it as evidence for the breakdown of a universe of justice.
On the other hand, he begins to participate in a new frame of
reference in which other dynamics may be experienced, dynamics of experience and meaning which cannot be contained
or fully accounted for within the categories of the first level,
though first-level categories may be used with poetic indirect-

ness to adumbrate them. Specifically, the conventional *conception* of justice is questioned and relativized, while the *sense* of justice remains strong and searches for a fresh and more adequate vindication. This new vision of justice, when it comes, will be seen not totally to deconstruct the old, but to relativize and to de-ultimatize it. The tension, then, between Job's complaints in 19:5–22, the vision of 19:23–27, and the warning of 19:28–29 is a tension arising through Job's participation in existence on several levels at once. This tension will not be abolished but will be sustained and placed upon a new footing at the very end of the book (see commentary on the epilogue).

Two Thematic Vectors Relevant to 19:25–27

Before we are in a position to appreciate the details of verses 25–27 in terms of resurrection, however, it will be helpful to trace briefly the thematics of the image of "dust," both outside and within the Book of Job. This theme is developed along two vectors.

(1) On the one hand there is the conventional biblical view, as "old" as the Garden story: "You are dust, and to dust you shall return" (Gen. 3:19). Narratively speaking, this sentencing comes after the eating of the tree of knowledge, and not prior to that prohibited act. This means that death and returning to dust are thematized in moral-historical rather than in ontological terms. That is to say, prior to the eating *two* possibilities are posed before the primal pair: possibilities for covenanting and for unilateral human existence. As in Deuteronomy 30:15–20, the two possibilities entail two outcomes which are embodied in the two trees: death and life. Nevertheless, *since* Eden (narratively speaking), the sentence "you are dust, and to dust you shall return" constitutes a settled fact and a settled existential horizon.

Job's consciousness of this horizon is manifest in his first response to calamity in the prologue, when he says "naked I came from my mother's womb, and naked shall I return there." (The "there" in the Hebrew of 1:21—not translated in RSV—is a euphemism for Sheol; compare the threefold reference to "there" in 3:17–19.) In the conventional (i.e., post-Edenic) biblical view, then, one is dust and one returns to it (Job 30:23; 34:15; cf. II Sam. 12:23 and Ps. 90:3). What of the other, vitalizing element, the breath of God in the dust? What of the other possibility once concretely if implicitly posed in the tree of life?

Insofar as Job shares the conventional view, that possibility exists only to be denied:

> "Remember that my life is a breath;
>   my eye [*sic!* contrast 19:27] will never again see good"
>   (7:7);
> ". . . he who goes down to Sheol does not come up,
> he returns no more to his house" (7:9–10);
> ". . . I go whence I shall not return,
>   to the land of gloom and deep darkness" (10:21);
> ". . . when a few years have come
> I shall go the way whence I shall not return" (16:22).

(2) On the other hand the conventional view is, however briefly and tentatively, countered by another. Reference has been made to Gordis' observation that, even as Job's spiritual agony arises from his clinging to a view of retributive justice, he moves toward a deeper sense of justice which survives to de-ultimatize the conventional view. In similar fashion, Job's repeated agonizing over the irreversibility of death is accompanied by another sense which surfaces only sporadically but which entertains another possibility: In 10:9, inquiring after God's creative purpose, he asks,

> "Remember that you have made me like clay;
> and will you return me to dust?"

Even if the question may be supposed to be rhetorical, in the context the sought-for answer surely is No. In 10:10–11 Job elaborates a description of God's fashioning of his body (note the terms: *skin, flesh, bones, sinews*), and in 10:12 he offers a suggestive exploratory meditation on God's breathing in of the breath of life, as he says

> "You granted me life and steadfast love *(ḥesed)*,
> and your care has preserved my spirit *(ruaḥ,* "breath").

Since his birth, God has graciously sustained and preserved his life/breath. *Was* this all just for the purpose of turning Job to dust again?

The niggling hope within the question in 10:9–13, in spite of such passages as 10:21–22, and in spite of 14:7–12, surfaces vividly in 14:13–17. Of course it surfaces only to vanish again in 14:18–22. But the alluring propositional energy of 14:13–17, though it vanishes from sight, does not cease to operate within

139

Job invisibly. This is suggested by the way in which it resurfaces in the affirmation of 16:19–21, and also by the increase in Job's existential energy attested in a general way in 17:3–10. The operation of this energy is attested more directly in 17:11–16 where, in the midst of darkness (the darkness of Sheol as in 10:21–22?), the desires of Job's heart sense light nearby. In view of that obscure illumination, he can no longer be completely confident of death as a final home. As he suggests at the end of chapter 17, his kinship is no longer solely and chiefly with death and its community. Were he to affirm it so, he would betray the hope which is at work in him. It is now not the pit and the worm but his new hope which is his proper father and mother and sister (or perhaps wife; cf., e.g., Song of Solomon 5:1). Even if he dies and descends to dust, in Sheol the merely dead will be no nearest kin, for his hope is his next-of-kin. It is such a transferred sense of alternate kinship and communal alliance which seems to run submerged under 19:8–22 (where all apparent divine and human community has vanished) and which surfaces again in 19:25–27.

Translation of 19:25–27 and Exegetical Comments

It is commonly acknowledged that any translation and interpretation of these verses is less than logically certain. (Perhaps such may be said to be the case with attempts to interpret any imaginative vision unconventional in its content.) The translation here offered will be followed with detailed exegetical comments on each line.

> For I know that my redeemer lives,
> and the last one will arise in behalf of dust,
> and after I awake, things will come around to this:
> From my flesh I shall see God,
> whom I myself shall see on my side,
> and whom my eyes shall behold, and not estranged.

The one to whom no single item in Job's present actual experience testifies, the one who apparently is not only totally absent but non-existent—his *go'el* or redeemer—lives for Job as imaginatively envisaged. The sentence is emphatic in Hebrew: "As for me, I know. . . ."

140

The second line begins with the word *'aharon*, which may be taken either adverbially ("at the last") or as a noun in synonymous parallelism with "redeemer." In Second Isaiah *'aharon* occurs as a noun to designate Israel's end-time divine source of redemption (Isa. 44:6; 48:12). In those contexts "I am the first and the last" refers to God as both creator and redeemer. We are inclined to favor the meaning "the last one" in Job 19:25; in which case this word (as in Second Isaiah) balances the many references to God as creator. But however the word is taken, a *future* reference is clear and the *figure* so referred to is clearly the redeemer. In turning from a bleak present toward a redemptively hopeful future, Job here participates in the sort of covenantally faithful act exemplified from Abraham to Habakkuk and beyond.

Many English translations render the Hebrew word *'apar* as "earth," in verse 25*b*. Elsewhere in the Bible the word is almost always translated "dust." Occurring 26 times in Job, the word in this book frequently functions to characterize earthlings as frail mortals while they live and as destined in death to return to dust. Especially noteworthy are 2:12; 4:19; 7:21; 10:9; 14:8, 19; 16:15; 17:16 and most especially 30:19 (see commentary at that place). In 19:2 Job has said that his friends pulverize him (or reduce him to fine dust) by their words. In 19:20 he portrays himself as already reduced to mere bones, a state which (as in Ezek. 37) is but one step removed from dust. With these observations in mind, we take the word "dust" in 19:25*b*, not in reference to the earth or ground upon which a redeemer shall stand, but as a graphic reference to Job-gone-to-dust. Such construal is supported by the poetic structure of the couplet, diagrammed as follows:

My redeemer lives
The last one in behalf of dust will arise

The reference to Job in the pronoun "my" is structurally balanced and existentially explicated by the noun "dust" in line two. The redeemer/last one lives and will arise on behalf of dust. The preposition (which RSV translates as "upon") can, of course, mean "on behalf of," as it does (suggestively) in Job 8:6. In the latter passage several elements are noteworthy: (1) Bildad assures Job that "if you are pure and upright, surely then he will rouse himself (*'ur*) *on your behalf*" (the same Hebrew preposition as in 19:25*b*). (2) Bildad goes on, "(he will) reward you with a rightful habitation." The word "habitation" here is the same as the word "habitation" in Bildad's second speech, in 18:15. Does the usage in 8:6 carry the same connotation as in

141

18:15, where (as we have seen) the language of tent and dwelling provides images for embodied existence? (3) Bildad continues, "And though your beginning *(re'šit)* was small, your latter days *('aharit)* will be very great." Bildad's two words here operate analogously to words for "first" and "last" in Second Isaiah; and, more proximately, the second term *'ăhărît* is cognate with the term *'aharon*, "last one," in Job 19:25*b*. (4) Later in chapter 8, Bildad portrays the calamity and subsequent restoration of the good plant, in imagery which Robert Gordis identifies as the possible inspiration for Job's words in 14:6–10. Bildad says in 8:19 (see commentary),

> Behold, this is the joy of his way:
> and from the dust *('apar)* later *('aher)* he will sprout.

Not only does this verse resume the theme and the term of futurity sounded in 8:7, but it combines the motifs of futurity and dust. Thus, by a delicious irony Bildad is seen to introduce in chapter 8 imagery which Job momentarily entertains in chapter 14 and then (after Bildad's negative twist on the imagery of habitation in chap. 18) takes up again and develops more fully in 19:25–27.

It is this thematic trajectory which provides one exegetical context within which to approach the interpretation of 19:26*a*, a line whose meaning has exercised the ingenuity and taxed the patience of scholars. In Hebrew the line is composed of four words, in this order: (1) The preposition *'aher*, (2) the word *'ori*, usually translated "my skin," (3) the verb *niqqepu*, which is puzzling, and (4) the demonstrative "this/like this."

"My skin" (RSV) straightforwardly translates the form *'ori*. By a very slight change in the vowel the text can be read *'uri*, "my awaking." The attractiveness of such a reading (suggested, e.g., in NIV margin) is that it picks up the verb which Bildad used in 8:6*b* and it picks up the general imagery and one of the verbs *('ur)* in Job's threefold question in 14:12. In the latter passage, post-mortem revival was presented (hypothetically) in terms of awaking from sleep—a sleep in which, Job went on to say in 14:14–18, he would rest and wait patiently until his change/renewal should come. This change, as we have seen, echoed the renewal which the hewn tree would display at the scent of water.

142

The verb in verse 26*a* is problematical. "Has been destroyed" (RSV) is a bland translation. The verbal root, *nqp* I, has the basic meaning "strike off," from which (with an eye to the root's meaning in Ethiopic, "peel, flay") it is possible to imagine Job referring in a peculiar image to his death. But in the Hebrew Bible the word elsewhere does not have this precise meaning; and indeed, the root occurs elsewhere only in Isaiah 10:34; 17:6; 24:13. Another identification of our problematical verb is much nearer to hand, the verbal root *nqp* II. This verb, occurring some 17 times in the Bible, has the basic meaning "to go around." Two figurative occurrences of this verb are particularly suggestive: In Isaiah 29:1 the verb indicates a temporal process come full circle "Add year to year; let the feasts *run their round*" (italics added). Similarly, in Job 1:5 the verb is used to indicate the point at which a meaningful temporal span is completed: ". . . when the days of the feast had *run their course*" (italics added), that is, completed the circuit from beginning to end. That such a usage of *nqp* II occurs already in Job should perhaps prepare us to recognize it again here. (The connection, in that case, may be not only semantic but literary: The use of the verb in 19:26 may evoke momentarily all the positive, life-affirming, celebrative overtones of 1:5.) The occurrence of the words "as/at the last" in verse 25*b* and "after" in verse 26*a* give further support to such a temporal construal of this verb.

The demonstrative "this" which follows the verb may then be taken as an adverbial accusative, to give the sense, "After I awaken, things will come full circle in this regard." In what regard? To that question the last three lines of the vision in verse 27 offer the imaginative answer.

In conventional biblical understanding and experience, the "full circle" of human existence is indicated by Genesis 3:19 and its thematic variations: "till you return to the ground, for out of it you were taken; you are dust, and to dust you shall return." But within Job's imaginative envisagement, the "full circle" is differently conceived: not from dust to life and back to dust; but from life to dust and back to life. The circle is completed when the embodied living person, having suffered the calamity of death and disintegration into dust, becomes once again an embodied living person in renewed relation to God. The verb "come around/come full circle," then, is seen to function here in the manner of the verb *ḥalap*, "sprout anew" in 14:7; 29:20 and in the manner of the latter's noun cognate *ḥalipa*, "sprouting, renewal" (RSV "release") in 14:14.

The precise character of the renewal in verses 26*b*–27*a* has

143

been variously interpreted, as either embodied or disembodied.
That we should translate the Hebrew "from my flesh" to mean
"from within my flesh" (and not, as would be grammatically
possible, "apart from my flesh") is suggested by two considerations. (1) The vision of verses 25–27 comes as an imaginative
reversal of the actual situation portrayed in verses 5–22. In those
verses, as we have seen, Job's sense of solitariness and abandonment to death comes to a climax in his description of himself as a
denuded skeleton (v. 20). That climax itself echoes (though from
a different perspective) Bildad's imagery of death-as-disembodi-
ment in chapter 18. The envisaged reversal (as in the imagery of
Ezek. 37) surely includes re-embodiment, at least at the level of
the imagery of renewal. (2) The language of these last three lines
themselves portrays Job as seeing God from a newly embodied
state. This is suggested by the poetic structure:

> From my flesh I shall see God
> whom I myself shall see on my side
> and whom my eyes shall behold, and not estranged

Eyes are, after all, part of one's embodied self. The phrases "my
flesh" and "my eyes," coming on both sides of the "naked"
emphatic pronoun in the second line, give a structural force to
Job's hope of a revived existence clothed in flesh: "my flesh
. . . I myself . . . my eyes."

Three further details of this imaginative vision remain to
be commented on. (1) The six lines display a chiastic or "envelope" structure. If the word *go'el* in verse 25a carries the connotations of kin redeemer, then the phrase in verse 27b
translated "not estranged" (or, alternatively, "not a stranger")
balances the word *go'el* structurally. These two words open and
close the six-line passage. The second and fifth lines (25b and
27a) are also paired by the way in which the prepositions express the redeemer's positive relation to Job: "in behalf of
dust / on my side." Lines three and four then constitute the
core of the envisagement, focusing on Job's waking and restoration to embodied existence from which he will see God. (2) Job's
hope is not just for himself but is thoroughly relational, one may
say covenantal. Resurrection here is not merely instrumental
to, nor is the redeemer merely an enabler of, Job's personal
well-being. It is the other way around: The redeemer acts, and
resurrection occurs, to serve the restoration of the relation between Job and God. It is not simply life that Job hopes for. As

144

the threefold repetition of verbs in the last three lines underscores (see, see, behold), Job's hope reaches toward a restored vision of God, a God no longer estranged from him. The vision is thoroughly covenantal; and in its emphasis upon beatific vision it is in the spirit perhaps of Exodus 24:9–11 (itself a narrative climax to a redemptive process begun in Egypt). (3) The last line of verse 27, "My heart faints within me," probably expresses the onset of "the profound dejection that follows the exaltation of the mystic experience" (Gordis, p. 207, and further references there).

Another Warning to the Friends (19:28–29)

The concluding verses resume the language of verses 5–22 (cf. "pursue" in vv. 28 and 22 and cf. "sword" in vv. 28–29 with the imagery in v. 12). Job now turns the language in a different direction. Within the exaltation of the visionary moment itself, Job saw God on his side. Now, with the visionary moment already fading, Job turns his gaze from God to his friends. If God will be on his side, it is now they who should fear. Do verses 28–29, expressing such a sentiment immediately following verses 25–27*b*, spoil the purity of the momentary vision? Perhaps they do for armchair purists. Yet such a conclusion to the chapter contributes to a realistic portrayal of the shifting lights and shadows of human consciousness in the unceasing concern to draw raw experience and ultimate meaningfulness into some kind of mutuality. The momentary vision has suggested to Job that beneath the appearance of divine injustice there lies a basis for hope in the covenant loyalty of God. When he turns to look again at his friends, he articulates that momentary assurance in the only theological vocabulary so far available to him (cf. also 13:9–12 and 17:4–5). His words and his categories of understanding are inadequate to his intuition. The lesson (often enough pointed out, but as often forgotten even by those who point it out) bears repeating, both in behalf of Job here and in behalf of the friends generally: For want of better language, we say lamely what we deeply feel; and when we are taken literally and in that form our words are rejected or turned back on us, we protest, "No, that's not what I meant to say." Yet in the same dispute we rarely listen sensitively for the other's deep intuition or credit the other with a genuine struggle to articulate authentic conviction through the imperfect means of such terms and frames of reference as are at hand.

145

A General Reflection on Hermeneutical Appropriation of 19:25–27

Two closely connected issues call for comment by way of an addendum to the preceding commentary. These issues have to do with understandings which may arise through reflection upon the results of exegesis, and which at the same time (given our exegetical heritage) underlie and shape the exegetical act itself. The first issue has to do with the relation between 19:25–27, taken as a vision of physical resurrection and the eventual denouement of the Book of Job in the divine speeches of chapters 38—41, the response of Job in 42:1–6, and the epilogue in the remainder of chapter 42. The second issue has to do with the relation between the vision in 19:25–27, taken as a vision of resurrection, and the witness of the community that produced the New Testament. The second issue may be put simply and practically in the following terms: Is one permitted, with a clear historical-critical conscience, to listen to Handel's use of this visionary text in the *Messiah,* not only with purely aesthetic appreciation but also with religious aspiration and affirmation?

First, then, the question of the relation between chapter 19 and the eventual denouement of the Book of Job. Even if one is willing to grant that Job can envision resurrection briefly in chapter 14 and then return to it again in chapter 19, does not the eventual denouement imply that chapter 19 forms no integral part of the final solution to Job's problem? And does this not imply that 19:25–27 is important primarily for its kernel of covenantal hope, a kernel from which, however, the husk of resurrection imagery may without loss be removed? Such a de-mythologizing procedure would seem to be supported and perhaps even required by the character of the eventual denouement as compared with the resurrection vision. (One thinks, for example, of 42:5*b* as a possibly de-mythologizing resumption of the emphasis on vision in 19:26*b*–27*b*.) Another hermeneutical possibility is open to us, however. This possibility calls for a willingness on the part of the reader to stay longer within the language of the text and to seek to discern analogical overtones which may in fact bind together the vision and the denouement.

146 One could, for example, take the epilogue as a sort of this-worldly analogue of what is envisioned in chapter 19. Or, what would amount to the same thing viewed from a different angle, one might suppose that the long interval of the dialogues, with

its persistent themes (on Job's part) of deep darkness and its sense of total absence, is itself a kind of Sheol or "death in life." Certainly some of Job's imagery conveys a sense of himself as already in such a state or "non-state." (In such a reading of the dialogues, Job's state throughout chapters 3—31 would be an extended parallel to the state of Jonah in Jon. 2:5–6; and the restoration of both Jonah and Job, in each instance quite this-worldly, would display the same sort of analogous relation to bodily resurrection.) The difference would amount to whether one views the epilogue as a this-worldly analogue to resurrection, or whether one views the dialogues as a this-worldly analogue to Sheol and the land of deep darkness.

If such a reading be thought to harmonize diverse texts too easily, another approach may be suggested. Let us agree that chapters 14 and 19 contain strange exceptions to a vector of religious query which, at the end of the book, arrives at a conclusion leaving the visionary elements in chapters 14 and 16 out of account. Why then has the author included these visions? Were we to have only chapter 14, with its negative conclusion, we might conclude that the author introduced such a possible resolution to Job's problem only for the purpose of dismissing it. Then why has the author returned to that vision in chapter 19, this time to leave it in the air, so to speak, without negating it? One might object that such a dramatic progress, with loose ends dangling, lacks coherence and narrative economy. But can we be sure that the sensibility articulated in Frost's poem "The Road Not Taken" ("Oh, I kept the first for another day!") is solely a modern one? Can we be sure that an ancient query into such a mystery as Job's does not find itself searching along more than one avenue of possibility at once? In the history of human inquiry and of human action, the way forward sometimes comes through a movement back into the past, to recover an alternative once declined or unexploited but now recognized as freshly germane. In such instances what makes the once-dangling possibility germane is the emergence of a new frame of reference. Once, to be sure, the declined possibility seemed a dead end, a *cul-de-sac*—but only because of the layout of the rest of the city. In the context of a comprehensive transformation of the city, the old *cul-de-sac* may become a thoroughfare.

This last point concerning the settled structures of one epoch, and the entertainment of discordant possibilities which may prove to find their accord within the structures of a different epoch, bears directly upon the question of how the Book of

147

Job is to be situated within the history of Israel's tradition. Job functions in general as one who challenges and overturns settled views, in the service of a new vision of which (in typically ironic fashion) he is only partly if at all aware. We may recall the sentences of F. M. Cross to the effect that the Book of Job belongs in that main line of evolution issuing in apocalyptic frames of religious thought and conviction.

Is it possible that death, as a kind of black hole in existential space from which there is no return nor trace of light (10: 21–22), belongs to a particular sort of world, a world established and/or conceived according to certain specific conventions which are, in the widest cosmic context, epochally specific and by no means ultimate? And is it possible that among these conventions the stringent processes of cause-and-effect retribution enjoy a certain pre-eminence? May it be that the possibility of resurrection turns on the question as to whether such a world (in biblical terms, such a "heaven and earth") is everlasting or whether such a world may be transcended by another "new" heavens and earth, a world construed and/or constructed according to transformed conventions? Might one suppose, for example, that Job's apparently gloomy conclusion in 14:12 ("till the heavens are no more . . .") is transcended (and at the same time affirmed within its epochal limits) by such later proto-apocalyptic texts as Isaiah 34:4; 51:4–6; 65:17–25 and 66:22, not to speak of their full-blown apocalyptic development?

To put this line of reflection another way: Is it perhaps the case that objections and resistances to the vision of bodily resurrection have their force within a world-view and a world-structure for which retributive cause and effect are integral? If the Book of Job consists in part in a radical critique (one might say an ironic de-construction) of that principle and dynamic, and of the world which it helps to constitute, does the Book of Job not implicitly open the way for an alternative world in which resurrection may be a constitutive dynamic and principle? Under the aegis of death-and-resurrection, the relation between these two worlds would not be one of simple continuity *or* simple discontinuity, but one of transformation. In such a relation, the new epoch would transcend the old, yet in such a way as to take the old up into it and in such a way that the old in some sense (language halting behind intuition) fleetingly and indirectly, or analogically, might adumbrate the new. In such a case, however, then perhaps after all the epilogue may be seen as haltingly reaching toward the same end as the vision of chapter 19.

The second issue to be considered in this general reflection may be posed in terms of the traditional Christian construal of Job 19 as a prophecy of the resurrection of Christ. Such a construal, which Handel in his day had no reason to doubt, allowed him to use verses 25–27 as he did in good faith. In our time, straightforwardly objectivist views of revelation which once underlay such construals of Old Testament texts generally have gone by the board in many sectors of Christian hermeneutical and theological reflection. Increasingly the Bible is approached as a construct of the human imagination and thereby as a means by which the human community through its gifted speakers and writers attempts to order the mystery of existence into a meaningful and navigable life-world.

The epistemological breakthrough proposed by such thinkers as A. N. Whitehead and Abraham Heschel opens fresh perspectives on this issue. What in Whitehead's thinking takes shape as his "Reformed Subjectivist Principle" is remarkably similar to Heschel's analysis of the structure of prophetic experience. In these two thinkers both merely objectivist and merely subjectivist approaches are inadequate. For Heschel, prophetic consciousness is to be described as a subjective human pathos arising in some kind of sympathetic conformation to and participation in the divine pathos, which itself arises within God in experiential relation to the world. In this view, while the biblical materials arise as a human construct based upon human experience, human experience and human pathos include within themselves some measure of sensitivity toward and sympathy with the pathos of God. It may be that the divine pathos arises within human consciousness in the form of imaginative feelings—precisely those feelings which have as their object and datum that which is nowhere quite the case in the actual world, but which can be adumbrated symbolically by means of the forms and the terms of speech belonging to the actual world (cf. the comments in the second-last paragraph, above). In such a view religious symbols, by the way in which they weave feelings of divine pathos upon images derived from feelings of the world, themselves are a form of covenanting between creator and creation.

149

What if it is the case that the divine pathos as imaginatively experienced is radically temporal (or historical) in character? And what if it is the case that the divine pathos displays a concern for humanity comprising not only so-called moral and spiritual dimensions, but a concern for the whole person and the whole created order, including those material and bodily dimensions which, after all, have been created by the same God? Is it unintelligible to suppose that prophetic—and in this instance Joban—participation in the divine pathos at some points may give rise to an imaginative vision of a future, in which the comprehensive divine concern for the creature and the world in all its modes and dimensions issues in such a comprehensive transformation as resurrection?

To suppose that we might know clearly what resurrection is, would be as literalistically foolhardy as it would be to rule out the possibility of resurrection on the basis of conceptions and dynamics whose currency is germane primarily to the current world order (cf. I Cor. 2:9–10). Anything approaching claims to proof or logical certainty on such matters would be folly. On such matters, one "proves" one's claims only in the way in which one answers existential questions: in living by their energy.

Such energy may arise through a perception of the felicity with which such texts as Job 19:25–27 resonate with the overtones of the resurrection testimonies of the New Testament. One is entitled (at one's own risk) to construe such a sense of felicity as indicating a divine covenanting intention only fleetingly intuited by Job (or the writer of Job), an intention coming to other modes of disclosure later. One is entitled, of course, to view such perceptions and such construals as infelicitous. One may then listen to the *Messiah* and one may read Job 19 in a variety of ways, finding oneself in that place where, as William James says, "we have the right to believe at our own risk any hypothesis that is live enough to tempt our will" (p. 29).

Job 20
Zophar's Second Response to Job: The Portion of the Wicked in a Moral Universe

150

Zophar continues the attack on the instability of evil by a portrayal of the wicked as insatiably greedy for an undue portion of the world's goods. As Zophar sees things, the wicked will find that before they have digested their ill-gotten gains they will be forced to expel them from their system. For, to those who have helped themselves to too great a portion of things, such a portion becomes poisonous within them. In short, a poisoned and frustrated appetite is the portion of the wicked. Like Bildad in the latter's second speech, Zophar attempts to show that judgment and retribution are intrinsic to moral evil and cannot be evaded.

* * *

What Job's Words Do to Zophar (20:2–3)

Guided in part by Marvin Pope, we offer the following translation, which discloses a chiastic sequence in the four lines of verses 2–3:

My disquieted thoughts give me answer,	(a)
because of the agitation within me.	(b)
I listen to your shameful rebuke,	(b')
and the spirit of my frame answers me	(a')

Zophar's "frame" is his embodied self. The "spirit of my frame" refers to the way in which his cultural feelings, thoughts, sensibilities, values—the heritage of generations of cultural shaping (see above, the "Reflection" at the end of commentary of chap. 8)—are so deeply ingrained as to form an organic extended part of his embodied self. In 18:4 Bildad had asserted that Job's claims would tend to threaten the very foundations of the natural order (as indeed they do, if my concluding "Reflection" on chap. 19 has any merit). In the present passage Zophar voices the same objection at the level of human culture as he is formed by it. What he hears literally shakes and jars his whole structure of existence. The protest of his whole being— the spirit of his frame, in its agitation—gives him his answer to Job. For in and through Job he feels himself threatened by a chaos which must be overcome.

A Refutation of Job's Vision (20:4–11)

In this part of his answer Zophar takes up the language of chapter 19 and turns it back on Job in a portrayal of the wicked. In 19:25–26 Job has said "I *know*. . . . And after I awake, things will come around to *this (zo't).*" Zophar counters with an appeal to the settled wisdom from the past: "Do you not *know this (zo't)?*" (20:4). Job has longed for an everlasting monument to memorialize his words—a way of perpetuating his good name (against Bildad in 18:17). Zophar retorts that the exultation and joy of the wicked is of short duration (v. 5), appealing perhaps to common memory of the ancient story of the tower of Babel (v. 6; cf. Gen. 11:4); and he goes on to show how the wicked suffer perishing (v. 7), scattering (v. 8), and oblivion (v. 9). The reference in verse 8 to the transience of dream and vision cruelly if indirectly dashes cold water on Job's vision of 19: 25–27. For Job has hoped, beyond death and dust, in a renewal of the sight of God. Zophar adopts the language of seeing to assert that the wicked will be seen no more. Job has entertained the prospect that his bones, though denuded by wasting and death (19:20), will be restored to flesh (19:26). Zophar counters this theme as well: The bones of the wicked, though for a time full of youthful vigor, that is, full of healthy flesh (cf. 33:19–25, esp. v. 25), will come to nothing. This destiny is signaled by a vivid reversal of Job's words in 19:25b. There Job has said "the last one shall arise on behalf of ('al) dust." Here Zophar counters, "[his vigor] shall lie down with him in ('al) dust." Though nowhere in this second response does Zophar directly accuse Job of being wicked (cf. 11:4–6, 13–14), the way in which he reverses Job's language and applies it to the wicked leaves little doubt as to what he implies.

The Portion of the Wicked (20:12–29)

In 18:4–21 Bildad had worked with the motif of place and had developed an extended figure of the wicked expelled from the tent—a figure which we construed as connoting also embodied existence destroyed in death. Zophar takes up a related motif, that of portion, as food and acquisitions, and develops it extensively through the remainder of this chapter. The figure is introduced already in verse 10, in the reference to the poor and to the wealth that the wicked must restore; and it is foreshadowed even in verse 7, where the reference to the dung of the wicked is seen in retrospect to have been to prepare the reader for the language of verses 12–15.

The opening line in verse 12 establishes the figure: "Though wickedness is sweet in his mouth." This figure picks up a motif which has appeared repeatedly since Job in 3:20 referred to the "bitter in soul" (see also 7:11; 10:1; 21:25; 27:2; as well as 6:5–7, 30; 7:16; 9:18, 21). The motif touches upon life as appetite for experience. Whereas Bildad has portrayed life under the image of indwelling (tent, home), Zophar portrays life under the image of ingestion (food and acquisitions). The parallels between chapters 18 and 20 are numerous:

Chapter 18	Chapter 20
wicked cast out of the tent (v. 14)	ingested food expelled from the wicked (v. 15)
death's firstborn gnaws on wicked's bones (v. 13)	wicked will be slain by the tongue of the viper (v. 16)
darkness is laid up for the wicked (v. 18)	laid up for the treasures of the wicked (v. 26)
tent of the wicked is destroyed (v. 15)	acquisitions of the tent consumed and dragged off (vv. 26c, 28)
"this is the habitation/tent of the wicked" (v. 21)	"this is the portion/heritage of the wicked" (v. 29)
the world abolishes all trace of such a one (vv. 15–19)	such a one comes under the expulsive straits and miserable force of that divine wrath which will divest of all ill-gotten gains (vv. 22–23)

In each case the world is, so to speak, a closed ecosystem (a "heaven and earth," 20:27; cf. 18:4) which has no room for the one who threatens its orders.

What is at the heart of such wickedness is an appetite whose acquisitive outreach is limitless in the deprivation to which it subjects others (vv. 10, 19). If the desire for place, turned wicked, finds its eventual place in the no-place of total obliteration (chap. 18), the desire for one's portion, turned wicked, finds its eventual portion in the no-portion of total deprivation. In each case the judgment fits the crime and its dynamics are internal to those of the form of wickedness.

Further Reflection on the Imagery of Bildad and Zophar and the Condition of Job in Chapter 19

The imagery of these two friends, Bildad and Zophar, corresponds in an interesting way with aspects of the language of the Satan in 1:10. For Bildad's imagery of the surrounding and enclosing structures of tent and body carries forward the Satan's reference to "a hedge about [Job] and his house . . .;" whereas Zophar's imagery of the filling and momentarily satisfying character of food and acquisitions carries forward the Satan's reference to ". . . all that he has, . . . his possessions, . . . all that he has." Job's two stages of calamity reverse the order

153

of the Satan's reference, as first "all that Job has" is given into the Satan's power (1:12), and only in the second instance is Job's own body afflicted (2:5–6). The result of these two afflictions is to leave him *divested* and *deprived,* a condition which has been only intensified by his dialogue with the friends.

The two needs, to be *warmed* and *filled* (James 2:16), have their basis, to be sure, in one's body—but they extend also to other levels of need, including the need to have one's experience enclosed within an intelligible frame of reference and to be embraced within the affection and support of others, and the need to be nourished with the comfort and affection of others. By the way they have interpreted Job's experience through their respective images, Bildad and Zophar not only deprive him of what they could give, but they increase his nakedness and his hunger. Framing chapter 19 as they do, chapters 18 and 20 throw the solitary visionary into bold relief.

Job 21
Job's Response to Zophar II:
The True Horror of the Fate of the Wicked

Bildad and Zophar have attempted to portray the destiny (whether place or portion) of the wicked in terms so horrible as to scare Job into repentance. He now shows them the true horror of the fate of the wicked: Such people live in unbroken enjoyment of the fruits of their wickedness and they die with impunity. So indifferent is God to matters of justice that the same destiny awaits the rich and the sated in body on the one hand and the poor and bitter in soul on the other. The friends' doctrine is so false as to be tantamount to idolatry.

* * *

In this chapter which concludes the second cycle of the dialogues, Job responds not only to Zophar but to the common doctrine of the three friends, drawing his language in turns from one or another of the three. Thus he opens with a reference to the friends' "consolations," broadening the scope of the term (from the root *nḥm*) by which Eliphaz in 15:11 had referred to his earlier report of a divine revelation. There Eliphaz had claimed divine inspiration for his message. Far from hear-

154

ing anything of divine origin in what they say, Job returns in 21:34 to the theme in concluding "How then will you comfort me [from the root *nḥm*] with empty nothings?" The "empty nothings" are literally "vapor, breath," a term often used to name what is futile. That is what he thinks of Eliphaz's revelatory "spirit" and indeed of all their mouthings. But the retort is perhaps sharper than this. For the term "vapor, breath" in the sense of "futility" sometimes is used to refer to false gods and idols (Deut. 32:21; Jer. 8:19; 10:8; 14:22; Ps. 31:6; Jon. 2:8). Is Job characterizing Eliphaz's "revelation," and the counsel of all three generally, as so much false religion and idolatry? In view of the frequency with which idols and false gods are called "lies" and "deceits," and in view of Job 13:4, 7, it may well be that Job concludes both the first and the second cycle of the dialogues with a reference to the friends' words as implicitly idolatrous.

If they truly would comfort Job, they would do well to pause in their mockery and listen to what he is saying. For he is not primarily interested in complaining against *them* (21:4); his "impatience" has a different object. In drawing their attention to this object, Job adopts the language of Bildad. In 18:20–21 Bildad has spoken of the horror with which people are appalled at the dire fate of the wicked. In 21:5–6 Job asks the friends to attend, not to his own condition, but to his alternate description of the fate of the wicked. If they have any moral sensibilities they will become speechless with horror. As for Job, when he thinks of what he is about to describe, his whole being shakes with moral indignation (v. 6; cf. Zophar's response to Job, as commented on above, at 20:2–3).

The True Horror of the Fate of the Wicked (21:7–34)

The *why* which opens verse 7 continues the force and expounds the content of the *why* of verse 4b: Job's complaint is against God and is over the fact that the wicked are not punished as the friends allege. Their fate, rather, is one of unbroken and untroubled prosperity followed by a quick and peaceful death (vv. 7–13). Zophar has attributed the prosperity of the wicked to their rapacious and grasping greed. Job in effect agrees with him, but goes more deeply in his diagnosis of their wickedness. It is rooted, he argues, in their impiety. This assertion is partially obscured by the translation of verse 16a as a question. In the absence of the interrogative particle, we take this sentence as

155

an affirmation, "Behold, their prosperity is in their hand." The diagnosis of wickedness in verses 14–16, then, is as follows: The wicked have no use for God, considering piety to be a waste of time. In the spirit of Deuteronomy 8:17 they are willing to believe that their own power and the might of their own *hand* has gotten them their wealth. Job retorts that human prosperity is not in fact a function of human power and that to think so is to live accordingly, with all the attendant social evils that such an impious attitude brings. Such an attitude and counsel (or "design") is not Job's, as he reverts momentarily to the creatural piety of his old days.

In verses 17–21 Job turns from a portrayal of the wicked to his complaint against God. He takes up in verse 17 Bildad's image in 18:5 and denies it. To the rationalization that God visits the sins of one generation upon their children (v. 19), Job objects that the wicked themselves need to be confronted with their judgment: There is an intrinsic need that moral obtuseness come to self-knowledge (vv. 19–20). Short of such self-knowledge and repentance, what would make the wicked care about their descendants' fate (v. 21)?

We should note that verse 19a, clearly a quotation of the views of the friends, is not directly so identified in Hebrew, which simply reads "God stores up their iniquity for their sons." We are to gather from what Job says that he is quoting their views to refute them. The same strategy, in our opinion, is employed in verses 22–26. Job imputes to the friends the charge against him: "Will he teach God knowledge, the one who judges on high?" (This verse is similarly translated, and taken as a summary of what the friends say against Job, by Gordis.) Then Job examines the efficacy of God's judgment, with the use of Zophar's language of satiation. The problem is that one person dies in *bodily* fullness while another dies in bitterness of *soul*, having never tasted of good. The shift in imagery is telling. Material well-being is presented as breeding a sense of security, which one may further identify as largely corporeal consciousness morally and spiritually somnolent. On the other hand, if material privation leads to intensification of inner awareness, the content of that awareness is bitterness. In Proverbs 30:7–9 the pious person prays for neither too much nor too little, but simply one's daily portion (what The Lord's Prayer calls "our daily bread"). Job sees no evidence for such an even-handed distribution from God (cf. Exod. 16 concerning the manna) as a sign of divine justice. The human condition is such that finally both the sated and the bitterly hungry become (as Hamlet's gravedigger observed) food for the worms. In describing the indiscriminate end of wicked and innocent with such an image of eating, Job refutes Zophar's extended figure of 20:5–29. In 3:17–19 Job had been eager for death as the great equalizer. He has, however, long since ceased to long for death and now its equalizing function in the face of the disparities of life only fills him with horror.

In verses 27–33 Job returns again to the imagery of Bildad in chapter 18. He asks his friends to inquire of those who come from distant parts (v. 29; cf. 18:20): Is it not true that the house and tent of the wicked (v. 28; cf. 18:6, 14–15), far from being destroyed at death, is replaced by a tomb which ensures his remembrance (v. 32; cf. 18:17)?

Having refuted the observations of the friends by his counter-observations, Job concludes, as we have said, by characterizing their comfort as so much empty wind (v. 34a). The very last line ends on a tell-tale note. Robert Gordis observes of the final word "falsehood" *(ma'al)* that "It is a priestly term occurring in the Priestly Code, Ezek. and Chronicles . . . in the meaning of 'violation of a sacred object'. . . . Here, Job declares the Friends' answers to be an act of faithlessness against the truth and by that token against God" (p. 236). (It may be noted that Gordis's interpretation of v. 34b and our interpretation, above, of v. 34a as a reference to idolatry, reinforce one another.) Once again, as in 13:9–11 and 17:4–5, Job betrays the conviction that however unjust God may be there is a divine concern for truth upon which he may rely against the friends.

On Job's Impatience (21:4) and "the Patience of Job" (James 5:11)

One may find in many commentators on the Book of Job an observation to the effect that James 5:11 does not accurately characterize the Job of the dialogues. Marvin Pope, for example, writes that James offers

> scarcely a balanced view, since it ignores the thrust of more than nine tenths of the book and appears to take account only of the beginning and end of the story. The vehement protests of the supposedly patient Job will surprise and even shock any who expect to find the traditional patient and pious sufferer throughout (p. xv).

That the issues are not so to be understood, however, is suggested by the following considerations.

(1) In chapter 3 Job cursed the day of his birth and longed for death. In his next utterance, responding to Eliphaz, he confessed to a lack of strength and an unwillingness to be patient, because of the loss of an end for which he might wait (see commentary on 6:11–13). In this utterance and in the following two, Job ended each time on the note of death as his end (7: 7–10, 15, 21; 10:18–22; 14:7–22). But by chapters 16—17 Job himself has begun to become aware of renewed resources of energy, so that by 17:11–16, and in the light of his tender shootings of hope and desire, he questions his former acquiescence in death. By chapter 19 he no longer ends his responses even with a query of death and instead spends his energy warning the friends concerning the consequences of the nonsense they are talking. As we have remarked above, the last lines of chapter 21 continue this vein. Somehow and from somewhere he has a resource of energy which enables him to more than sustain his side of the dialogue. In view of the existential connection which in 6:11–13 he had drawn between strength and patience, this energy of persistence should lead us to reconsider what the terms "patience" and "impatience" really describe.

(2) Job's expression "impatient" (qṣr ruaḥ, "short of breath/spirit") has recently been analyzed, along with its close synonym qṣr nepeš ("short of nepeš") by Robert D. Haak, who comes to the conclusion that the expression contains two distinct meanings: "The first connotation is a kind of 'weakness.' The second connotation is the commonly cited one of 'impatience'" (JBL 101:167). Such passages as Job 6:11–13; Isaiah 40:28–31, and the Book of Habakkuk as a whole suggest that "weakness" and "impatience" are not two distinct meanings, but two dimensions of one existential condition, either of which can be highlighted in a given context but neither of which is totally absent when the other is present. It is as though one's energy is derived in part from the future viewed in hope, and that patience (like William James's "seriousness") is "the willingness to live with energy, though energy bring pain" (*The Will to Believe*, p. 86). Where the future seems devoid of hope there is loss of energy and corresponding sense of weakness; and there is impatience, to be understood as the desire to give up on life, to give up the ghost (or *ruaḥ* or *nepeš*), to resign oneself to one's fate (as, e.g., in Exod. 6:9). As we have observed,

158

Job's early display of despair and of weakness has steadily given way to enactments of energy and even of sporadic hope. Consequently, we should not be misled by Job's reference to "impatience" *(qṣr ruaḥ)* in 21:4. Even in chapter 17, where Job said "my spirit *(ruaḥ)* is broken, my days are extinct, / the grave is ready for me" (17:1), he immediately manifests renewed reserves of energy (17:9–10) and goes on to call in question the grave as his true next-of-kin, in view of the desires of his heart (17:11–16). If faith is not simply the total opposite of doubt, but rather is that existential act which takes doubt up into itself and transcends it in courage (after Paul Tillich), likewise patience may be described as that existential act in which one (in this instance Job) acknowledges one's lack of spirit to go on, and then (one knows not how) goes on.

Further, Job's word "complaint" (21:4) is a common term for devout meditation or complaining address to God (see commentary on 12:8 and 15:4). Insofar as he continues at great length to complain against God, and insofar then as his so-called impatience is poetically paralleled by this word for prayerful utterance (however complaining) does not Job exemplify the spirit of the importunate friend of Luke 11:5–9 and of the importunate widow of Luke 18:1–8? This Lukan comparison brings us to the context in which James alludes to Job.

(3) In James 5 the analogues to "patient Job" are identified as (a) laborers who cry out to God for redress (James 5:4); (b) farmers who, having planted, now must wait for rain (5:7); and (c) the prophets whose suffering patience (as exemplified by Jeremiah and Habakkuk) is no mere serene quietism but a strenuous wrestling with one's doubts and with God. These three analogues to Job portray persons enacting a refusal to give up on God in spite of all evidence to the contrary, whether that counter-evidence be in the form of stingy employers (James 5:1–7), disappointing weather (5:7*b*–8), or delayed vindication (5:9–10), that is, whether it fails to be manifest in the human, natural, or divine realm. If James concludes such a gallery of heroes with Job (5:11), surely it is because James was not looking solely at the figure of the prologue and the epilogue! Rather, it is because precisely in Job's turbulent and energetic refusal to give up, James saw a generic resemblance to the oppressed laborer (Job 7:1–3; 14:14), the anxious farmer (6:15–20; 37:1–13; 38:25–27), and the righteously indignant prophet (21:7–33; cf. Jer. 12:1–4).

159

INTERPRETATION

If such a view of patience is in fact offered to us in Job and in James, then we may recover a sense of patience as a strong theological virtue; and in our efforts to acquire and to exercise such a virtue, we may be delivered from the false guilt of supposing that patience must always be serene and tranquil (a supposing that seems to be implicit, for example, in the remarks of Pope quoted above). Finally, such a view of "patient Job" enables us to appreciate another connection between this book and subsequent apocalyptic self-understanding. The one who wrote "I John, your brother, who share with you in Jesus the tribulation and the kingdom and the patient endurance . . ." (Rev. 1:9) surely would have found in Job a kindred predecessor.

PART FOUR

Dialogue: Third Cycle
JOB 22—27

Job 22
Eliphaz's Third Response to Job:
Direct Attack and Renewed Appeal
for Submission

Eliphaz now lays direct and specific charges against Job, in an attempt to bring him to an admission of his (supposed) wickedness. Then he concludes as he had done in his first speech—he appeals to Job to repent and to submit to God. Who knows? He who now is useless to God may, through repentance, become profitable to the divine governance of the world, perhaps as an intercessor on behalf of the guilty.

* * *

Why God Reproves You (22:2–20)

Job has accused the wicked of questioning the profit in serving God (21:14–15). Eliphaz turns the question of profit around: Does Job suppose that any human can profit God (22:2–3)? Is it not the human who is profited by one's own wisdom? Yet, once again a rhetorical question is subverted by the ironic undertow set in motion by the prologue. The reader knows that Yahweh has everything to gain—a whole new mode of covenanting relation—if Job remains blameless. That we are to read Eliphaz's rhetorical questions ironically, against the background of the prologue, is suggested by the placement upon Eliphaz's lips of the terms "blameless" and "your fear of him" (cf. 1:1, 8). The verb in verse 4, which Eliphaz no doubt uses in its meaning "reproves," can also mean, more widely, "to prove, adjudicate." The answer to verse 4 is, then, yes! It is indeed concerning Job's piety that God is proving Job and entering into that arena in which *mišpaṭ* (v. 4*b*, RSV "judgment")—the nature of one's dealings with another—is the issue. Deaf to this deeper import

161

of his own words, Eliphaz goes on (v. 5) to identify the cause, as he thinks, of Job's condition: his wickedness.

At this point Eliphaz does what no friend earlier has done: He no longer engages in third-person indictments of the wicked in general, nor does he venture a brief second-person accusation (cf. 15:5–6); rather, he launches a brutally specific and extended direct attack on Job's character (vv. 5–20). Job has oppressed the weak and the poor (vv. 6–7, 9) and favored the powerful and rich (v. 8); that is why Job is in his present plight (vv. 10–11). Beginning in verse 12, Eliphaz then reaffirms what Job had ridiculed in irony (21:22): God who is in the heights *does* judge justly. (V. 13 should begin "and you say . . .;" the conjunction is not "therefore," but ordinary "and.") If even the high stars are visible (v. 12b), then what makes Job think that God cannot see through the cloud cover to human affairs (vv. 13–14)? (On the association of God's shining presence and the light of the stars, see 10:21–22 and commentary; also chap. 25.)

In 16:6 Job had asserted that it will make no difference to his condition whether he speaks or remains silent. There we suggested that such a situation enables Job to show disinterested piety toward God. Eliphaz misconstrues Job's words, however, as an impious attack on God. In so speaking, according to Eliphaz, Job shows himself to be in the very company of the wicked whom Job has accused of seeing no profit in serving God (22:15–18; cf. 21:14–16). Eliphaz's sarcastic repetition (v. 18b) of Job's vehemently sincere line, "But the counsel of the wicked is far from me" (21:16b), only underscores his attempt to retort Job's argument on his head. Such wicked persons, including Job, do in fact come to their deserved end (v. 16), and Job's own experience is a case in point (vv. 10–11). The righteous will live to rejoice in this fact (vv. 19–20).

Submit to God and All Will Be Well (22:21–30)

As though sensing that he will have no further opportunity to speak, and desiring to end on a conciliatory note, Eliphaz returns to the appeal with which he had concluded his first response (5:8–26). He opens (v. 21) with the same verb which he has already used twice in verse 2. This verb *(skn)* means "to be of use or service, to be a steward; to benefit or profit." Often it describes the action of subordination as a faithful servant. Followed by the verb *šalam*, "be at peace," which likewise in this context may refer to formal submission, *skn* here serves to call

162

for Job to subordinate himself to God and to be of such use to God as a faithful servant can be. So construed, verse 21 introduces a theme which will bring this passage to a conclusion in verses 27–30. If Job will receive instruction from God (v. 22) and return to the Almighty, he will be built up (v. 23a, RSV marginal note; Pope translates "healed").

What does such subordination call for? The imagery of verses 24–25 portrays such subordination in terms with which we have in part already become familiar. The terms form a contrast, with gold, Ophir, precious silver, and the Almighty on one side and dust and stones on the other. Dust of course is common earth—such as humans are made of. Gold and silver, though also of the earth, are not common earth; they are exceedingly valuable. They are associated with kings, and are used to make crowns and other royal ornaments (e.g., Ps. 45:9; 72:15; I Kings 10:11). Job has lamented that God has stripped him of his glory and taken the crown from his head (19:9). Yet, Eliphaz implies, Job's language in general betokens the sort of boasting one might hear from a rebellious petty king. Let Job give up his claims for himself; let him submit to God by laying his "gold" in the dust. (Cf. the related image from a royal psalm: "thou hast defiled his crown in the dust," Ps. 89:39.) For Job himself is dust (cf. 4:19). If he will forsake his own claims and make the Almighty his gold—ally himself unquestioningly and subserviently to God in the latter's divine rule and judgment—then all will be well.

Formally we may note the rhetorical rhythm of Eliphaz's argument. Three times he repeats his "if . . . then" affirmation of the need for submission and the results of such an act. The aim of such repetition, of course, is to engage the hearer's feeling self in the force and movement of what is being urged and thereby to move the hearer to make such a response. The device is well known to preachers. Once such a submission and restoration has taken place, then Job may indeed be of some use after all to God (vv. 27–30), as a loyal servant whose intercessions on behalf of others will be effectual. Marvin Pope's translation of verses 29–30 clarifies this outcome:

> when they abase, you may order exaltation;
> And the lowly of man he will save.
> He will deliver one not innocent,
> who may escape by your clean hands.

Job will become a faithful intercessor in the mold of Abraham (Gen. 18:21–33) and of Moses (Exod. 32—34).

We may observe now that Eliphaz's third speech ends the way it began, on a note of dramatic irony. Whereas the rhetorical questions of verses 2–4 are subverted by the ironic undertow set up by the prologue, Eliphaz's intention in the affirmation of verses 21–30 is subverted in retrospect by what is shown in the rest of the dialogues and the epilogue. For one thing, Job is vindicated, not through his self-abasement in the dust, but precisely as a prince with God. (On 22:24–25, see 23:10; 31:35–37; and 40:10; also, commentary on 42:6.) It is as such a vindicated royal figure that Job will intercede for those not innocent—the friends (42:7–10a)! From the point of view of the dramatic progress of the dialogues, one senses here a shift from prologue as background to the end of the book. In similar fashion we shall see how Elihu's whole speech (chaps. 32—37), climaxing in the language of storm theophany, is undercut by Yahweh's immediately following speech from the whirlwind.

Job 23—24
Job's Response to Eliphaz III:
A Search for God in Space and Time

Job begins to turn away from the friends, as he now searches anew for God in space and in time. Could he find where God is, he might find a hearing; but he finds only terrifying darkness. Were God to appoint times of judgment, the cry of the oppressed would be redressed; but God hears nothing amiss. Job's complaint calls into question whether the traditions of the Exodus and the burning bush have any truth. At the same time, by the language he uses, Job may set the stage for a reading of the divine speeches and Job's response as an analogue of the scene at the burning bush; and by this language as well, Job lends his complaint to appropriation by subsequent apocalyptic sensibilities.

*   *   *

164   Job's first utterance after his calamity (chap. 3) took the form of a soliloquy. Even in his second speech he turned directly to the friends only at 6:14. From then on, however, each of Job's responses has opened with a direct reference to what

they have been saying to him, characterizing it with sarcasm or irony. Now, in chapters 23—24, Job begins to turn away from them, addressing them only obliquely, and returning largely to interior dialogue. Even God no longer is addressed directly in the second person, as Job enters more deeply into the solitariness of his situation. In chapters 23—24 Job searches for God first in the present and in terms of space (23:3, "where, . . . his seat;" v. 7, "there;" vv. 8–9, "forward, backward, left, right"), and then in the future in terms of time (24:1, "times of judgment, his days"). In chapter 23 Job is preoccupied with his own case, whereas in chapter 24 he enlarges the scope of his concern to embrace all who in one form or another share his plight.

Complaint-as-Rebellion as Piety (23:2)

We read this verse in accordance with Revised Standard Version marginal notes: "Today, indeed, my complaint is rebellion; / my hand is heavy on account of my groaning." In 15:4*b* Eliphaz had used the word *śiaḥ* to refer to meditation before God and as a synonym of "piety" or the fear of God in 15:4*a*. Job took up this word in 21:4 with the connotation of "complaint," to indicate that his argument was with God. Now in 23:2 he continues this statement and he goes on to characterize his complaint as rebellion. In 22:21–30 Eliphaz has counseled submission and peace-making with God. Job will not sue for peace under the present circumstances. In Jeremiah's terms, that would be to say "Peace, peace" when there is no peace (Jer. 6:14). Somehow, a peace on those terms would be a betrayal of the divine-human relation. By a strange paradox, the only loyal act under the circumstances is rebellion. Someone in modern times has written to the effect that "prayer is the only form of revolt in which man remains upright." The second line of 23:2 shows that Job's "rebellion" takes the form of a prayer for justice: "my hand is heavy on account of my groaning." The posture is one in which Job extends his hands in prayer to God (cf. Pss. 28:2; 77:2 and Exod. 17:12). That such a rebellion is an act of loyalty is indicated not only by the posture of the hand outstretched toward God in prayer, but by the content of Job's yearning in the following verses.

A Search for God in Space (23:3–17)

The idiom with which Job speaks in verse 3 may be translated literally, "who will give that I might know where to find him?" Half a solitary wish, it yet has overtones of a prayer which

165

reaches out in all directions for help. As such, it continues the thrust of the previous verse and the terms "my complaint, my hand (heavy in prayer)."

Job here longs, as he had done in 9:33–35, for a tribunal where his case would be truly heard. In this "utopia," this "no-place" (for he cannot find it), Job would not only be heard but would be addressed in a manner that he could understand. Formally we may notice that the utopian vision is opened and closed with similar terms: "my case" *(mišpaṭ)* and "arguments" *(tokaḥat)* in verse 4 are balanced in verse 7 by "reason" or "argue" *(nokaḥ)* and "my judge" *(šopeṭ)*. By an often-proposed emendation involving only a change in vowels, verse 7b may in fact repeat the word "my case *(mišpaṭ),* in which case the line may be read, "and I could successfully *bring forth* my case." The verb then (as in 21:10b where it refers to a cow birthing a calf) vividly expresses the relief Job would attain at finally getting his inner concerns—so long bottled up and hidden inside him for want of a hearing—lodged in someone else's understanding. In such a reading verses 6 and 7 form a repetition of the sort a-b-a'-b', in which "he would give heed to me" is the counterpart of "I could successfully bring forth my case." Once again we may observe that the awareness of simply being heard, of having one's case lodged in the understanding and sympathy of another, is already an experience of deliverance; while the lack of such a hearing forms one large part of the solitariness of suffering. Job's imaginative search for such a place contrasts cruelly with the results of his actual outreach. In verses 8–9 the Hebrew text should be read as follows:

> "Behold, I go forward, but he is not there;
> and backward, but I cannot perceive him;
> on the left where he works, but I cannot behold him;
> on the right, where he is concealed, but I cannot see him."

In this "going," Job now affirms (v. 10) he himself will be found blameless: "He knows the *way* that I take; when he has tried me, I shall come forth as gold" (italics added). Then in verses 11–12 Job continues the figure of his conduct as a way, in such a fashion as to claim for both his past life and his present "rebellion" the status of loyalty to God. Now the image of gold in verse 10 is used with telling effect. It comes as a direct repudiation of Eliphaz's counsel in 22:24–25. There Eliphaz had advised Job to lay his claims in the dust, since the latter is a truer

166

measure of human status before God. In affirming that he will come through God's ordeal as gold, Job touches upon the thematics of royalty which we have noted from time to time in the dialogues. In 19:9 Job had interpreted his sufferings to indicate that God is stripping him of his royalty, but now 23:10—perhaps inadvertently—betrays a shift in his consciousness, wherein his sufferings become the conditions under which his royalty truly emerges (cf. 31:36–37).

In verse 10 Job gives a peculiar twist to the biblical sense of life as something lived out before the transcendent God— before the One by whom one is known but Whom one does not know except through the walk of loyalty. Such a twist occurs again in verse 13. There, "unchangeable" (RSV) interprets a Hebrew text which reads literally "he is one." It is possible that we have here an allusion to one of Israel's epithets for Yahweh (cf. Deut. 6:4; Zech. 14:9; and see Job 31:15*b*). In such a case it would appear that, all the while the speakers have been referring to God by the pre-Mosaic terms "God" *('eloah)* and "the Almighty" *(šadday)*, it remains the Yahweh of the prologue and of the speeches from the whirlwind and of the epilogue that they are discussing, a Yahweh whose proper name is suppressed while the divine character is under re-examination. That Job in 23:13 is giving a turn to a Yahwistic affirmation is suggested by a comparison with Isaiah 43:13: "I am *He* [in Second Isaiah a common synonym for "I am Yahweh"], . . . I *work* and who can *hinder it (yešibenna)* (italics added)?" Job asks, "He is *One*, and who can *turn him (yešibennu)* (italics added)? What he desires, that he *does."* The hiddenness of God consists not only in the fact that Job cannot find the divine seat, but also in the way God's purposes for Job are hidden in the divine mind (23:14; cf. 10:13).

The contrast between Job's utopian vision of 23:3–7 and his unvisionary sense of his life is vividly signaled by a repetition which closes this chapter. In verse 4 Job imagines the open access to God within which "I would lay my case *before him* (literally "to his face," *lepanayw*). But in view of God's hidden working (v. 9), which will carry on unhindered to its completion (vv. 13–14), Job's feeling is pronouncedly otherwise: "Therefore I am terrified *at his presence (mippanayw,* "before his face"), . . . I am indeed cut off *by (mipne,* "in the face of") darkness, and *before my face (mippanay)* is a covering of thick darkness" (23:15–17, italics added). All is shrouded in a terrifying hiddenness of divine action and purpose. This theme of hiddenness both ends Job's personal plight in chapter 23 and opens his portrayal of general injustice in the following chapter.

A Search for God in Time (24:1–25)

The first verse, translated somewhat literally, reads:

> Why are not times hidden by the Almighty,
> and why do those who know him never see his days?

We shall examine this verse more closely below. For now it will suffice to note that what Job has in mind is the notion that God might entertain, within the hiddenness of the divine counsel and purpose, a timetable according to which at some appointed day the injustices in the world would be set right. That such is not the case is indicated by what Job goes on to say in verses 2–12. In chapter 21 he had set forth his bewilderment—indeed his horror—at the prosperity of the wicked. In response, Eliphaz in chapter 22 had asserted in general categories Job's wickedness as the basis for his suffering (22:5–9). It is significant that such an itemized (if general) accusation triggers Job's heart-rending picture in 24:2–12. In contrast to the stereotyped terms of 22:5–9, Job's portrait of the sufferings of the innocent is agonizingly particular and deeply moving in the sensitivity and freshness of its observation. Such a picture can be painted only by a consummate deceiver or by one whose moral outrage is its own evidence for the speaker's moral integrity. How can the reader (or the friends) hear what Job describes, know that it is all too true, and still sleep contentedly at night or eat with contentment during the day?

If that question can be asked of ourselves, what is to be said for God? The dying groan and the wounded cry for help—and God sees nothing amiss. The last line of verse 12 merits closer examination. The verbal idiom is the same as that in 23:6b and in Isaiah 42:25 where it appears in its full form: to take or lay to one's heart. In Job's utopian vision God would take to heart Job's case; but in real life God does not do so, in the case of Job or anyone else. The last word of 24:12c (RSV translates "their prayer," by a slight emendation of the Hebrew) is *tipla*, the same word with which 1:22 ended. There Job did not charge God with *wrong*. Here God does not see that anything has gone *wrong* despite the groans and cries. Eliphaz had credited God with the ability to judge through deep darkness (22:12–14). This

168

God, Job now says, seems not to detect the skulking crimes which the wicked perpetrate whether in the night *or* in the day. The emendation of verse 14*a*, from Hebrew "at the light" to "in the dark (RSV)," overlooks the fact that, given how God sees nothing wrong in verses 2–12, evil is emboldened to work its way in both light and darkness. If indeed the wicked do show a slight preference for the cover of the night, this only serves further to distinguish Job as having a clean conscience. For he does not share their fondness for the dark. This is signaled by some verbal connections between 23:15–17 and 24:15–17: (1) Job is *terrified* at God's presence; for the Almighty has *terrified* Job with the darkness. But the wicked are friends with the *terrors* of deep darkness. (2) The threefold negative reference to the (hidden or covered or dark) *face* in 23:15–17 is contrasted by the way the wicked cover and disguise their *face* (24:15). Also, (3) those who rebel against the light are not acquainted with its *ways* and do not stay in its *paths*. Job, however, has kept God's *way* and not turned aside; his foot has held fast to God's *steps* (23:11). In verses 18–20 Job quotes the views of his friends (as he has done in 21:19 and, perhaps, in 21:22). He then refutes those views with what he says in 24:21–24. As he had argued in 27:33, so now again he argues that the wicked prosper in their life and then come to a quick and painless end.

Near the beginning of this speech, Job had introduced his utopian vision with the idiom *"who* will give that I might know?" He closes with the same interrogative pronoun in 24: 25: "who will make me out a liar?" The last sentence of the chapter contains the third occurrence in this speech of the idiom "to take (to heart)," as Job says "If it is not so, who will make me out a liar, / and take my words as nonsense?" As in 23:6 and in 24:12, he continues to search for anyone who can perceive the moral dilemma of the world for what it is. Such a search may be rebellion (23:2), but it is a moral rebellion.

Reflection on Job as Critique of the Exodus Tradition

One standard characterization of the Book of Job is that it offers a critique of the reward-and-punishment theology of the Book of Deuteronomy. A more radical form of this characterization would have it that the Book of Job calls into question not only the Deuteronomic theology but the covenantal relation itself as inaugurated at Sinai. After Job, who any longer can believe in the covenant of Sinai? Yet the Book of Job goes

169

deeper in its critique, to call in question the Israelite testimony to God's saving acts as enacted in the Exodus. This observation takes as its point of departure the theme in 23:2 of complaint and groaning as loyal rebellion.

The classic instance of such a rebellion is presented in Exodus 2:23–25. There Israel has come to the end of various stratagems designed to subvert the oppressive policies of Pharaoh. The death of the king of Egypt and the change in rulers offers a propitious opportunity for revolt or escape. What do the Israelites do? They groan *('anaḥ)* under their bondage; they cry out *(za'aq)* for help; their cry *(šaw'a)* comes up to God; and god hears their groaning *(na'aqa)*. This fourfold prayer of revolt is *heard,* with the result that God determines to save. In closest conjunction with this determination to save comes the revelation of the divine name at the burning bush (Exod. 3:14).

Despite his groaning *('anḥa)*, which has gone on so long that his arms have become wearied with reaching out to God, Job does not find his experience answered in the manner of the Exodus; the problem is yet wider in scope. If Exodus 2:23–25 portrays the plight of the oppressed of Egypt in lapidary terms, Job portrays the plight of all oppressed people in wrenching particularity of detail, ending on the theme with which 23:2 begins: "the dying groan *(na'aq)*, the wounded cries for help *(šiwwa')*." Thus, in 23:2 and 24:12 we have three of the four terms found in Exodus 2:23–24. In contrast to Exodus 3, however, God does not think anything wrong (24:12c). Where is the God of the Exodus? Where is the God of the burning bush? Where is *Yahweh?* If Job's despairing testimony in 23:13 that "he is One" touches upon one of the Israelite epithets for Yahweh, then it is not surprising that just such a suppressed reference to Yahweh should appear in the dialogues exactly at the point where not only the covenantal traditions of Israel, but the redemptive traditions of the Exodus, are challenged by the nature of Job's experience. For the unchanging God of 23:13 and the unmoved God of 24:12 resembles unfeeling and unresponsive Pharaoh more than the hearing, remembering, seeing, knowing, and delivering God of Exodus 2:24–25 and 3:7–8. Or does such a reading of chapters 23—24 prepare us to view the divine speeches of chapters 38—41, and Job's response in 42: 1–6, as some kind of analogue to the scene at the burning bush?

A final word is in order concerning the language of 24:1. Three pairs of terms are noteworthy: (1) There is the pairing "the Almighty / those who know him." The concern voiced in this verse is a concern which is especially agonizing on the part of a special group. (2) There is the pairing "times / his days." The motifs articulating the theme of divine providence in history, and of divine intervention at appointed times to judge and to save—these motifs are of course at home in a variety of Israelite traditions. But the term "times" comes to recurrent and special usage in Apocalyptic writings, e.g., Daniel 8:17; 11:13, 35, 40; 12:4, 9; also Ezekiel 21:30, 34; 35:5. (3) There is the pairing "hidden / see." What God has *hidden in store* for the appointed time should one day be *seen* (cf. 21:19). Though Job's words here call all this in question rather than affirming it, yet one notes the use of language which in time will become standard apocalyptic coinage, and which indeed will provide the very image signaled by the meaning of the term *apocalypse* —"un-hiding." Such a linguistic tendency in Job is of a piece with what was observed in relation to the language of the imaginative reaches of Job in chapters 14 and 19. It is under circumstances such as Job's, and at the time in which the Book of Job was written, that the seeds of apocalypticism were sown.

Job 25—27
The Dialogue Breaks Down

The dialogue, which up to this point has proceeded in an even alternation of speakers, suddenly breaks down. Job cuts Bildad's opening remarks (chap. 25) short with an interruption of his own sarcastic retort (26:1–4) followed by a mimicking completion of Bildad's words for him (26:5–14). Then Job utters the first of two oaths concerning his own innocence (27:1–6) and an imprecation against his enemies (27:7–12), before he anticipates Zophar by uttering what he expects the third friend to say (27:13–23). The dialogue, clearly, is over.

* * *

It has become a commonplace view among critical scholars that the third cycle of the dialogues is badly disarranged, whether accidentally or as some scribe's (or scribes') "deliberate attempt to refute Job's argument by confusing the issue" (Pope, p. xxvii). That the third cycle "cannot be meaningfully interpre-

171

ted in its present form," says Gordis, "is beyond question" (p. 534). One wonders, however, whether the hypothesis of deliberate rearrangement can be taken seriously. Any scribe bold enough to attempt to deface Job's position by tampering with his words would surely have to rearrange more than the text of chapters 25—27. Would not chapters 29—31, left intact as they are, render the supposed rearrangement of chapters 25–27 ineffectual? As for Gordis's assertion, we may remind ourselves that absolute negative statements have problematic descriptive force and serve often to objectify the speaker's confession of inability to interpret meaningfully. In his recent commentary on Job, Francis I. Anderson attempts to interpret the text as it stands; and while one may or may not agree with its analysis, one cannot call it meaningless.

In this commentary, no attempt will be made to reconstruct a third cycle in which the alternation between Job and friends proceeds exactly as it has done up to now. If in fact the text has secondarily suffered disarrangement, the fact remains that the only clues to who originally said what are clues which every reader can acquire from a careful reading of the dialogues in chapters 3—24. Perhaps there is something to be said for leaving an ancient work partly in ruins and for allowing each reader to reconstruct the outlines of the original edifice with the use of one's own imagination, informed as it may become through careful study of what still remains intact.

There is another possibility which, though it is not here adopted, may be mentioned simply to enlarge the reader's sense of the options. It may be that the author has deliberately dissolved the otherwise orderly sequence of statements and counter-statements into a confused tangle of incoherent voices —a formal way of paralleling the argument of Job that the hedge against chaos has given way and that disorder and evil in the world make clear understandings impossible. Such a device would admirably prepare the way for the skeptical statement in chapter 28, before Job recovers himself with the integrative verbal actions of chapters 29—31.

We propose, however, the following interpretation of chapters 25—27. Already at several points in recent chapters, Job has quoted snatches from the friends arguments ironically or sarcastically. Some of these quotations are generally recognized; but in other instances commentators, failing to identify them as polemical quotations and finding them unlikely as expressions of Job's own views, have excised them as perhaps the insertions of scribes who, horrified at Job's impiety, have attempted to put more acceptable words on his lips. Is it not possible that the same Job who earlier has quoted lines and verses from his opponents' speeches finally engages in such a stratagem wholesale?

That such a thing may be the case is perhaps supported by the shape of the friends' argument to this point. By chapter 22 Job has heard Eliphaz conclude with the same appeal for repentance and conversion as ended Eliphaz's first speech in chapter 5. Before such a reiterated appeal at the end of chapter 22, Eliphaz launched against Job a personal attack which differed from all the other of the friends' personal attacks only in its directness, explicitness, and force. The manner of Eliphaz's third response, then, signals to Job the vanity of any hopes he may still entertain of hearing anything new from his friends. That the other two friends have taken their arguments to their respective rhetorical extremes is also clear. Bildad had introduced his own central metaphor of the house/dwelling of the wicked in chapter 8 (vv. 6, 15, 18, 22); and one can hardly imagine how Bildad could elaborate further on the development of that metaphor given in chapter 18. Likewise, Zophar in chapter 20 has unsurpassably exploited his central metaphor of the ingested acquisitions of the wicked, a metaphor introduced in chapter 11 (with 11:14a cf. 20:10b, 18a; with 11:14b cf. 20:26c, 28). That the second and third friends, like Eliphaz, have exhausted their possibilities for argument becomes evident from the way in which Bildad begins his third response. When he adopts the structure of the argument which Eliphaz had used in 4:17–19 and 15:14–16 (cf. 25:4–26), Job can stay to hear no more. He interrupts impatiently and angrily attacks Bildad's words with their implicit claim to inspiration (26:1–4, on which see below); and with a rhetorical flourish which improves on the form while retaining the substance, he finishes Bildad's speech for him (26:5–14). The awed tone of Bildad's brief speech, as an invocation of God's grandeur, is reproduced with an angry sureness of eloquence and tone which is reminiscent of Cyrano de Bergerac's response to the bumpkin who accused him of having a big nose.

173

Then (27:1–6) Job responds to such an argument with his own counter-argument. In the face of the friends' predictable views, Job's words now take a new turn. He takes a first solemn oath as to his innocence. Then, following directly upon the self-imprecation which forms part of his oath, Job calls down an imprecation upon his enemies/friends in 27:7–10 (cf. 13:9–11; 17:4–5; 19:28–29). Finally, Job completely preempts Zophar's third speech by making it for him. Verses 13–23 doubtless are Zophar's sentiments, beginning as they do with the conclusion in 20:29 (cf. 27:13) and continuing with the metaphor of the acquisitions of the wicked. The speech clearly is Zophar's; but it is Job who makes it for him—Job who, we may say, by now can reconstruct Zophar's words as surely as any biblical scholar.

More clearly than any other indication could give, the rhetorical device of having Job finish his friends' arguments for them signals the end of the dialogues. Job will no longer listen to the friends; he knows already what they will say. The friends see that they have nothing more to say, or that there is no point in trying to say it. Now Job turns to a long soliloquy (chaps. 28 —31), formally balancing the soliloquy with which he began in chapter 3 but containing a quite different tone and atmosphere. From such an overview of the contents of chapters 25—27, we may now turn to a closer examination of the parts of the text.

Bildad's Third Response to Job: A Variation on Psalm 8 (chapter 25)

That Bildad's third response in 25:4–6 borrows from Eliphaz's words in 4:17–19 and 15:14–16 is readily apparent. Bildad, however, weaves this borrowing into his recurrence also to Psalm 8 which Job had parodied in 7:17–18. By this means Bildad seeks to counter Job's accusation (24:1) that God does not keep times of judgment nor act to deliver the innocent.

Bildad's opening word (a form of the root *mašal*) is not well translated by the word "dominion" (RSV, Pope, Gordis). Elsewhere, the form of this verb which is used here describes not the *exercise* of rule but sovereign *delegation* of rule to an inferior ruler. Such also is the meaning of the verb in the present instance. The bestowal of rule, and the power to command respect ("fear"), belong to God. It is God who "makes peace," that is, who is the source of cosmic order and stability, from the lofty eminence of high heaven. (Cf. Ps. 8 where God, whose glory is above the heavens, ordains strength to still the enemy and the avenger and delegates to humankind dominion over creation.)

174

The theme of the ordering power of God is continued in
25:3 by the use of motifs which become clear by comparison
with Isaiah 40 and Genesis 1. First, there is no *numbering* his
armies (25:3*a*). These armies (or "troops") are the stars, as suggested by Isaiah 40:26, where the heavenly "host" brought out
by *number* is the heavenly *ṣaba'* or military force. Similarly in
Genesis 1:14–19 the sun, moon, and stars are described in their
ruling function by the verb *mašal*—a form of the verb which
we have just identified in 25:2.

The import of the first three lines of Bildad's response now
becomes clear. In 10:22 Job had described the land of the dead
as a place where there are no constellations and where the
divine light is itself absent. In 22:12–14 Eliphaz had asserted
God's effective and just rule of earth, by means of the language
of stars and God high in the heavens. In 23:17 and 24:12*c*, Job
had denied Eliphaz's assertion. Bildad reasserts Eliphaz's argument, in 25:2–3. In this line of interpretation, 25:3*b* may be
understood in terms of God's action in ruling justly. In such a
context the verb and the preposition in this line may be translated in one of two ways. The Hebrew expression may mean
here, as often elsewhere, *"against* whom does his light not
arise?"* In this case Bildad is describing God's action against the
wicked whom Job has just described in 24:13–25. Or the expression may mean here, as in 19:25 (on which see commentary),
"On behalf of whom does his light not arise?" In this case Bildad
is affirming God's action in behalf of the innocent, an action
which Job has denied in 24:1–12*b*. That we should adopt the
latter possibility is suggested by two considerations: (1) Bildad's
verbal expression in 25:3*b* echoes Job's in 19:25; (2) the latter
way of reading the line has Bildad inadvertently foreshadowing
how God will act on behalf of Job.

Meanwhile we may note that the reference to God's light
in verse 3*b* joins the reference to moon and stars in verse 5 and
the reference to high heavens in verse 2 to emphasize the
divine order by means of the imagery of the heavens and the
heavenly bodies—a theme prominent on the fourth day of
Genesis 1 as well as in Psalm 8.

The logic of Bildad's argument now begins to emerge.
Twice Eliphaz has asserted that before God even the heavenly 175
subordinate rulers (the "servants/angels" of 4:18; the "holy
ones/heavens" of 15:15) are impure. Bildad restates this theme
in terms of the moon and the stars. If even they are not bright

and clean alongside God's own sun-like light, how much less the mortal (*'enoš*, vv. 4*a*, 6*a*), the offspring of a woman (v. 4*b*), the child of earth (*'adam*, v. 6*b*), who is but a maggot and a worm. This last characterization as maggot and worm identifies human existence not only as earth-bound but as earth-destined through death and decay. This is suggested by the fact that wherever worms and maggots as such are mentioned their function is to consume dead tissue. Where they are used as a figure for human being (Ps. 22:7; Isa. 41:14; Job 25:6), the force of the figure is to describe human being as earthy in its eventual or imminent destiny. In Psalm 22 the speaker is self-described as already, and for practical purposes, dead and by consumption become a worm (cf. Job 17:14). In Isaiah 41 the exiles are viewed (with gentle divine humor) as "dead" with regard to how they feel about their own hopes (cf. Ezek. 37:11 in context). In Job 25 the figure underscores the condition of humankind as mortal. This interpretation is supported by the resulting parallel between 25:6 and 4:19–21.

Yet Bildad has missed the point of the comparison in Psalm 8. In his own comparison, to be a mortal is to be even less pure and clean than the moon and stars, who themselves are not bright in comparison with God (the sun?) in the high heavens. In Psalm 8, however, while the comparison begins to arrive at the same conclusion, it then goes on to achieve a different vision of human vocation. When the psalmist considers the heavens and the moon and the stars, the psalmist is led to wonder what status a mortal can have. But that wondering is answered by the recognition that this mortal, seemingly minute and earthbound before the stellar bodies, in fact has been given dominion (*mašal*) over the works of God's hands. Both Job in chapter 7 and Bildad here are shown as offering variations on Psalm 8. Bildad recasts the comparison in Psalm 8 to denude humankind of the royal honor and vocation bestowed on it by God. If Job in chapter 7 ironically reinterprets the special attention for which the God of Psalm 8 has singled out humankind, he nevertheless sustains a sense of that special attention and vocation. The resolution of the Book of Job will suggest that Job's reinterpretation of Psalm 8 was right but in a different sense than he realized; whereas Bildad's own reinterpretation is simply wrong. Human suffering no doubt is connected with human mortality and frailty; but it is also connected with the human vocation to royalty under God. In affirming merely the former

176

connection and not also the latter one, Bildad is thoroughly conventional in his religious sensibilities. But he is simply wrong.

Job's Response to Bildad III:
A Parody of the Friends' "Inspiration" (chapter 26)

Job will hear no more of what Bildad has to say and cuts in with savage sarcasm. To Bildad's characterizations of humankind as mortal, born of woman, maggot, child of earth, and worm, Job adds his own list: powerless (26:2*a*), strengthless (v. 2*b*), and unwise (v. 3*a*). Whereas Bildad's contrast was between lowly, impure humankind and the lofty purity of the God who makes peace and keeps order, Job's characterization of himself shifts the contrast in keeping with what he had said in 9:2–4: the reason one cannot be just before God (cf. 9:2) is that one cannot match God in strength or in wisdom understood as ability to succeed in action (cf. 9:4).

To this point in the dialogues, the friends have made little claim to divine inspiration. Eliphaz had done so once explicitly in 4:12–17; and in his second speech he had more briefly indicated the revelatory source (as he saw it) of his advice in his phrase "the consolations of God" (15:11; see 15:14–16 and commentary above on all these verses). Though Bildad makes no explicit claim to speak by inspiration, such a claim may be implicit (or may have been heard by Job) in Bildad's borrowed use of Eliphaz's argument. Job directly challenges any such claim. (Is it this challenge which Elihu feels he must overcome in his repeated claims to inspiration in chapters 32—37?) Not all who claim the spirit possess it; or perhaps (with an eye to the issue as posed in I Kings 22:5–24) not all spirit phenomena are a guarantee of truth. To refute the claim to inspiration, Job proceeds to show that he can crank out the same sort of verbiage (26:5–14), and yet with a flair that shows up the rhetorically inferior quality of Bildad's words. If the poetic concreteness and freshness of 24:2–12 attests the authenticity of the moral sensitivity and passion of Job (see commentary above), the dexterity of 26:5–14 in the service of ridicule may attest the problematic character of claims to speak by inspiration.

It may be that the reappearance in this parody of some of Job's earlier images helps us to hear Job's own voice behind the view he ascribes to Bildad. Compare, for example, (1) "naked/no covering" in 26:6 and 24:7*a*, 10*a*; (2) "pillars tremble"

177

in 26:11 and 9:6; (3) "covers astral bodies" in 26:9 and 9:7; (4) "the sea" in 26:12*a* and 9:8*b*; (5) Rahab in 26:12*b* and 9:13. (The last four points of comparison link chapters 26 and 9; we may recollect the observations in the first paragraph of this section concerning the connections between 26:2–3—itself indubitably Job's speech—and 9:2–4).

The portrayal in 26:5–13 is then concluded in terms which again ridicule the claim to inspiration. In 4:12 Eliphaz had said, "now a word *(dabar)* was brought to me stealthily, / my ear received the whisper *(šemeṣ)* of it." Job echoes this language, as he says "these are but outskirts [distant sounds] of his ways, / and how small a whisper [*šemeṣ dabar*] is heard of him" (26:14*ab*). That the word *šemeṣ* occurs only in these two places in the Hebrew Bible emphasizes the connection between them.

Over against such a whispering revelation Job places his own—a revelation borne in upon him by his own experience, one which in comparison with theirs may be called the thunder of God's power. That 26:14*c* expresses Job's own view is suggested by the following consideration: The word "power," in its only other occurrence in the book up to this point (12:13), is used along with the words "wisdom," "counsel" or "purpose," and "understanding." In 12:13 these four words come together in a description of divine actions which, displaying power and know-how and purpose, embody an "understanding" which, as 12:14–25 go on to show, is in fact beyond human understanding. Thus, to the friends' claim to speak by an inspiration which is given esoterically and in the night, Job responds by pointing to the voice of God speaking publicly in and through Job's suffering and other similar human calamities.

If our connection between 26:14*c* and 12:13 is valid, then we may further observe how verse 14*c* forms an inclusion with 26:2–3. For in the words "counseled" and "wisdom" of verse 3 and the words "power" and "understand" of verse 14*c* we have the four terms of 12:13. Moreover, though different Hebrew words are used, the common theme of "powerless" and "strengthless" in verse 2 and "his thunderous power" in verse 14*c* further supports the identification of an inclusion between verses 2–3 and verse 14*c*. This in turn supports the identification of 26:5–14 as part of Job's speech in this chapter, and not as a speech which is to be transferred to the lips of a friend.

A Short Note on Thunder. With only two or three exceptions, references to thunder in the Hebrew Bible always con-

178

note God's action in revelation or actions of deliverance and judgment. (In this connection, it is interesting to note that in Ps. 96:11 and 98:7, in a context of cosmic praise of God, the call goes out, "let the sea thunder!" One is intrigued by the parallel in George Herbert's poetic figure for prayer as "reversed thunder." Are praise and prayer, then, likened to reversed revelation?) In Job the verb occurs in chapters 37 (verses 4 and 5) and 40 (verse 9) and the noun in chapters 26 (verse 14) and 39 (verses 19 and 25). From this we see that it is Job who introduces the figure; whereupon Elihu takes it up and repeats it twice as he develops the portrayal of divine revelation in a storm. The word is then taken up in the divine speeches, first to describe the more modest creaturely forces of power (the word "strength" in 39:19*b* is *ra'ma,* forming an inclusion with the masculine form *ra'am,* "thunder" in 39:25*c*), and then to describe the divine revelation through action in 40:9. By means of the strategic use of the term "thunder," then, we are led to read the divine speeches against the background of what Elihu has said, and what Job has said, as well (in view of 26:14) as what Eliphaz said in 4:12–17. Thus various claims to speak on the basis of revelation are adjudicated and finally resolved. For, to anticipate, Job in 42:3*b* shows that he spoke the truth in 26:14*c*.

Job's First Oath and Anticipation of Zophar III (chapter 27)

Job's first oath exhibits a densely textured and highly integrated poetic structure. Therein it symbolizes the very thing it is about. For the oath both enacts and exhibits a good conscience, that is, a testifying state of consciousness in which all the ingredients of consciousness are mutually affirming and reinforcing. In this oath self-consciousness is rendered prominent by the way in which, in line after line, first person verbs and pronouns stand over against the (dis-confirming) presence of God and the friends. The poetic structure of the Hebrew is somewhat obscured in the translations, which in various ways strive for good English but at the cost of formal exactness. The following translation is a wooden attempt to indicate the Hebrew structure of the oath:

I

2.*a* By the life of God who has put away my justice,
  .*b* and of the Almighty who has embittered my soul,
3.*a* all the while my breath is in me
  .*b* and the spirit of God is in my nostrils—

179

II

4.*a* if my lips speak falsehood.
  .*b* and my tongue, if it mutters deceit,
5.*a* may I become profane if I declare you right.

III

  .*b* May I die, I will not put away my integrity from me,
6.*a* My right I hold fast and will not give up,
  .*b* nor pricks me my heart concerning my days.

We begin with observations on the formal features of this oath:

(1) Three solemn oath formulas may be discerned, one in each of the three sections of the oath: "By the life of El (or God)," one of the most common oath formulas; "may I become profane," a form of self-imprecation in the event the denied possibility were in fact the case; and "may I die," where the Hebrew preposition in the expression "until I die" has not only temporal force, but the moral force of a self-imprecation. (Interestingly, one meets with another solemn threefold oath in Rom. 9:1 where Paul affirms, "I speak the truth in Christ; I lie not; my conscience bears witness with me in the Holy Spirit." Both Job and Paul, in their respective ways, implicate the divine spirit in their oaths; in both, false speaking is explicitly repudiated; and Paul's oath is introduced with a reference to Christ, participation in whose sufferings and vindication has formed the topic of Paul's preceding words in Rom. 8.)

(2) The three references in section one to Job's interior life (soul, breath, spirit) are balanced by the three references to his organs of speech and breath (nostrils, lips, tongue). No longer is Job's body a witness against his inner self, in contrast to 16:8.

(3) In verses 4*a*–5*a* the "if" clause which forms the conditional part of the oath is repeated three times.

(4) In verses 5*b*–6*b* the asseveration following the self-imprecation "may I die" is made with three negatives (not, not, nor).

(5) What Job defends by these oaths is his justice (v. 2*a*), his integrity (v. 5*b*) and his right (v. 6*a*).

(6) The three verbs "put away" (twice) and "give up," in verses 2*a*, 5*b* and 6*a*, are reversed semantically by the single verb "hold fast" in verse 6*a*.

180

(7) The three sections of the oath shift their focus as follows: section I focuses on God (who is named—fittingly—in threefold fashion), and on God's action of putting away Job's right; section

II focuses on the friends, whose testimony is declared false and deceitful; section III focuses solely on Job himself and on his integrity and right which he holds fast, refusing to put it from him like God and refusing to give it up as his friends have urged him to do. We may note that the one positive verb in section III, "hold fast," by its collocation with "integrity" in the preceding line, evokes the language of 1:3 "He still holds fast his integrity" and 1:9 "Do you still hold fast your integrity?"

Alienated from God and from his closest human community, Job seemingly cannot bind himself to anything but himself. To agree with God and with his friends would be to put away his integrity; and to do that would be to lose his very being. He comes down to his final affirmation: "my heart does not prick me concerning my days." The term "heart" here designates one's inner processes of consciousness and thought, while the verb designates what seems to be a wide-spread figure for the experience of the conscience when it is "bad": we speak of the prick of conscience; we recall the voice which said to Paul "it is hard for you to kick against the goad"; and we recall the fairy tale in which the prince was given a ring which pricked him slightly whenever he told a lie. With this oath, then, we have come to a new stage in that exploration of solitary consciousness which was initiated in the soliloquy of chapter 3 (see the section "On Soliloquy and Consciousness" under Job 3:24–26). It is appropriate to reflect on the significance of the oath at this juncture and in the wider setting of the Joban experience.

A Reflection on Conscience and Oath as the Most Solitary and the Most Social of Moral Actions

It has been argued that moral existence has its mystery in the fact that moral relations cannot be grounded or fully explained outside themselves, either in the empirical or in the rational realm. S. T. Coleridge held that acts and convictions in the moral realm are postulates of humanity. This is to say that moral acts and convictions are those self-grounded acts upon which one's humanity is founded and by which one enters into moral relations with others. Elsewhere Coleridge defined faith as "fidelity to our own being—so far as such being is not and cannot become an object of the senses; and hence, by clear inference or implication, to being generally, as far as the same is not the object of the senses" (S. T. Coleridge, p. 425). In his refusal to betray his deepest sense of himself, which he calls his integrity, Job displays faith in the sense in which Coleridge defines it.

That such self-attestation and self-directed fidelity is not mere blind egotism, nor overwhelmingly self-centered presumption and arrogance, is shown in the fact that Job makes his oath not only *in the presence* of God, but by the life of God and by the spirit/breath of God which is in his own nostrils. To speak falsely would be to betray not only his own life but also that spirit within him which is God's. (In passing, we may note the contrast between the reference to the spirit of God in 27:3 and the spirit in 26:4. Indirectly one may take Job's language in the oath as setting forth the claims of a clear conscience in contrast to the friends' claims to inspiration as attested by conventional spirit phenomena.) What is so striking about Job's oath here is that, deeper than the fact of his alienation from God by God's injustice toward him, there is the fact of the existential bond between God and himself, a bond signaled textually by the progression, "the life of God . . . my breath . . . the spirit of God in my nostrils." If Job's oath displays fidelity to his own being, it displays at the same time fidelity to the being of God as the divine ground and source of his own life. The measure of his covenanting fidelity is seen in his loyal oath taken in the strength and spirit given him by the One who, it appears, has deserted him to his solitariness.

At a depth where existence seems solitary and free, and where nothing in Job's experience justifies a loyal response—at this depth—Job freely binds himself by God to God. In that act Job postulates himself toward God and the world, as it were *ex nihilo*. Nothing in experience and in reason urges such an act. He creates himself, as it were, as one who is willing for a loyal relationship even with a reality which seems to have betrayed him. Therein he "answers" to, and displays, that divine reality of which he is the human image, that divine reality which first postulates itself ("I will be who I will be") and then brings into existence a world grounded in such an act ("let there be . . .").

Our reflection on the oath so far has explored Job's relation with God. Further light will be shed on the significance of oath-taking if we reflect for a moment on its human social dimensions. One may suppose a witness taking an oath as to the reliability of one's testimony. In this instance the witness is vouching for a truth-correspondence between what is said in testimony and the original event concerning which testimony is being given. In such an instance it is the original event itself concerning which knowledge is desired. The testimony is secondary to the event itself and reliable only in its correspondence with it. In the case, for example, of a murder in the library, society may well prefer the evidence of a hidden camera over the testimony of a human witness that the butler did it. The point of the oath here is to assure the truthfulness of the human testimony. What does the oath add to the content of the testimony? It adds nothing, beyond the testimony already given, to the understanding of what happened in the library.

However, the oath, adds a great deal to our estimate of the reliability of the oath-taker. For, unlike empirical events like murders in libraries (which could be picked up by hidden cameras) and unlike rational relations like mathematical equations (which can be verified by anyone who knows the correct procedures), moral acts in their interiority cannot be verified empirically or rationally. Moral acts both constitute, and issue from, the solitary individuality of the moral agent. The oath is that moral act which at one and the same time is the most solitary of acts and the most social of acts. For the oath is that moral act undertaken with the most solemn intention by the fully gathered and concentrated self; it is an act taken in full view of, and in the knowledge (con-science) of one's past experience as remembered, or in intended fidelity to what was experienced and is now forgotten (27:6 "my days"). In that sense the oath is a social act as unifying oneself in reference to all one's experiences, memories, and intentions. But the oath is a social act in another and equally important sense. In the oath one binds oneself not only to oneself but also to others. The self-imprecation in such an oath touches upon the fact that, in binding oneself to others through an oath, one posits one's integrity upon the truth of the oath. To lie under oath, therefore, is by that very act to destroy one's own moral integrity, in both its individual and its social, its solitary and its public, aspects.

The gravity of the oath, then, rests in the fact that it destroys the primal bond which unites God, society, and the individual, that bond which, deeper than all specific moral norms, is the existential basis for existence. This is why the oath is the sacred touchstone of communal existence: It is how individuality and communality, solitariness and publicness, are both enacted and attested. For all its institutional enforceable sanctions, society finally depends for its well-being upon the frail mystery of the enactments of the moral self, enactments which can become public in that one form in which they remain solitary; enactments which, made in the solitariness of one's conscience, in that very act display themselves publicly—those enactments we call oaths.

It is in such an enactment, now, that Job gives the lie to the Satan's charge and shows himself as fearing God freely and without cause. In the first lines of our commentary on the prologue, we quoted Robert Alter's words to the effect that the Hebrew narrators' preference for dialogue "is finally a technique for getting at the essence of things." In a manner which gives sharper point to his observation, the oath of 27:1–6 allows the writer to expose the very inner essence of Job, as one whose covenant loyalty is unimpeachable.

What, however, is the evidence for the truth of such an oath? Where the oath backs up testimony concerning events external to the witness, then of course other testimony or evidence may corroborate or disconfirm the truth of an oath. Where the only "evidence" is the oath itself, contradicted by the opinions of others, what evidence can there be except the ring of truth in the attestation of one or the other party? And what is the basis on which one detects that ring of truth? Is that basis not in part the truth of the moral being of those who hear the oath? In such a case there is no proof, and can be no proof, outside the moral realm. Proof here is available in the only form in which it exists: deep calls to deep. It is to the moral being of the reader that the Book of Job addresses itself. Our assessment of the truthfulness of Job's oath, and of the message of the book as a whole, will rest finally on our response at that level.

A final word may be offered by way of situating one of the themes of 27:1–6 in the context of the dialogues to this point. It has been observed that consciousness and conscience are intimately related to the extent that they are not synonymous. Earlier (chap. 3 and 12:22) consciousness has been imaged under the figure of "light." That consciousness functions as such a light is attested in such places as Romans 1:21 and Ephesians 4:18, where darkness characterizes the degenerate moral self. Such a figure is interestingly presented in Proverbs 20:27: "The spirit [nešama] of 'adam is the lamp of Yahweh, /searching all the inward parts [or chambers]." Bildad in chapter 25 has spoken of God's judgments from the external perspective of God as lofty cosmic overlord, whose examination of earthly

184

actions comes as a shining light (25:3*b*). Job, of course, in many places has denied that God's light shines at all upon the human scene with any moral illumination or judging action. He repudiates Bildad's latest words as so much misguided claim to inspiration (*nešama,* 26:4). When Job, however, makes his oath by the use of this same word *nešama* ("breath," 27:3*a*) as the presence of God's life within him, we may identify a divine light which shines within his clear conscience. At a time when the light of moon and stars is gone out (25:5; cf. 10:22*a* and its reference to obscured constellations); at a time when God's own beaming approval seems to be obscured so that God's own shining is as darkness (10:3*c*, 22*b* and commentary there); at such a time the divine light of revelation, and the divine spirit of inspiration, is to be seen in Job's conscience. If, in swearing by the God who seems to have deserted and betrayed him, Job thinks that his deep is calling out to the divine deep, the reader may see his deep, rather, responding to the calling out to him of the depth of God.

Job's Anticipation of Zophar III

In the interpretation of chapters 25—27 here offered, we have suggested that in chapter 26 Job interrupts Bildad's third speech with a sarcastic challenge to Bildad's sources of inspiration and then finishes his speech for him. In chapter 27 Job follows his solemn oath with equally grave words of imprecation against his friends as a group (27:7–12). Then he concludes his engagement of his friends with a parody of what he might expect to hear from Zophar. That Job's own oath might issue in such a parody of Zophar is perhaps indicated in the following correlations between the oath of 27:1–6 and Zophar's first words in 11:1–6. Job's "my lips will not speak falsehood" in 27:4*a* is reminiscent of 11:2*b* which literally reads "should a man of lips be vindicated?" and of 11:5*b* with its reference to God's lips. The overall claim of Job in 27:1–6 to a good conscience is in accord with the views which Zophar attributes to him in 11:4, and is in contradiction to what Zophar says in 11:6 *c.* In 11:2–6 Zophar contrasts what Job says (with his lips) with what God would say (with his lips) if God were to disclose what is hidden in the divine wisdom, and this would be that Job's guilt is even greater and deeper than he is conscious of. But Job's oath by the life and in the spirit of God, in which his conscience is the presence of the light of God, gives the lie to Zophar's

185

claim to a vast discrepancy between what Job says and what God would say. In this way of looking at it, verses 1–6 of chapter 27 are an exact if belated answer to 11:1–6, while 27:13–23 are a caricature of the acquisitive imagery which Zophar initiated in 11:13–20 and elaborated so fully in chapter 20.

PART FIVE

Soliloquy
JOB 28—31

Job 28
A Meditation on Wisdom

The dialogue with the friends concluded, Job now enters into a meditation on the human search for wisdom and its apparent inaccessibility. Humans can mine the earth for its hid treasures, and they can trade among themselves for the precious products of the earth; and in such activities they may be said to display a wisdom of sorts. The wisdom which Job seeks cannot be found or bought. God alone has access to such wisdom, for it is found and displayed only in the enactments by which creativity brings cosmos into existence. Job concludes that humankind may perhaps approximate such wisdom, if at all, in acts of piety and uprightness. Ironically, he fails to appreciate that by such acts as exemplified in his conduct since his calamities his own life may stand as a close analogy and image of the divine creativity.

* * *

Commentaries and scholarly studies generally reflect a wide variety of views as to the origin of this chapter and its function in the Book of Job. Ultimately, the issue turns on two factors: how one reads the Book of Job generally and how one reads chapter 28 in particular. In the context of the reading of the whole book which is offered in this commentary, and given the understanding of the chapter here presented, we find it plausible to read the chapter as part of Job's own utterance.

Introductory Comments and Short Outline

In chapter 3 Job had broken his seven days of silence with 187 a soliloquy at the center of which lay a series of questions both specific and general. Implicit in those highly immediate questions lay a desire and a search for wisdom. That desire and that search, together with the apprehensiveness that it faced no sure prospect of satisfaction, has carried Job through the dialogue and to this point. Now, the dialogue terminated with chapters 25—27, Job ends as he began, in monologue. In chapters 29—31 he turns entirely inward, assessing his own past and present and then placing both past and present within the solemn seal of a second extended oath. In these three chapters there is no explicit search for wisdom, though in the light of the approach taken to chapter 28 one may suggest that chapters 29—31 present to the reader one form of wisdom's enactment.

Prior to these three chapters, then, we have in chapter 28 Job's summation of the outcome and the further prospects of the human search for wisdom in the context of human travail. Given the failure of the friends to satisfy him, given God's failure to speak, given Job's implicit assumption as to the relational and covenantal context within which wisdom should emerge, his solitary monologue in this chapter comes to the one conclusion left to him: Wisdom in its primal and ultimate character is withheld from humankind and its functional equivalent for humans is piety and uprightness. Such a conclusion (28:28) may strike one as disappointingly conventional, not to say banal. On the other hand it may be that such a view, once freshly entertained but become banal through superficial or thoughtless repetition, is here presented as renewed and refreshed through the searching reflection in which Job and the reader have been engaged since chapter 3. Not all explorations issue in the discovery of totally new terrain. Sometimes, exploration issues in the discovery, as though for the first time, of terrain in which one has always lived. In such cases, this terrain may be occupied by conventional minds and by those newly wakened. The question then (and it is not easily answered) becomes: In what sense do they inhabit the same terrain and in what sense are they worlds apart? In terms of 28:28, one may ask whether this conclusion (at this point in Job's search) is crushingly banal or fresh with chastened profundity. It may depend on how one comes to the conclusion and how one entertains it.

It is possible that contextual factors indicate such a transformed understanding. On the one hand, the phraseological connections between 28:28 and 1:1, 8 and 2:3 may serve to indicate that up to 28:28 Job has survived the test and continues to be God's loyal servant in spite of the removal of the hedge of which the Satan had spoken (1:10). On the other hand, it may be the case that chapters 29—31, by the way in which they follow immediately upon 28:28, show Job continuing to display the task of "fearing the Lord and departing from evil," as he now understands these matters. Such an understanding, then, is formally continuous with what Job displayed as in 1:1; but materially it is quite different from the piety displayed in 1:21.

The chapter as a whole falls neatly into three sections. *Section I:* Verses 1–11 contain a meditation on the practical wisdom (wisdom as "know-how") displayed in human technological and exploratory endeavor in the search deep within the earth for precious metals and stones. This section concludes (vv. 12–13) with a question as to the place from which wisdom can be mined. *Section II:* Verses 15–19 contain a meditation on the practical wisdom displayed in human capacities to assess the value of, and to trade in, the precious metals and stones which human ingenuity has mined. This section concludes (vv. 20–22) with a question as to how wisdom can be acquired. In the conclusions to both sections 1 and 2, the answer comes: No creature knows. *Section III:* Verses 23–28 contain a meditation on the divine creativity and the recognition that only in that divine action can one identify the "place" of wisdom to impress one deeply with their pronounced unlikeness. Under the impact of such an impression, one can only include that wisdom in its primal reality, as original and originating in God, is inaccessible to earthlings (v. 28, *'adam*), who therefore are to occupy themselves with such wisdom's earthly and creaturely analogue: piety and uprightness.

Chapter 28 and Genesis 2—3: The comments in the preceding paragraphs lead naturally to a brief comparison with the theme of human access to wisdom as presented elsewhere in the Hebrew Bible. We have already noted some of the themes and motifs common to the prologue of Job and to Genesis 2—3. In the latter passage the serpentine temptation is to suppose that wisdom can be gained by unilateral human action involving a finding and an assessing ("good to make one wise") —a unilateral raid on those secrets reserved to the divine self (cf. also Gen. 11:1–9 and Deut. 29:29). In contrast to this unilateral approach, the garden story implies another approach which is relational and covenanting in character. One is not to seize wisdom as by a raid on the inaccessible but to enter into

189

wisdom's realm through the practice of a piety and an uprightness defined in terms of human response to the divine trust. For
the command in Genesis 2:7 is not chiefly a prohibition or an
imposed rule as the basis for divine-human relations. More
deeply, the gift of the tree of the knowledge of good and evil
and the warning not to eat it is the gift of freedom by the
opening of a *moral* alternative and thereby the creation of the
need for a *moral* decision. (The plurality of trees in Gen. 2:9
otherwise poses only *sensual* alternatives, giving rise only to
aesthetic decisions.) This gift is both a test and a trust, placed
in the keeping of humankind.

The structural analogy between Job and the Garden couple
may be pursued a bit further. *In the Garden* we find two prominent types of tree: the one "every tree that is pleasant to the
sight and good for food" and the other "the tree of the knowledge of good and evil." (The tree of life is, of course, also there,
and is the most important tree of all. Significantly, little attention is given to it at the outset, perhaps because access to it turns
on how one relates to the other two types of tree.) Were humankind to find itself amidst only the first type of tree, all decisions
would be sensual and aesthetic and piety would have the character of a conditioned response at the sensual level, in the form
of gratitude for satisfied appetites. The introduction of the second type of tree introduces a moral dimension into the Garden
and the choices of humankind. Whereas sensual choices are
heavily conditioned by the force of physical appetite, moral
choices governed by a prohibition are conditioned at a different
level and in terms of the sense of "ought" and "ought-not."
Even here, the snake's words come as a divinely commissioned
and sanctioned means by which the otherwise overwhelming
moral weight of the "divine parental superego" may be neutral-
ized to increase the reality of the freedom to be enacted in the
human decision concerning the trees in the Garden. The full
force of the existential situation is reached in the Garden when
humankind finds that it has been addressed concerning the tree
by two different voices saying contradictory things. As in
I Kings 22:5–23, the dilemma created by hearing two contradictory words has to do, not simply with whether one shall obey,
but with the more critical judgment as to what sort of action will
constitute genuine covenanting response.

In the Book of Job we find an analogous situation. Now the
moral life considered as cause-and-effect, action-and-conse-

190

quence, has itself come to resemble the plurality of the first kind of trees in the Garden. For, while one may choose uprightness or a life of evil, a life of uprightness (as the Satan points out) is still to some degree conditioned by its outcome. Conventional divine imperatives to such a life predispose the prudent person to piety. It is necessary that the divine voice (and the logic which it carries) be countered by another voice. The equivalent in Job to the tree of temptation in the Garden is the experiences which he undergoes. The equivalent in Job to the voice of the snake in the Garden is the voice of his friends urging him to repent. In the Garden story the couple yield to the persuasiveness of the snake's words. Thinking to find wisdom by their unilateral efforts, they discover in the end only that they are naked; and they try to hide from God. In the Book of Job the central figure does not yield to his friends but remains faithful to what, in our comments on 27:1–6, we have identified as the silent voice of God speaking in and through his own conscience. In that act he does not hide from God but seeks all the more intensely a meeting with God face to face. At no point has Job sought for wisdom unilaterally, but for a wisdom which God would share with him or disclose to him. Not having found such a wisdom so far, Job in chapter 28:1–27 has the courage to confess his failure, and in 28:28 displays even greater courage in reaffirming his sense of what is called for. By a strange paradox, the confession of 28:28, rightly heard, may betray the presence in Job of the very wisdom which he believes to be inaccessible to him. Such a possibility lies under the surface of the imagery of chapter 28 as a whole, to which we may now proceed.

First Meditation: Bringing to Light Precious Materials from the Dark Dust (28:1–14)

The portrayal of human activity and ingenuity in mining is framed by verses 1–2 and 10–11. The close connection between these verses will be highlighted by the following translation:

> 1.*a* There is a mine *(mosa')* for silver,
> .*b* and a place where gold is drawn forth;
> 2.*a* Iron is taken from the dust *('apar)*,
> .*b* and copper is extracted from stone *('eben)*.

191

The four lines name four kinds of product: silver, gold, iron, and copper. The first two lines refer to the locus of this product:

mine, place. The last two lines refer to the earthly substance from which the product is taken: dust, stone. The motif of place and mine (*moṣa'*, literally "place of coming forth") runs through chapter 28, whereas the contrasting motifs of dust on the one hand and the precious metals on the other have appeared repeatedly throughout the dialogues.

> 10.a He splits open rivers of precious ores,
>   .b his eye sees every rare thing;
> 11.a He pries free springs of shining wealth,
>   .b what is hid he brings forth to light.

Again the four lines name four kinds of product, indicated here by solid or broken lines. Lines 10.*a* and 11.*a* describe the activity of mining, while lines 10.*b* and 11.*b* describe the result in what meets the assessor's eye. The general similarity between verses 1–2 and 10–11 is accentuated by the way in which the word for mine (*moṣa'*) in verse 1.*a* is balanced by its verbal counterpart "brings forth" (*yoṣi'*) in verse 11.*b*. However, there is a difference between verses 1–2 and 10–11. In contrast to the specific metals named in verses 1–2, verses 10–11 tease the imagination with their reference to unspecified precious things. The reader is being set up for the extended catalogue in 28:15–19. Meanwhile, between these opening and closing pairs of verses, comes a celebration of human ingenuity and prowess, in terms which connect suggestively with the thematics and the imagery traceable in chapters 3—27.

To begin with 28:2, we note that the precious commodity iron has its source in *dust.* Moreover, to the miner the subterranean darkness is no longer a forbidding and fearful mystery. Miners put an end to *darkness;* they *probe (ḥaqar)* to the farthest *bounds,* where they dig for stones amid *gloom* and *deep darkness (ṣalmawet).* The root for "probe" (*ḥqr*) has occurred often in the dialogues (the *verb:* 5:27; 13:9; see also 28:27; 29:16; 32:11; the *noun:* 5:9; 8:8; 9:10; 11:7; see also 34:24; 38:16). The word "bounds" has occurred at 11:7 and 26:10. Nouns for darkness of course form a leading motif in Job. Particularly important is the way in which the word for "gloom" (*'opel*) elsewhere has occurred only on Job's lips (3:6; 10:22; 23:17; and see 30:26). The combination of the three words for darkness (darkness, gloom, and deep darkness) comes elsewhere only at 10:22, where Job's descent into the earth is of a different sort and is unaccompanied by the hope of finding any light. It is as though, in describing the hazardous but worthwhile human quest for the precious resources which lie hidden within the dust, Job unwittingly resorts to the language of his own current experience! Or is it, rather, that in describing the human occupation of mining, with its results as named in verses 1–2 and 10–11, Job is unwittingly providing an interpretation of his experience? Such a reading of 28:1–11 would place this part of Job's speech in a direct line of continuity with 23:10.

The correspondence between the miners' locus and activity and Job's experience extends also to the portrayal in verse 4 of the solitary isolation of the miner, far from human habitation or traffic. The contrast between common human life and the miner's task is continued in verse 5, which is to be understood as follows:

> "As for the earth, from it *comes forth* bread,
>   but its depths are changed like fire."

The verb in the second line can refer to a transformation, as in the case of Saul's heart in I Samuel 10:9. The comparative phrase "like fire" is taken to indicate not the process but the result of the change or transformation: "fire-stones." The point of the verse is that while the surface of the earth produces bread, in its depths are produced precious stones. The connection between "fire" and precious stones is indicated by 28:11a with its description of shining wealth, and by Ezekiel 28:13–15 and the reference there to precious gems as "fire-stones." (We shall have occasion to return to Ezekiel shortly.) Thus read, verse 5b is then amplified in verse 6. Just as 28:2 identified dust and stones as the earthly source of iron and copper, so verse 6 identifies stones and dust as the source of sapphires and gold. (Again one thinks of 23:10.)

Not only are these depths far from human habitation and travel, but the path to them is hidden from the sharpest bird's eye and is barred to the proudest animal (vv. 7–8). One is reminded here of the imagery in 11:7–9, where the terms are remarkably close, including the root *ḥqr*, "deep things," in 11:7, the noun "limit, bounds" in 11:7, and in 11:6 the reference to "secrets of wisdom" where the word for "secrets" anticipates 28:11 "the thing that is hid." Only the miner can find such hidden treasures at the roots of the mountains (v.9), and bring to light all manner of precious things (vv. 10–11). That we are to read 28:3–11 against the background of Job's agonizing

193

search is suggested by the following earlier articulations of Job's concern: In 3:21 he analogizes his longing for death to those who dig for hid treasures, and the finding of the grave to those who find such treasures. In 10:22 Job characterizes the underworld as a land of darkness, gloom, and deep darkness without stars or God's light. In 12:22 Job accuses God of uncovering deeps out of darkness in order to bring to light deep darkness (the very deep darkness, perhaps, into which Job has gazed in 10:22). But in 28:3–11 the miner is shown penetrating into just such a darkness, gloom and deep darkness (v. 3) in order to bring to light the hidden riches which lie there (v. 11). The similarity between 12:22*b* and 28:11*b* is particularly striking.

Yet Job seems to be oblivious to the hermeneutical connection between the picture he has painted in 28:1–11 and his own experience. Or if the connection is intentional, he does not see that his own "mining" experience since the double calamity has given results analogous to those he has just described in the present passage. For he concludes that in the search for wisdom all creatures are ignorant. No one knows the *place* of wisdom (cf. v. 1), nor the way to it: it is to be found neither with the living nor with the dead. ("Deep" and "Sea" in v. 14, as mythic emblems of chaos and destruction, are the counterpart of "Abaddon" and "Death" in v. 22.) In the prologue of chapters 1 and 2 the reader was given access to the proceedings in heaven, and thereby to some understanding of Job's experience; but Job himself underwent that experience without benefit of the perspective given the reader. Likewise, we propose, by the way in which themes and images previously appearing in the dialogues are employed in 28:1–11, the reader is invited to adopt a somewhat different understanding of Job's words here than that which he himself has. Irony again is at work in a positive direction.

Second Meditation: The Futile Attempt to Buy Wisdom (28:15–22)

If the first meditation compared the search for wisdom with the human ingenuity and prowess displayed in mining for the precious products of the earth, the second meditation compares that search with the human sense of worth and skill in negotiation displayed in activities of trading for precious metals and gems. Formally two features of the passage are worthy of note. Verses 15–19 in Hebrew contain precisely seven verbs, all with the negative particle. (Verse 17*b* in Hebrew has no verb nor negative particle.) All the more strikingly, the extensive catalogue of precious things numbers only thirteen. Yet a moment's reconsideration discloses that there is a fourteenth—it is the wisdom of verse 18*b*. Whereas all other valuables can be ranked and thereby evaluated comparatively, wisdom cannot even be put on the scale; and whereas all other valuables can be obtained by requisite amounts of yet other less valuable items, wisdom cannot be purchased. Thus the two practical activities in which human wisdom excels—technology and commerce—bring one nowhere near wisdom in its intrinsic character as the art of living meaningfully.

This meditation of course draws on themes already present in the tradition; but it elaborates those themes both formally and reflectively. The comparison of wisdom/understanding with gold/silver occurs for example in Proverbs 16:16; 20:15; and 31:10 (see also, interestingly, 17:16). A most suggestive treatment of this theme, however, occurs in Proverbs 25:11–12:

> A word fitly spoken
>   is like apples of gold in a setting of silver.
> Like a gold ring or an ornament of gold
>   is a wise reprover to a listening ear.

This proverb envisages the wise offer of counsel to someone who is in need of reproof. The root of the word "reprover" (*mokiah*) has, of course, occurred often in the dialogues of Job; and this proverb invites us to view 28:15–19 as a figurative way of viewing the verbal interactions, or "transactions," in the dialogues. In their arguments back and forth, Job and his friends have been engaged in that form of commerce, of verbal exchange, in which they have hoped to find true wisdom. According to Job their best and most precious exchanges have not succeeded, for the "price of wisdom" (v. 18*b*) is above the best they have to offer. The human plight, in such an endeavor, might be summed up in the words of Proverbs 17:16: "Why should a fool have price in his hand to buy wisdom, / when he has no mind? (Mind here translates *leb*; cf. Job 11:12–13 and commentary.)

Yet Job's melancholy conclusion concerning the outcome of the dialogues is not entirely accurate. We have attempted to trace, in his own words and at times in the words of his friends, elements which the resolution of the book will bear out as true,

195

though often in a sense which they did not intend. Moreover, Job's words have betrayed a gradual transformation in him, which gives weight to his affirmation in 23:10 that "he knows the way that I take; / when he has tried me, I shall *come forth as gold*" (italics added). In the commentary on this verse, we noted that it came as a response to Eliphaz's urging in 22:21–25. There Eliphaz had (1) urged Job to receive instruction from God's mouth, and lay up his words in his heart *(leb);* (2) urged Job to lay his own gold in the dust; and (3) urged Job to make God his gold and silver. The relation between the three parts of this urging suggests that Eliphaz was drawing the stock wisdom analogy between wisdom and precious metals and moreover that (in the spirit of Prov. 25:11–12) he identified his own counsel and that of his friends with the divine wisdom so analogized, whereas Job's words he accounted as worthy only to be returned to the dust and the stones. In light of the pairing of dust and stones in 28:2, 6, are we to understand Eliphaz in 22:21–25 as counseling Job to return his "gold" to the mine from whence it came? That would be a figurative way of telling him to eat his words and to embrace instead what God (and they) had to say. That Job's retort to this urging, in 23:10, may include a reference to his own *speech* is suggested by a comparison of Proverbs 17:3, "The crucible is for silver, and the furnace is for gold, / and Yahweh tries the *hearts*" (italics added), with Proverbs 27:21, "The crucible is for silver, and the furnace is for gold, / and a man is judged by his *praise* [or boast]" (italics added). Job in 23:10, then, may be claiming that when he is tried, the "arguments" which he has made before the friends and which he seeks to lay before God (23:4) will be vindicated. That this is not an idle boast is confirmed in the epilogue (42:7, 8).

We shall reserve a further comment on the overtones of the catalogue of precious things until we have attended to the third part of this chapter.

Third Meditation: Wisdom's Place in God's Creative Activity (28:23–28)

The final meditation opens in a manner which formally continues motifs earlier employed: God understands the *way* to wisdom (see v. 13*a;* and v. 7, the mine shaft as a "way" to the place of gold); and God knows its *place* (see vv. 1, 12, 20). The resulting image, however, is theologically startling to conventional religious sensibilities. One would have supposed that wisdom is "in" God as a divine attribute; yet this verse suggests that even God must "find" wisdom by following a path that brings God to a place where it exists. This strange figure, however, is illuminated by the verses which follow.

The scene in verses 24–27 focuses on the creative activity of God. As in Genesis 1:1, the terms "earth" and "heaven" together are the biblical way of referring to the whole cosmos. The verbs "looks to" and "sees" may portray God's search throughout the cosmos for the place of wisdom. Yet that does not suit the overall picture. These two verbs in Hebrew sometimes describe an activity of attending to something or of furnishing and providing something (as when in English we speak of "seeing to" or "attending to" a matter). It may be that we should read verse 24 as follows: "When he attended to the ends of the earth, / and saw to everything under the heavens." This most general reference to God's creative activity is then followed by a more specific focus on four creative activities in which wisdom is most mysteriously "present" in a manner unfathomable to humankind: the "weight" of the wind, the measure of the primordial waters, the seasons and locations of rain, and the way of lightning. These superterrestrial phenomena baffle mere humans (cf. chap. 38). But this meditation goes on to observe, it was *when* God created the heavens and the earth, it was *when* God determined the strange orders and patterns of celestial phenomena, it was *in* these creative activities that God saw and named and established and searched out (*ḥaqar*, a word which has occurred so often in Job in reference to the search for wisdom) wisdom in its interiority. Formally, one may suggest that the four verbs in verse 27 correspond to the four most mysterious creative activities mentioned in verses 25–26, as if to associate in the closest way the divine *knowledge* of the way to and place of wisdom and the divine *activity* of creating cosmos.

All of this goes to imply that true wisdom is found "in" the creative act; and the "way to" wisdom is entry into such an act. Wisdom is not something entertained conceptually and contemplatively apart from action and then applied or brought to bear upon a situation secondarily—as though one could work out a theory and then apply it in practice or as though one could meditatively penetrate to the realm of eternal and unchanging structures of wisdom and then bring them into the world of

197

action. In the dynamic world of biblical thought, where even the name of God mysteriously somehow points to activity and purpose ("I will be who I will be"), wisdom emerges "in" the creative act, as it were at the edge of the knife, the point of the chisel, the tip of the brush or (cf. 10:3, 7, 8, "hands") the fingers. To create by a wisdom available before the act would be mere mechanical reproduction or copying of eternal forms—a conception at home perhaps in Plato or in the mythic world of Canaan and Mesopotamia. As the poem in Proverbs 8:22–31 affirms, wisdom itself is something created, albeit the first of the "ways" of God. To say that the wisdom by which each creative act is carried out is created in that very act of creation is to affirm, on the one hand, the freedom of the act of creation; and on the other hand, it is to affirm the dynamism of history as essentially ongoing creation, in which no prior action or pattern of meaning is totally adequate to each new challenge, but the wisdom for the moment must in some degree arise *in* the moment. Such a view of wisdom is at home within the biblical world view, where the emphasis is upon *praxis,* upon the faithful enactment of what may come into existence as an emergent value—the enactment, so to speak, of what may be brought forth into the light. It is at home within a world view where even the divine creator must first create and only then inspect and pronounce good (Gen. 1), a view within which only negative statements ("it is not good . . .," Gen. 2:18) may be pronounced categorically in advance.

This provides the clue to the reason for wisdom's inaccessibility. For all the inventive craft of human wisdom, as displayed for example in technological ingenuity and commercial canniness, such wisdom spends itself on the *products* of divine creativity (the earth and its treasures). Only by a dim analogy does such human activity participate *in* the creative process itself. To that degree humankind remains outside the place of wisdom and knows not the way to it. In such a situation, the nearest one may approximate to the wisdom of the creator is to adopt a posture of piety and moral rectitude before the creator (v. 28).

Clearly the speaker in chapter 28 must be taken as intending an expression of the sense of wisdom's inaccessibility to humankind. Yet if we read chapter 28 in the light of chapters 1—27 (and, retrospectively, in the light of chapters 38—41), it may be suspected that there is more to the matter than the speaker realizes. It may be, therefore, that the author is inviting us to read chapter 28 ironically. If the speaker is Job, we may remind ourselves that Job is in the very midst of his trials; and this, by the very view of wisdom which he has just set forth in verses 23–27, means that he is not yet in a position to "see" himself. He is still in the process of enacting his response to what has been laid on him, a response which, in its departure from conventional models (as represented by the friends), may be said to be creative.

In 28:1–11 human ingenuity is exercised upon the products of the divine creativity—earth and its treasures of gold and the like. In 28:15–19 human canniness is exercised upon those same products. As we have seen, gold is not only the result of divine creative activity, and the earth is not the only dust (28:1, 6) from which gold "comes forth" (v. 11*b*). There is that other dust which is Job himself; and he is engaged in a suffering process in and through which, we may say, his depths are being changed like fire (cf. 28:5*b*, and translation above) with the result that "he knows the *way* that I take; / when he has tried me, I shall *come forth* as gold" (23:10, italics added). This is a gold which God cannot create; or rather, this is a gold which God can create only with the cooperation and co-creative activity of Job. If Job may be viewed as inhabiting the place and treading the way of wisdom, then we may take his "I shall come forth as gold" as also a hope that he will finally come to the point where he will know wisdom for what it is.

An Additional Reflection on Gems, Precious Metals, and Wisdom

In an earlier section of commentary on chapter 28 ("Chapter 28 and Genesis 2—3"), we touched briefly on some connections between the Book of Job and the Garden Story in Genesis 2—3, regarding the latter's treatment of the question of wisdom. There is in the Hebrew Bible another portrayal of a human figure in "Eden, the garden of God" which touches suggestively on the Joban theme as presented in chapter 28. This portrayal is given in Ezekiel 28. The following features are relevant to our reflection: (1) Ezekiel is addressing the prince (28:1–10) and king (28:11–19) of Tyre, i.e., a royal figure. (2) That figure is human (*'adam*, v. 2) but considers himself as God, or as wise as a god (vv. 2, 6). (3) In his wisdom, so understood, that figure through trade and commerce acquires great treasures of

199

gold and silver. (4) But such "wisdom" is unrighteousness, and merits God's judgment, issuing in the prince's death and descent into the Pit. Such is the first portrayal of the royal figure. In 28:1–10, then, we have a critique of human pretensions to wisdom, in a royal context, and against the background of the serpentine temptation of Genesis 3:5–6. In Ezekiel 28:11–19 the critique is both more detailed in its connections with Genesis 2—3 and more complex in its analysis of the connection between wisdom, royalty, and humankind. Here wisdom is not something to be grasped at, nor are precious treasures something to be acquired by trade. The primal figure in the garden is created full of wisdom. Moreover that figure was "covered" with every precious stone and metal. That the "covering" is not a secondary garment, but the stuff of which the figure is made —so that this "adam" is not made from the dust of the ground but from the post precious of earth's treasures—is suggested by the fact that the "covering" in Ezekiel 28:13 probably is from the same root as the verb "knit together" which describes the formation of the human body in Psalm 139:13, and from the same root which we have in Job 10:11 where Job speaks of being "clothed" with skin and flesh and "knit together" with bones and sinews. In Ezekiel 28:11–15b, then, the precious body of the primal figure is the material embodiment of the moral integrity (28:15) and fullness of wisdom (28:12) of that figure. Such a figure walked with impunity on the holy mountain of God and amid the stones of fire. Only when the practice of trade corrupted this figure was it cast from God's mountain, cast to the ground and turned to ashes, where all who looked on would be appalled (Ezek. 28:17–19).

In the first phase of this garden scene of Ezekiel, then, we have a positive connection between humankind, wisdom, royalty, and precious metals and gems. It is in the course of historical action that this original positive relation is corrupted and issues in death. With this additional perspective on the primal situation in the Garden of God, we may look to chapter 28 of Job with renewed appreciation that the sense of the chasm between divine wisdom and the human condition is not ontologically determined and unbridgeable, but has arisen historically and therefore, perhaps, may historically be bridged. The Book of Job in general, and such passages as 23:10 in particular —and even chapter 28, when read on the many levels at which it operates—may be taken as tracing the *path* along which, and as identifying the *place* at which, God and humankind may meet in wisdom. It is the path and the place where Job now finds himself.

Job 29—31
Job's Summing Up:
Recollection of Things Past,
Recognition of Things Present,
and a Final Oath

Job concludes the dialogues, as he had opened them, in soliloquy. These concluding words show the transformation which he has undergone in the process. In chapter 3 he had cursed the day he was born, longed for Sheol, and identified his present miserable condition. In these concluding chapters he affirms the goodness of his past life, portrays the misery of his present condition, and in full view of both undertakes an oath as to his own innocence in society and before God. In chapter 3 he had implicitly identified himself as part of the company of slaves *vis-à-vis* royalty. Now he affirms his own princeliness in and through his oath. Isolated as he is from God and society by their treatment of him, he nevertheless binds himself to them in and through this act of conscience.

* * *

In his first words in chapter 3, after the arrival of the friends, Job uttered three things: a formal curse against the day he was born, a longing to have gone from conception or birth directly to Sheol, and a brief but vivid characterization of his present state. In his concluding words in chapters 29—31, before Yahweh finally speaks, Job again utters three things. The difference between the latter and the former utterance testifies to the difference which has come about in Job through his ordeal. More than any explicit claim he may make on his own behalf (as, e.g., in 23:10), the nature and the tenor of his latter utterance both discloses and verifies his integrity—his existential and religious wholeness. For in these three chapters he expresses a deep and unqualified longing for his past life, and

201

thereby manifests a deep and genuine acceptance of it (chap. 29); he expresses a detailed and unflinching recognition of his present misery, and thereby manifests a realistic acceptance of it (chap. 30); and in the full presence of his total self so "convened to consciousness," he searches his assembled self in the full light of conscience and binds himself to God and the community in a solemn oath (chap. 31).

Formally, then, Job's opening words in chapter 3 and his concluding words in chapters 29—31 are similar; but materially they signal a profound change within him. The first words are filled with raw emotion, while the last are full of deep but resolved feeling ordered through reflection and considered action. The first are charged with a spirit of rejection, while the last are infused with a spirit of acceptance which is not to be confused with approval. In the first the imagery of royalty (3: 14–15) and slavery (3:17–19) occurs side by side, but in a manner that suggests which Job finds most apt for his situation: slavery (cf. also 7:1–6; 14:1–6). In chapters 29—31 Job comes down on the other side: in the past, when Job enjoyed God's blessing (29:2–5), he was like a king (v. 25); now, though God has stripped him of royalty and cast him into the miry clay (30:19), Job continues nevertheless to display a royal consciousness (31: 35–37).

Chapters 29 and 30 merit the closest comparison and study in the light of one another; for, much like Milton's poems *L'Allegro* and *Il Penseroso,* they are mirror opposites. Only some of the connections can be observed here. It may be remarked that such a comparative study supports the present form of the text and suggests the unwisdom of various attempts at re-ordering or deletion.

Job's Recollection of Things Past (chapter 29)

Job opens with the wish that he might be as once he had been. In chapter 3 he had found God's gift of light and life so cruel in the face of subsequent darkness that it would have been better for that light never to have been given. Now he celebrates that light (29:3). If verses 2–6 celebrate his one-time personal well-being under God, verses 7–11 celebrate his one-time reputation and status in the community. His very presence elicited respect: Eye and ear blessed him and testified (v. 11*b*) in his favor. All this was not merely because of his personal power or affluence, but because of his beneficent actions in the

community (vv. 12–17). These actions had the character of righteousness *(ṣedeq)* and justice *(mišpaṭ)* (v. 14). The imagery in
verse 14 merits closer examination. Literally the Hebrew text
reads, "I habited myself in righteousness and it habited itself in
me; my justice was a robe and a turban." (For the second half
of the first line, cf. Judg. 6:34: "the spirit of Yahweh was clothed
with Gideon.") In light of the two dimensions of "habiting"
presented in the first line, we may wonder how the second line
is to be taken. Are Job's acts of justice the robe and turban
(insignia of royalty?) which *he* wears? Or are they the concrete
and incarnate robe and turban which *justice* wears? Perhaps
both are the case. In any event, the verse indicates the inner
moral and spiritual reality embodied in his relations with
others.

As a concomitant of Job's benevolent actions on behalf of
the powerless and the unfortunate, he entertained thoughts
concerning his own future (vv. 18–20). Such a life as his surely
would end in a peaceful death in his own home, "old and full
of days." Thereafter would he not somehow, like the phoenix
(reading thus with Pope and Gordis in place of RSV "sand"),
have his days multiplied? In verses 19–20 he recurs to the hopeful imagery of chapter 14: Like a tree whose roots and branches
are given ample water (14:8–9), his glory would be refreshed
and the bow in his hand would also be renewed *(taḥlip;* cognate
with 14:7 *yaḥlip,* "sprout," and 14:14c *ḥalipa,* "renewal, relief"). Was such a hope and prospect entertained explicitly and
with vivid consciousness? Or was it at first a non-specific and
implicit tonality, an unreflective sense of his life opening out
positively into a future much like his past under the kindness
of God? Was it only his calamity that threw this tonality into
sharp relief, in the form of those sporadic outbreaks of hope
which we have called the outreach of his imagination? In any
event, by the manner in which verses 18–20 are tucked away
in the midst of verses 7–25, we may take them, not as deduc-
tions consequent upon his beneficent actions, but as an internal
concomitant of them.

Job resumes in verse 21 the description of his status and his
actions in the community as begun in verses 7–17. Now the
language in which this description is continued takes on a no-
ticeably royal connotation, ending in the words "chief" and
"king" in verse 25. The royal connotation of the language
becomes clear when we compare verses 21–25 with Psalm 72.

In that Psalm the king is given God's justice and righteousness that he may judge the people—especially the poor—in keeping with those virtues. His reign of righteousness and peace comes down like rain on the grass and like showers on the earth (72: 5–7); for he delivers and redeems the poor and needy from oppression and violence (72:12–14). Blessings are directed to him continually (72:15b; Job 29:11). Prayers are offered for his longevity—that he may live as long as the sun and moon (72:5); that he may be imperishable like gold (72:15a); and that his name may endure forever like the sun. Given the royal language implicit in Job 29:7–17, 21–24 (Hebrew *mošab* in v. 7 is perhaps not just a "seat" [RSV], but a royal throne as in Ezek. 28:2), and explicit in 29:25, the "thought" of 29:18–20 correlates nicely with the motif of royal longevity in the psalm.

The imagery of light in verse 24 is particularly felicitous. Formally it makes an inclusion with the reference to light in verse 3. The connection between the two verses continues the suggestion that Job mediated God's beneficent rule to the people. The phraseology of the second line echoes that of the priestly blessing in Numbers 6:25–26 and the latter's many evocations in the psalms. Like Moses (Exod. 34:29–35), Job's face shone with God's own light. The result was that when those who had lost all capacity for belief in life's goodness felt his gaze upon them they could not discount and cast aside the upspringings of hope and meaning which he kindled within them. Thus, their own hopes in Job's presence were analogous to those which he entertained in regard to his own life (vv. 18–20).

By the way in which the royal portrayal of Job comes to such a compassionate climax in verse 24, we may assess the felicity with which the concluding verse sets forth his past eminence: not primarily in his decisions for the conduct of his people's internal affairs, nor yet in his leadership of his troops in war, but in the overall way in which he brought comfort *(nḥm)* to the mourners. That this line should not be re-translated or deleted and that 29:21–25 properly conclude chapter 29 (contrast Pope, Gordis, JB, NEB) is indicated by the mirroring contrast between the conclusion of 29:25 and that in 30:31: On the one hand Job comforted mourners; on the other hand his own lyre is turned to mourning and his pipe to the voice of those who weep. The question which 29:25 and 30:31 leave for Job and the reader is whether the one who thus gave comfort and who himself has come to mourn will himself eventually receive comfort. The answer to that question comes in 42:1–6.

Job's Recognition of Things Present (chapter 30)

The contrast between what Job recollects and what he now experiences is emphasized by the threefold repetition of the word "now" (vv. 1, 9, 16). This word also introduces the first three sections of the chapter, while the fourth and final section is introduced by the contrastive particle "yet" in verse 24.

A Senseless Disreputable Brood (30:1–8). Verses 1–8 give a shocking picture of human beings whom one would disdain to have associate with one's dogs (v. 1), those who are driven out of human society (v. 5) and left to forage like animals in the wild regions of the land (vv. 3–4, 6–7). Their social uselessness (vv. 1*cd*, 2), their treatment at the hands of society (vv. 5, 8*b*), and their own brutish behavior (vv. 3–4, 6–7) all arise from a root fact: They are "a senseless, disreputable brood." It is difficult to find a translation adequate to the extreme lengths to which the Hebrew terms here take the reader's moral imagination. The first term, "senseless," represents Hebrew *bene nabal*, "foolish ones," where the term *nabal* reminds the reader of how Job responded to his wife in 2:10. As the comments there indicated, the term identifies the absence in persons of any moral or religious sensibilities or any social habits and behavior rooted in them and making social intercourse possible. The second term, "disreputable," represents Hebrew *bene beli šem*, "nameless ones," an expression which compounds the force of the preceding one. In human society, where social relations are rooted in sensibilities of primal sympathy having moral and religious overtones and where individual identity arises partly through embodiment of recognizable common values and partly through the individually distinctive way in which those values and sensibilities are embodied and enacted, how *can* one discover or make contact with anything personal or individual in a *nabal*, a fool, much less give a personal name? The very namelessness of such a brood is already their alienation from the community.

What are we to make of such a portrayal? Does it not give the lie to Job's claims in chapter 29 to such social compassion that he even searched out the cause of those unknown to him (29:16)? No doubt Job's lack of feeling for them establishes the

205

limit within which his righteousness and justice (29:14) were operative. Job is after all a creature of society. All that he claims in chapter 29 is that within the context of his society (within that particular "hedge," we might say) he was known to be extraordinarily compassionate and upright. If 30:1–8 implicitly criticizes Job's moral and religious stature, that stature nevertheless is at home in the moral and religious frame of reference which it has been the business of the Book of Job to bring under reexamination and critique generally. If these senseless, nameless "humans" exist only to be driven beyond the pale of society, beyond the hedge and into the wilderness, yet they are introduced here to set the stage for a portrayal of Job under even worse conditions.

One Whom God Has Humbled (30:9–15). Verses 9–15 now depict Job's condition in comparison with that which he has just painted. For these very "fools," supposedly devoid of any capacity for moral and religious discrimination, look at Job and hold him up to scorn (v. 9). "They abhor me" in verse 10 does not fully convey the force of the Hebrew verb. The Hebrew noun "abomination," with which the verb is cognate, names those objects or practices which lie under the gravest taboo and interdiction in Israel. No more solemn judgment can be levied than to call something "abomination." Such a judgment, of course, arises in the context of a clearly defined and socially shared moral and religious sensibility. The irony of verse 10 now becomes clear: These senseless ones whom society repudiates finally have found a fellow human being who offends and violates their supposedly deficient sensibilities! *They* recognize in him one whom *God* has humbled; and they, accordingly, dissociate themselves from him. This ironic reversal may be set forth in similarly forceful terms in verse 12. The term translated "rabble" (RSV) may in fact come from a homonymous root which describes the outbreak of leprosy and similar eruptions. "On my right hand the leprous arise, / and they drive me forth," then, portrays Job as unfit even for the company of lepers, and he is treated by them as they are normally treated by society.

206   This section closes with a pair of words which contrast with the pair which opened the section: "my honor" and "my prosperity" contrastingly balance "I, their song" and "I, their byword." The word "honor" connotes generosity, nobility, in a

phrase *noblesse oblige*—the very character recalled in 29:7–25. In Isaiah 32:5–8 the fool and the noble are vividly contrasted. In 29:7–25 Job was held in honor by the princes and the nobles (vv. 9–10); here he is ridiculed by the foolish. Once higher than the highest, he has become lower than the lowest.

I Liken Myself to Dust and Ashes (30:16–23). Verses 16–23 now shift the focus of Job's plight from human "society" to God. Fittingly, the section opens with a reference to his *nepeš*, in an idiom frequent in psalms of complaint; and it continues with language which, at every point, echoes (or rather recalls and amplifies afresh) language already heard in his complaints in chapters 3; 6—7; 9—10; and 12—14. In verse 18 we should read God as the subject of the verbs (following Pope): "With violence he grasps my garment, / seizes me by the coat collar." As an introduction to verse 19, verse 18 then resumes the imagery of 9:31 and 19:9 and contrasts with 29:14. Verses 16–23 thus portray Job's present treatment at God's hands in contrast to how God earlier had watched over him (29:2–6). There is in fact an interesting thread which runs from 29:3–4 through 30:11*a* to verse 23. In the first passage the friendship of God was on Job's tent. In 30:11*a* the foolish see that God has loosed Job's cord— literally, his tent-cord—a figure for bodily death, as indicated by the usage in 4:21. Because of the character and the significance of God's action (30:18–19, on which see comment below), Job concludes: "I know that you will return me to death, / and to the *house* appointed for all living" (30:23, italics added). Dust and ashes signify death as Job's destiny. (Contrast 19:25, in our analysis, which also opens with the affirmation "I know.") The conclusion in 30:23 ("I know") comes in contradiction of the hope expressed in 29:18–20 ("I thought").

It may be observed, however, that this melancholy conclusion is predicated upon the sense that, for all Job's calling out in distress, God does not answer (v. 20). What will happen to this conclusion if it should turn out that God after all does finally respond (cf. 14:15)? Is this conclusion by implication reversed? Is the conviction of 29:18–20 in some sense vindicated? Such an outcome, we suspect, is signaled by the verbal connection between 42:6 and 30:19. The connection between these two verses is underscored by the fact that, though the term for dust occurs some two dozen times in Job, and though the term for ashes also occurs sporadically, the pair of terms occurs only in

207

these two places in the book, and elsewhere in the Hebrew Bible only in Genesis 18:27. In this and in other respects 30:19 merits closer attention.

The two parallel expressions, "mire // dust and ashes," connote a theme already familiar to us. "Mire" occurred already in 4:19 ("clay") in reference to the human body as mortal; and in 10:9 Job said, "remember that you made me of *clay*; / and will you return me to dust again?" Verse 19 of chapter 30, while it echoes such statements and so anticipates 30:23, also carries other more pointed connotations. These are conveyed in the two verbs, each of which carries a double meaning. The verb translated "cast" also means "point out, instruct, teach," and the verb "I am become" also has connotations of making or drawing a comparison and likeness, so as to produce a parable or similitude. When these two verbs occur together—in a book which is traditionally classified as "wisdom" literature—we can hardly fail to hear the following connotation: In God's action of plunging Job into the mire through the latter's suffering and imminent death, there is, so to speak, an enacted parable. There is a point to be gathered from such an action. (It is typical of wisdom teachers to instruct their pupils by "directing" them to the observation of nature and its processes.) Job is, then, the observant pupil who "gets the point;" and in the manner of a budding "maker of parables" (cf. Ezek. 21:5), he says "I liken myself to dust and ashes."

For their part, dust and ashes are an apt figure for human destiny. The difference between dust and ashes is only that ashes are the residue of what was once organic life; so that "dust and ashes" speaks of humankind in respect to origin and destiny. Taking his cue from God's treatment of him (v. 19*a*), Job recognizes with renewed poignancy the finitude and status of humankind in the total scheme of things.

The Total Scheme of Things (30:24–31). Verses 24–31 now amplify the theme of verse 20—Job's cry to God. This theme both opens the final section (v. 24) and closes it (v. 31). Before we consider this section more fully, a final observation may be offered on the expression "dust and ashes." In its one occurrence outside of Job, it is used by Abraham to indicate (one may say, to parabolize) his stature *vis-à-vis* "the judge of all the earth" (Gen. 18:25–27). The expression conveys Abraham's lowliness before God, as but nothing more than common clay.

208

Yet this is a strange form of humility; for this "dust and ashes" has the temerity to argue with God over such an august divine prerogative as *justice,* indeed, over whether God will destroy the righteous with the wicked. Though not on his own behalf, Abraham here voices the very concern which we have been hearing on the lips of Job. That dust and ashes should have the temerity so to address God on such a matter is surely one part of what it means to be human *('adam)* from the ground *('adama),* to be dust in the image and likeness of God. When in 30:19 Job reinterprets his sense of who he is, it is as though he momentarily relinquishes the image which he bears in favor of mere unqualified dust and ashes. Yet the fact that he recurs to the mode of questioning God in verses 24–31 (as if to ask, "Does the judge of all the earth do right?") and that he goes on to his princely oath in chapter 31 displays the divine image still present and seeking confirmation.

Job now contrasts his treatment of others with God's treatment of him. His soul was grieved for the poor (29:12, 16); but when he looked for good, evil came (30:25–26*a*). Others who had lost hope recovered it in his smile and the light of his face (29:24); but he waits for light, and darkness comes. Others in the gate (29:7) received the refreshment of Job's words as rain on parched souls (29:23); but he waits in vain in the assembly (30:28), and instead of rain feels on his face the searing heat of the sun (30:28, 30). He had been a father to the poor (29:16); now, he is brother to jackals and companion to ostriches (30:29), those hapless creatures of the wilderness. He had comforted mourners (29:25), but his lyre is turned to mourning and his pipe to the voice of those who weep.

In the imagery with which Job concludes the doleful portrayal of his present condition, we have yet another instance of dramatic irony. He intends his "wilderness" imagery of verses 28–31 to signal the hopelessness of his plight. To be a brother of jackals and a companion of ostriches is like calling the pit one's father, or the worm one's mother or sister (17:14; cf. also Ps. 88:18*b*). For, with only one exception, everywhere in the Hebrew Bible where jackals' voices are mentioned they are presented as giving forth lamentation or mourning—as though they existed to give voice to the desolation and sterility of the wilderness. Only in Isaiah 43:20 is this situation changed, when the jackals give forth praise because of Yahweh's eschatological transformation of the wilderness into a garden land. The deli-

209

cious irony in Job's language of 30:28–31 is that, in the divine speeches of chapters 38—41, the wonder and goodness of God's creation is detailed almost totally in terms of the creatures of the wild—including the ostrich, who this time is presented as laughing (39:18). Thinking himself to have been driven beyond the pale of human society and of the structures supportive of life (cf. comments, above, on vv. 1–8), Job in fact is situated precisely in that place where he will receive a new revelation from God concerning the total scheme of things and concerning the "place" of humankind in it.

Job's Second Oath (chapter 31)

The picture in 30:25–31 achieves unusual intensity in the way in which, on the one hand, it situates Job in the midst of the community (v. 28, "I stand up in the assembly"); and on the other hand it portrays Job there as terribly solitary, in an existential wilderness (v. 29, "I am a brother of jackals, /and a companion of ostriches"). If, as we suggested in the commentary on 27:1–6, the oath is at one and the same time both the most solitary and the most social of human acts, then we may appreciate how the last part of chapter 30 sets the stage for chapter 31. To such a stage Job has brought his total self, past and present, in the vivid consciousness of all of his experience.

Recent analyses of Job's oaths have emphasized the formal character and the legal setting of such verbal acts. The result is an interpretative procedure which examines the text within strict categories of social behavior and principles of moral or legal logic. Some have gone so far as to suggest that, by taking an oath so understood, Job coerces God into answering. A somewhat different understanding of the oath is presupposed in this commentary; and it will be helpful, therefore, to sketch some additional features of that understanding as a preface to the interpretation of chapter 31 here offered.

A Reflection on the Ground and Character of the Prick of Conscience and the Self-imprecation

It is sometimes argued that conscience is a faculty by which we come intuitively to know moral principles which can then be stated in the form of rules and laws. In this view conscience functions as a sort of internal tribunal or courtroom, examining our behavior against the specific rules and laws by which conscience is informed. The pain or "prick" of conscience is then the condemnatory awareness of having violated a rule. A somewhat less transcendental and impersonal, somewhat more immanent and social account of conscience-as-relation-to-norms, can be developed along Freudian lines. The conscience is not a faculty for intuiting absolute moral principles, but simply the human psyche displaying the activity of the super-ego, the internalized voice of the norms of society as mediated through parents, teachers, and other significant social figures. The "prick" of conscience here has much the same character as in the first view, except that there may be a more concrete sense of responsibility to personal others rather than to abstract principles or categorical laws as such. (We may remind ourselves that 27:6 says literally "my heart does not *prick* me" (italics added), where the verb *ḥarap,* "reproach," means literally "to say sharp things against.")

The prominence of courtroom language in Job (e.g., chap. 9) attests the appropriateness, in some measure, of the tribunal as a metaphor for conscience. The friends' frequent recurrence to tradition and the lore of the ancestors (e.g., 5:27; 8:8–10) likewise attests the appropriateness, in some measure, of the internalized voice of the elders as another metaphor for conscience. Both metaphors, and the views of conscience which they sponsor, leave out of account a deeper factor in both the rise and the operations of conscience. That factor is what we here call primal sympathy. In this view, the original confused sentience which characterizes an infant's awareness, barely, if at all, distinguishes between self and mother. Presumably most especially in the womb, but even in early post-natal experience, primal sentience, feeling, or "pathos" is massively attuned to the "pathos" of the mother, in primal sympathy. This primal sentience gradually takes the form of conscience ("knowing with"), in the process of the polarization of awareness into a sense of self and others, a sense of "I" and "Thou." Concurrently, through the polarity of feelings in primal sympathy, one becomes aware of oneself and others as having appropriate needs and claims. The moral imagination, wherein one transcends narrow self-interest and whereby one turns to others for help in time of need, operates through the analogies made in terms of primal sympathy. The sympathetic wince of pain at another's misfortune (or the shaking of the head, as when Job's friends come to condole with him in 2:11) is an act of moral imagination grounded in primal sympathy: One "knows" how

211

the other "feels," for one feels with the other. The prick of conscience is a similar act, with this one difference: The pain which one feels in that prick is a recapitulation within oneself and a sympathetic sharing in the pain which one has caused the other, together with the awareness of one's responsibility for the pain.

Such an analysis allows us to imagine how views of moral retribution might arise, not just at the level of abstract *theorizing* about moral acts and their consequences, but at the level of human *experience.* The moral imagination, grounded as it is in primal sympathy, knows itself to share in the fate of others. Especially where one's own acts are concerned, the moral imagination knows that it *ought* to share in that fate. The prick of conscience is an internal symbolic act of identification, goading and spurring in the depths of one's solitariness to enact that identification in overt acts of solidarity.

Primal sympathy and the claims of the moral imagination, of course, generate social customs and rules of conduct which in time take the form of abstract norms and principles. In the process, the experiential awareness of sharing in the fate of others who suffer one's actions also takes on more abstract form, until images of cause and effect (e.g., of sowing and reaping, of conceiving and bringing to birth) express formal doctrines of action and consequence, sin and retribution, reward and punishment. As thus formulated, the dynamics of life become increasingly rigid and brittle, until an experience like Job's is subject to misinterpretation both by his friends and by himself. What is called for is a return to less highly abstracted modes of consciousness and conscience and to more primal modes of awareness, a return to what is here called primal sympathy, but a return undertaken in full consciousness and intentionality, as an enactment of covenant commitment. It is a return, perhaps, to what the Hebrews called *raḥamim,* "tender mercies," the feeling of a mother for the child of her womb and of children for their siblings; and it is a return, perhaps, to *ḥesed,* "steadfast loving-kindness," the social bond which is prior to law and at the base of law. Such a display of primal sympathy (implicit in Job's self-portrait in chap. 29, and prominently withheld from him in chap. 30) comes now to vivid expression in the terms of Job's second oath.

Job's Manifold Self-Imprecation (31:1–34). Several features of this self-imprecation may be noted. (1) As Robert Gordis has observed, the chapter lists fourteen sins from which Job insists he has been free (p. 542). This "double heptad" or "twice-seven" is perhaps an emphatic way of signaling a complete catalogue. In 28:15–19, the device listed all possible candidates for value; here it is used to formalize Job's claim to an exhaustive self-examination in the light of conscience. There may be another aspect to the significance of the double heptad. The Hebrew verb "to swear, take an oath," is developed secondarily from the word for the number "seven," so that the act of swearing involves, in some way, the act of "sevening." Insofar as swearing includes the aspect of self-imprecation, it has the character of a curse or penalty invoked upon oneself in case of perjury. Thereby one formally and juridically and publicly affirms what the prick of conscience (or its absence) internally and solitarily and primally signals: that the guilty does and ought to share in the suffering which has been caused and that the innocent does not and ought not to be held accountable for a given crime. Often the oath in practice omits the self-imprecating part, so that the uncompleted statement "If I have done so-and-so, . . ." becomes in effect an emphatic way of asserting "I have not done so-and-so." In chapter 31 a number of the sentences have this uncompleted character; but the self-curse is explicit in verses 8, 10, 22 and 40 and is backed up by the general statement in verse 3.

(2) The catalogue of possible offenses portrays sin as the violation of concrete social relations—indeed, as the unfeeling disregard of primal sympathy as educated into social and moral sensibilities—rather than of abstract principles. In 24:1–12 Job's portrayal of the plight of the powerless, by the freshness and detail of its elaborations, testified to a lively social sensibility rooted in primal sympathy. The vivid detail in Job's present catalogue of offenses and in his invocations of self-judgment is imbued with the same feeling and offers the same kind of testimony. The customary formality of the oath is thereby re-grounded in the primal awareness out of which it originally developed. Job's self-imprecations are not to be interpreted, therefore, merely at the level of abstract moral logic, and as re-statements of a rigid reward-punishment dynamic which he has earlier both denied and presupposed. These self-imprecations, rather, serve to affirm Job's loyalty to the human community and to God, and to lay the basis for his appeal to an answering loyalty from God.

213

(3) In the first oath (27:1–6) Job grounded his words in the

very God who had taken away his right and embittered his soul. Likewise in this second oath Job repeatedly invokes God as ultimate ground of his behavior and sanction for his oath (vv. 2–4, 6, 11–12, 14–15, 18, 23, 28, and esp. 35–37). Two of these references to God are of particular interest:

> "Did not, in the womb, my maker make him?
> And in the womb did not One make us?"
>   (v. 15, author's translation).

The word "One" in the second line does not only serve to identify a common maker, though it does do that; as in 23:13 it echoes the Hebrew epithet for Yahweh as One (Deut. 6:4; Zech. 14:9). The second word for womb, *reḥem*, vividly underscores the verse's portrayal of the basis for social feeling and proper social relations in compassion and tender mercy. This primal feeling binds together not only human beings, but human beings and God (especially where the divine-human relation is imaged in terms of the parent-child relation, as in personal religion).

A similar sensibility is reflected in verse 18 which (like 29:14) comes as a general explanatory statement embedded within a detailed description of social awareness (31:16–17, 19–21). The precise meaning of this verse is disputed. If we translate the verbal part of the second line as a passive "I was guided (in Hebrew terms: *'enaḥenna*, *niphal* with energic ending, in place of the text's *'anḥennah*, "I guided her"), the verse reads as follows (much as in JB):

> "From my youth he [God] reared me as a father,
> and from the womb of my mother I was guided"
>   (author's translation).

Again, then, Job takes his awareness of God's parental nurture of him as the feeling-ground for his own treatment of the widow and the fatherless (vv. 16–17). Thus the religious imagery implicit in verse 15 and explicit in verse 18 is in accord with the meaning of Job's own name, "where is the (divine) father?" That Job continues to use this imagery for God in chapter 31 is significant, given his sense (as in chap. 30) that he has been abandoned by all human and divine kin and left to associate with the jackals.

214

Job's Signature and New Royal Habit (31:35–37). To his elaborate oath Job now affixes his signature, thereby grounding his own identity in the truth of what he has just said. He calls

for God to hear him, answer him, and present the divine indictment against him. In an anticipation of such a document, he
takes yet another oath (vv. 36–37 in Hebrew continue in the
form of an incomplete self-imprecation, "If I would not carry it
on my shoulder, . . ."): He will wear that document as a crown.
In 19:9 he had complained that God had stripped him of his
glory and crown (cf. 30:19). Now he finds another crown to wear
(one in keeping with the turban in 29:14). That crown will be
an indictment empty of true charges. For he remains convinced
that when God has tried him he will come forth as gold (23:20).
Even if God should bring against him a bill of particulars, they
will be so patently false a list of reproaches, of "pricks," that he
will wear them proudly as, one might say, a crown of thorns.

The claim of verses 35–37—indeed, the boast—can be
taken as the assertion of an unbridled presumption. Or it may
be taken as Job's faithful stewardship of a covenanted conscience. That it is not a unilateral self-proclamation, but a self-
binding within a relationship, is signaled by the way in which
verses 35–37 give way to one more self-imprecation.

Job's Evocation of the Garden Story (31:38–40). These
verses commonly are transposed to a place within the catalogue
preceding verses 35–37, on the ground that they belong with
the other oaths and that they are anti-climactic and inappropri-
ate as a conclusion. We have seen that the similarly common
transposition of 29:21–25 in fact destroys the parallel structure
which chapters 29 and 30 display through their contrasting
endings. In chapter 31 likewise it is advisable to attempt an
intelligible interpretation of the text as it stands, before resorting to rearrangement.

Formally, we may suppose that verses 38–40 are the words
with which Job would approach God, and the means by which
he would give an account of all his steps. For we must not
overlook the fact that verse 37 envisages further speaking on
Job's part, following God's charges. In light of the primal imagery which forms the content of verses 38–40, these verses make
a most fitting way for Job to end.

The "primal imagery" of these verses is, specifically, the
garden imagery of Genesis 2—3. The conditional part of the
self-imprecation contains two asseverations, one pertaining to   215
Job's treatment of the land and its furrows and one pertaining
to Job's relations with others who "own" and work the land for
its yield—literally its "strength" (as in Gen. 4:12). The first asse-

veration (v. 38) has its force against the background of the human commission to till or work the ground and to *keep* it (Gen. 2:15), that is, to tend it nurturingly and not to abuse it. Job here shows himself to be bound in a covenant of primal sensitivity with the earth from which he has sprung (cf. 5:23). The second asseveration (v. 39), nevertheless, defines those relations in close connection still with the ground. In Genesis 2:18 human society is given its basic task as one of mutual *help* in tilling and keeping the garden. That help, one may assume, extends to a fair and just sharing of or compensation for the products of the ground. Job here acquits himself of a possible charge (cf. 20: 18–21; 22:6–9) that he has committed the primal wrong of stealing the fruits of the ground from others and (for so the Hebrew reads) of causing them to breathe out their life *(nepeš)* in despair or in death. One detects here a reversed echo of Genesis 2:7. In this way of reading verses 38–39 we can see how all the specific sins of verses 5–34 are gathered up for recapitulation (in vv. 38–39) in the more encompassing "mythic" language of Genesis 2—3. The same may be said for the self-imprecation of verse 40 as a recapitulation of the self-imprecations in verses 5–34.

For the language of verse 40 thematically draws upon the curse of Genesis 3:17–19. We have already seen how the theme of the return of the human dust to the ground (Gen. 3:19) recurs throughout the Joban dialogues. That theme is present also in 31:40 by implication, as Job invokes the ancient judgment upon himself in case of perjury. This verse in Hebrew reads, "Instead of wheat, let there come forth thorns, / and instead of barley, foul weeds." Even in the very last word "foul weeds," in Hebrew *bo'ša,* we may hear an inverted echo, by a play on word sounds, of the garden story. In Genesis 2:25 the last sentence "and they were not ashamed" includes the verb *boš.* Given the move in Genesis 3 to the depiction of the primal couple's shame, and finally to thorns and thistles, the final word in 31:40*b* may carry overtones of shame.

In 31:6 Job had used a word by now familiar to the reader: "and let God know my integrity *(tumma)."* The subscription which follows Job's final speech (or is it Job's own formal signal that he has nothing more to say?) runs as follows: "The words of Job are ended *(tammu)"*—completed, finished, and—like himself—blameless *(tam).*

PART SIX

A Voice for God, the Voice of God, and Job's Response

Job 32:1—42:6

Job 32—37
The Sudden Appearance of Elihu as an Inspired Young Prophet

Appearing like an Elijah from nowhere, and like a prophet claiming divine authorization, Elihu speaks to set everyone straight. Yet several features of his presentation work to subvert his own claims to speak for God. In fact he serves the narrative progression in a manner analogous to the snake in the garden story and the many prophets *vis-à-vis* Micaiah in Kings. For his "inspired utterance" stands alongside the following divine speeches to require Job to decide which is the authentic word of Yahweh. Elihu thus not only intensifies the issues at work in the Book of Job, but also implies a critique of the prophetic tradition.

*   *   *

Introductory Comments on the Status of Elihu in Job

The speeches of Elihu have often been held to be a secondary insertion into the Book of Job. Objections to the speeches as original turn on four considerations: structural, stylistic, linguistic, and theological. It is observed, for example, that (1) Elihu is mentioned nowhere else, not even in the epilogue, his long speeches interrupt the continuity between chapters 31 and 38, and he contributes little if anything to the content or dramatic movement of the book; (2) the literary style is diffuse and pretentious, inferior to that of the rest of the book; (3) the linguistic usage differs from that in the rest of the poetry; and

217

(4) the speeches offer an alternative resolution to Job's problem from that of the (baffling) divine speeches.

Yet there is little agreement, from one scholar to another, on details of analysis. The argument from style is difficult to control: As F. I. Anderson observes, the author may deliberately be portraying the self-inflated young man as a prolix and as a less than inspiring preacher. When such scholars as Gordis and Freedman argue that the Elihu speeches are from the hand of the author of the dialogues, but from a slightly later period in the author's life, one wonders whether the linguistic argument is not a counsel of desperation. Structural and theological arguments depend for their weight upon how one construes the book as a whole. In the construal being developed in this commentary, the Elihu speeches present no critical problem, though they do tax the reader's patience. We see no cogent reason to view them as other than integral to the book, and we will consider them in that light.

Elihu's Claims to Inspiration

Elihu opens his words, and frequently bolsters them, with an appeal to divine inspiration. He reiterates the claim to possess spirit *(ruaḥ)* and breath *(nešama)* at 32:8 and 18, and at 33:4. The vivid image for the divine afflatus in 32:19–20 is reminiscent of the image in Jeremiah 20:9. In the light of this "inspiration" he claims to speak a "knowledge" which is not derived merely from experience and observation and tradition (as so often in the case of the friends), but from divine revelation under the conditions of inspiration. (The word *dea'*, "knowledge," occurs in 32:6, 10, 17 and in 36:3; 37:16; while the cognate *de'a* occurs in 36:4. RSV "opinion" in 32:6, 10, 17 obscures the force of Elihu's claims for his own utterance.)

It is noteworthy that this is only the second emphatic claim to such a source of knowledge on the part of the friends. We have suggested that in 15:11 Eliphaz appealed to his earlier inspired word and that in chapter 25 Bildad may implicitly have made a similar appeal. Yet chapters 32—37 are the first extended counsel explicitly claiming inspiration since Eliphaz in 4:12—5:7. Structurally, then, chapters 32—37 may be taken to form an inclusion with chapter 4. The intervening chapters present the friends' arguments as based on the general grounds of normal human experience and observation, while these arguments are bracketed and enclosed

218

within two appeals to the specific ground of revelation through inspiration.

The Subversion of Elihu's Claims to Inspiration

Several features both within the text of Elihu's words and in the wider context of his words conspire to subvert his claims to speak the divine word by the unambiguous help of the divine spirit:

Job's Words. Job's words in 26:1–4 (and in 27:1–6), by the way in which they have undercut the friends' claim to inspiration, work by anticipation also to undercut Elihu. At the very least, Elihu's appeal to the spirit and the breath behind his words is matched by Job's appeal using the same words in 27:3, following as these latter words do upon 26:4.

The Divine Speeches. By the way in which they ignore what Elihu has said and "speak over his head" with a different kind of answer, the divine speeches in chapters 38—41 retrospectively undercut what Elihu has claimed to say in God's name.

The Epilogue. The final subversion (narratively speaking) of Elihu comes in the epilogue. Along with Satan, he is not even mentioned there. Since what he has to say in fact succeeds only in reiterating the arguments of the three friends, he is not even deemed worthy of separate mention in 42:7–9.

From Within. The preceding subversions of Elihu's words all come from the wider context in the Book of Job. Several other aspects of his words, in addition to his claims for inspiration, also work to subvert his speeches from within:

We have already pointed out how Elihu's claims to inspiration repeat similar claims on the part of Eliphaz and how these claims are subject to the same critique that Job leveled against Eliphaz. In that connection, Elihu's words share a formal similarity with those of Eliphaz in chapter 4. In their content, however, Elihu's words are overwhelmingly in agreement with the advice and the argumentation of the friends. Gordis has argued that "Elihu contributes a very significant idea—that 219 suffering often acts as a discipline, or, in biblical language, that God sends suffering as a warning in order to safeguard man against sin" (p. 550). But, as Pope points out, that view is anticipated already in 5:17–26. When Elihu, therefore, advances the assertion to the friends that "I will not answer [Job] with your speeches" (32:14*b*), this assertion is undercut by the way in which his speeches do repeat theirs. If this is the case, then the reader is warned that Elihu is being presented as someone who does not understand himself or his role in the dramatic context. This means that Elihu is presented in the mode of dramatic irony.

Similarly, Elihu's claim to speak impartially for God, in 32:21–22, is undercut by Job's words in 13:4–12, 13–16.

Again, Elihu's presentation of an "intercessor" in 33:23 suffers the same subversion which Eliphaz's statement of the intercessor theme in 22:27–30 suffers. For the reversal of intercessory roles in 42:7–9 shows them to have been talking nonsense in their case against Job.

In 35:1–8 Elihu repeats Eliphaz's denial (22:2–4) that Job's righteousness could make any difference to God. The prologue (which shares with the reader a perspective hidden from Elihu as well as from the friends and Job) has already shown us that God has a huge stake in Job's righteousness. Elihu's argument in these verses rests on conventional assumptions about God that persist to the present day, both as general religious convictions and as formal theological propositions. According to these assumptions, God is all-sufficient in such a way that nothing any mere mortal might do can make any difference to the divine life or the divine knowledge. That such a view is placed on the lips of Eliphaz and Elihu is not the best advertisement for its soundness! Moreover, in the light of the prologue we may be permitted to assert that it is simply wrong, at least from the point of view of the Book of Job.

In 35:10–11 Elihu says (perhaps following up on Job's complaints as in (24:1–12),

> But none says, "Where is God my Maker,
>   who gives songs in the night,
> who teaches us more than the beasts of the earth,
>   and makes us wiser than the birds of the air?"

220   The second line in this passage more recently has been translated "who gives strength in the night," as a result of the discrimination in Hebrew of homonyms with the different meanings "song" and "strength." It may be, however, that we need not choose between these meanings as mutually exclusive. Like

the intrinsic existential relation between hope and strength (see commentary on 6:11–13), there may be an intrinsic existential relation between strength and singing. In the midst of a dark night of pain or confusion, the ability suddenly to sing brings with it a renewal of one's energies and resources. Conversely, when in such a condition one is visited by sudden up-springings of strength, they may well overflow in vocal expressions of gratitude or hope, or even of praise (cf., e.g., Acts 16:25; or Jer. 20:13 in its context). Does this in fact not describe exactly what we have been witnessing in Job? From his early expressions of weakness (e.g., 6:11–13), Job has grown in strength (e.g., 17: 9–10 and commentary) until in chapters 29—31 his spirit is nothing if not strong. Also, his imaginative outreaches, erupting sporadically out of the midst of his deep gloom of mind and spirit, have much of the tonality of songs in the night. Again, then, Elihu's argument as a whole is subverted by the way in which his words contain a truth which he does not intend.

There is at least one more suggestion of ironic subversion. Elihu has claimed to speak from a divine inspiration which fills him like new wineskins about to burst (32:19–20). What he does not admit, what he perhaps does not himself realize, but what the narrator takes pains to point out no less than four times in a very short space, is that Elihu is speaking out of his own anger (32:2 [twice,] 3, 5). He may suppose (or the reader may be tempted to suppose) that, like the prophets of Israel's tradition, he is the messenger of God's anger. The reader, however, knows that God is not angry with Job. The fourfold identification of his motivation in speaking, then, can only signify the subversion of his own claims to speak by inspiration.

Why Then Is Elihu in the Book of Job?

In the view here being presented, Elihu is introduced at just this point in the book for reasons integral to the plot and as a further means of bringing under critique certain longstanding religious attitudes and traditions. The way in which Elihu's appearance at this point serves the plot has to do with the fact that Elihu's words are offered under the aegis of the claim to inspiration.

Apart from Eliphaz in 4:12—5:7, Job and the friends have pursued their questions on the basis of human experience and observation. Repeatedly Job has longed for, requested, and even demanded a confrontation with God, in which God would

221

speak to him. We may indeed appreciate the force of those objections to Elihu's presence, which argue that after chapter 31 one would most naturally expect to hear the divine voice of chapters 38—41. Yet, further reflection suggests that such a sequence would offer too unambiguous a resolution.

Which Address Is from God? At various points in the commentary on previous sections of the book, we have referred to the garden story in Genesis 2—3 and to the scene in I Kings 22:5-22 for narrative analogues to the issues in Job. Another such reference will help us to understand how Elihu is to be taken. Both in the garden story and in the episode in First Kings, a human is confronted with the voice and the directive of God and then with another voice which also claims to speak for God. In the instance of the garden story, the snake's counsel is not offered in direct opposition to that of God, but rather as an alternate communication of what God knows and wishes the humans to know. Similarly in the scene in First Kings, both Micaiah and the group of prophets claim sincerely to speak on behalf of God—and Micaiah even goes so far as to affirm the group in its claim to speak by inspiration! What he goes on to point out, however, is that their inspiration serves a purpose other than that which they understand.

In both of these narratives the reader enjoys a perspective denied the main characters. (For the woman was not present when God spoke to the man; and the King of Israel was not present in the divine council.) From this vantage point the reader is able to appreciate that the one who has to make a decision is confronted with *two* claims to divine truth. The question now is not simply whether or not to obey; the question is, Which is the genuine voice of God? In such a situation the hearer (the first pair; the King of Israel) is cast back upon one's own inner moral condition: The decision as to which voice is the true divine voice itself discloses the inner moral and spiritual reality of the hearer and responder.

We have already seen this dynamic at work in the prologue (where the loyal wife plays the devil's advocate to Job) and in the dialogues (where the loyal friends fulfill the same role). Precisely because the wife and the friends largely argue from observation and experience, if the final words of Job in chapter 31 were followed solely by the divine revelatory speech in chapters 38—41, the alternative claims of the friends on the one

222

hand and of God on the other would be an unequal contest. By their claim to divine inspiration, the Elihu speeches stand immediately alongside the divine speeches in order to pose vividly, inescapably, and excruciatingly to Job the need, one more time, to weigh what is said to him upon the scales of his conscience and his spirit. That such a task is not easy is suggested by the experience of a figure who in other respects too is not unlike Job. This figure is the prophet Jeremiah. This prophet could publicly deny the truth of what the many false prophets had to say; and he could expose the inadequacy of baalistic religion in such words as these:

> they have forsaken me,
> the fountain of living waters,
>   and hewed out cisterns for themselves,
> broken cisterns,
>   that can hold no water (2:13).

In private, however, and in the presence of God, Jeremiah could call his own prophetic experience into question, in terms of both of the above public stances: "Wilt thou be to me like a deceitful brook, like waters that fail" (15:18)? Such inner doubts are presented as coming later, after Jeremiah's initial call to his task. Job enjoyed no such initial call. By what criterion, then, should he be expected to identify the true divine word when it finally but unambiguously came to him, first through another person (as often in Israel) and then within his own consciousness? We may suppose that the trial of Job's piety and of his uprightness reaches a climax at this point. Such, then, is the function of the Elihu speeches in the Book of Job, coming as they do between Job's last words and the divine speeches from the whirlwind: They stand beside the divine speeches to create a situation in which Job must decide which "revelation," which address, is from God.

Preparation for Theophany? In passing, one may note how the latter part of Elihu's fourth speech (36:24—37:24) introduces many of the themes and images which are then taken up into the divine speeches. If, as we have suggested, Elihu is in fact speaking by a particular sort of inspiration (the sort portrayed in I Kings 22), such an introduction to chapters 38–41 becomes more readily understandable. Having begun to speak in the heat of his own anger, but claiming to speak by God's breath and spirit, he tiresomely repeats words which we have

223

already heard all too lengthily from the friends. But in the end he does serve to set the stage for his divine successor. Is the reader to imagine that Elihu's imagery in chapter 37 functions in Job's mind in such a way as to prepare him for theophany?

Wider Critique? The Elihu speeches may serve also the purpose of a wider critique. They may serve the critique of Israel's prophetic tradition, at a time (the exile) when that tradition would be heard in the light of Israel's devastating experience at the hands of Babylon. There is much evidence to suggest that the experience of exile confirmed in many minds the correctness of the prophetic preaching concerning sin and judgment. To that extent the old teaching concerning moral retribution would tend to be consolidated. Yet such passages as Jeremiah 31:29–30 and 45:1–5, as well as passages in Ezekiel exploring the particularity of divine justice as applied to individuals, indicate that many in the exile were troubled by the implications of a simple "retributive" deduction from experience in the light of earlier prophetic teaching.

The dilemma may be posed in terms of the use of one particular biblical figure, the hiding of the divine face. In the psalms this figure is always used in the context of the complaints of the innocent, and the anguished queries as to why God deals in such a way with the innocent. When this figure occurs in prophetic contexts, on the other hand, it always occurs to serve the prophetic judgment upon the community for its sinfulness. These two contrasting uses converge (not surprisingly) in Isaiah 53:3. There, "we" despised the servant figure. How? "Like one from whom the face is hidden." As in Job, the religious community viewed the suffering one in terms of the figure in its prophetic usage, as one from whom the divine face is hidden in judgment. The community now sees that if the divine face was indeed hidden it is because the suffering one underwent the mystery to which the psalms of complaining innocence have pointed. (In terms of Isa. 45:15, God was not hidden *from* the suffering one as guilty but hidden *in* the innocent sufferer.)

If Isaiah 52:13—53:12 in such fashion brings under critique a narrow and facile retributive interpretation of exilic experience in the light of previous prophecy, then we may appreciate yet another connection between Deutero-Isaiah and the Book of Job. For, by re-presenting the simple retributive doctrines of the friends as inspired (prophetic) utterance in the mouth of

Elihu, and then by subverting that "inspired" utterance through its contrast with God's own speech to Job in chapters 38–41, the Book of Job helps to make a critique of the prophetic tradition in the degree to which that tradition over-moralizes the mystery of suffering.

Job 38—41
Yahweh's Questions from the Whirlwind

God finally answers Job. But the answer, unlike those of the friends, gives no reason for Job's sufferings. It is as though those sufferings are simply left enshrouded in the mystery of their givenness, their having happened. All God does is to deny Job's charges of dark purpose and indifference to justice and to ask Job three sorts of questions: Who are you? Where were you? Are you able? On the face of it these questions are rhetorical and have the specific force of impossible questions to which the proper answers are, I am nothing, I was not there, and I am not able. Yet again and again throughout the divine speeches, images and motifs and themes from earlier in the book are taken up and re-presented in such a way as to engender the suspicion that these apparently rhetorical questions are to be taken ironically, as veiling genuine existential questions posed to Job. The questions, as from another burning bush, have to do with the issue of Job's willingness to enter upon human vocation to royal rule in the image of God, when the implications of that image are intimated in terms of innocent suffering.

* * *

On the Diversity in Interpretations of the Divine Speeches

We come now to what one may reasonably expect to be the climax and denouement of the Book of Job. Yet the divine speeches have generated interpretative responses which seem as diverse and as irreconcilable as the disputes between Job and his friends. If Yahweh's words to Job, and Job's words in response, finally bring all the doubts and questions to a resolution, it would appear that we the readers require a similar direct divine word to us, to resolve our doubts and questions concerning the way in which to understand how Yahweh's and Job's words answer each other. Short of such a fresh theophany, each of us is left to make of chapters 38—41 what seems most fitting within the context of the book as a whole, the Old Testament as a whole, and existence as a whole. In what follows there will be no attempt to survey the many options already available in the interpretive literature. Rather, we will simply set forth the interpretation arrived at by bringing to bear on chapters 38—41 the general approach taken in this commentary and the exegetical results achieved to this point.

Two types of interpretative conclusion seem inherently improbable, and accordingly are set aside from the outset. On the one hand, it is improbable that the divine speeches serve simply to reassert conventional wisdom on the issues with which the book has been occupied. One expects, rather, a word which establishes some new position. On the other hand, it is improbable that the divine speeches serve to subvert not only conventional wisdom but any and all wisdom. One expects a word which establishes a position within which one may *stand*.

The point of the preceding paragraph may be posed in the terms of Wayne Booth's study of the rhetoric of irony (see the Introduction, under "Approach to the Interpretation of the Text"). As we have noted, Booth sees irony as having the function of subverting the very view which it seems to affirm, in order to establish a different view to which, then, the hearer or reader is invited. We will argue that the divine speeches, while appearing to reaffirm certain kinds of conventional wisdom concerning creativity and creatureliness, and the wisdom appropriate to them, in fact at several points drop hints of the subversion of that conventional wisdom for the sake of a deeper wisdom implicit in the understanding of humankind as the divine image. These hints will invite Job (and the reader) to adopt a new position on, and indeed a new mode of participation in, the realities of creatureliness and creativity, light and darkness.

Though we disagree with his interpretation of the new perspective thus offered, we think Matityahu Tsevat is correct in his suggestion as to why the message of the divine speeches is stated obliquely. He writes,

226

. . . the very radicalism of the book's answer, shattering a central biblical doctrine and a belief cherished in ancient Israel, would itself demand the protection of a veil. . . . the answer of God, presenting a doctrine as radical as it is new, . . . may never have been tolerated or preserved for us but for the protection of its

form, its eschewal of the direct, categorical pronouncement
(*The Meaning of the Book of Job* p. 103).

We agree with Tsevat concerning the writer's strategy *vis-à-vis*
the writer's readers amid the conventional community. However, we would take his point into the book itself. The rhetorical
strategy is to be attributed not only to the writer *vis-à-vis* the
reader, but, within the book, also and primarily to Yahweh
vis-à-vis Job.

By means of rhetorical questions used ironically, Yahweh
addresses Job at two levels—the level of the questions taken as
rhetorical questions and therefore as a form of assertion; and
the level of the questions taken as genuine, once their supposedly rhetorical character has been seen to be subverted by
their ironic tone. Whereas in Genesis 2—3 humankind is given
its dreadful freedom, and its fateful invitation to participate in
the drama of existence, through two distinguishable voices (the
voice of Yahweh and the voice of the snake), in Job 38—41 Job
receives the same gift and the same invitation from the one
voice of Yahweh, speaking at two levels. By the ironic mode of
Yahweh's speaking, the twin options formerly posed by Yahweh
and the snake (in the Garden) or by Yahweh and the Satan (in
the prologue to Job) are still heard, and heard for the last time.
There is, however, a reversal of roles in this last instance. In
Genesis 2—3 and in Job 1—2 the snake and the Satan subvert
the claims of Yahweh, claims which for their part are offered
straightforwardly. In chapters 38—41 the supposedly straightforward import of the rhetorical questions is subverted ironically and the genuine questions of Yahweh emerge only when
the ironic subversion is recognized.

A question now arises, however, concerning the function—
one could say the ontological status and significance—of irony.
If irony can subvert position *A* in order to establish position *B*,
what is to prevent the reader from suspecting (fearfully or with
absurdist glee) that position *B* is vulnerable to the same subversion by *C*, and *C* by *D*, *ad infinitum, ad absurdum, ad
nauseum?*

A vivid awareness pervades some aspects of contemporary
literature, drama, and philosophy, and recently some ventures
in Joban interpretation, to this effect: Any and all affirmations
are subject to infinite subversion by the power of doubt or ironic
"de-construction." Such a sense of the infinite vulnerability of

all statements to subversion may be said to be the hermeneutical dimension of the sense of existence itself as absurd. At bottom, the meaningless void endlessly subverts the meanings which we humans spin (like a hedge) for ourselves. In this context, the question arises as to whether and how we can distinguish between stable ironies (those which subvert one position in order to establish another which the writer intends to be taken as itself a stable and unsubvertable ground), and unstable ironies (those in which every position is in turn a candidate for subversion).

In our view, the contemporary debate on this issue is one form of the two voices in the Garden, the two voices in heaven in the Joban prologue, and the two levels of divine speech in chapters 38—41. Ingeniously, these last two modes of address, in chapters 38—41, offer Job two options for self-understanding; and by their delicate balance of rhetorical weight force Job (and the reader) to choose freely (*ḥinnam*) between them. If the interpretation offered in this commentary is at all near the mark, then a fresh theophany to the contemporary reader of Job, giving the meaning of the divine speeches, would only repeat the options, leaving the reader with the need for "morally active engagement" (Booth) in the act of interpreting the divine questions to Job. It is, then, part of the literary success of the author of Job, in which *how* the Book of Job means is part of *what* it means (John Ciardi), that interpreters differ as to the meaning of the divine speeches and of Job's response and that they differ, accordingly, in their understanding of the meaning of the book as a whole. Interpreters not only will but must divine the meaning of the speeches, the response, and the book as a whole in the context of their own reading of existence. The diversity of interpretations matches the diversity which is displayed in our respective interpretations of existence. *All* positions, nihilist and absurdist no less than affirming and covenanting, are irreducibly confessional.

Some Salient Features of the Divine Speeches

Before considering the divine speeches in close detail, we may note the following salient features of the speeches as a whole:

228

(1) In keeping with the thematics which were sounded emphatically in chapter 3, but which were implicit already in

chapters 1—2 and which have recurred throughout the dialogues, the divine speeches have to do primarily with the creator, creativity, and creatureliness.

(2) The portrayal of creation in chapters 38—41 is reminiscent of Genesis 1, not only in its similar catalogue of the regions of the cosmos and their denizens, but in its light/darkness alternations. The sequence of day/night/day/night in Genesis 1 is partly paralleled in chapters 38—41. In chapter 38 verses

4-7   celebrate the creations of the earth, with a paean of praise from the morning stars;

8-11   celebrate the birth of sea (which, as we shall see, is not devoid of ethical and spiritual connotations of darkness);

12-15   again recur to the motif of morning light;

16-18   speak again of sea and darkness;

19-20   conclude with a unified presentation of light and darkness.

(3) Strangely, though the two speeches otherwise catalogue the cosmos and its denizens with representative thoroughness, no attention is given to humankind as a creature. As a corollary to this absence, all the creatures which are presented are wild creatures untamed by human intervention.

(4) Yet humankind *is* present in chapters 38—41, not in the catalogue of creatures described by Yahweh, but as the addressee to whom Yahweh offers the descriptions. This means that Job (or humankind generally) is not, as some have concluded, so insignificant a creature as to be overlooked in the general cosmic picture. Rather, humankind is that part of creation whom God addresses with questions concerning the rest of creation. Herein we see another way of presenting the two dimensions of the divine image: To be a human being is to be a creature who is yet God's addressee and whom God confronts with the rest of creation vocationally.

(5) The whole scene of creativity is posed to Job in the form of two sorts of questions: "Who are you?" and "Where were you?" It may already be observed that a matter-of-fact inclusion of humankind within the creaturely catalogue would implicitly answer the questions as to the status (who?) and the place (where?) of humankind *vis-à-vis* creativity and the creation.

(Cf. the commentary on chap. 28, esp. the section on 28:23–28 and the "Additional Reflection.") As it is, the omission of humankind, together with the questions "Who?" and "Where?" and "Can you?" already serves to open the human question to the possibility of new answers. Such questions direct Job and the reader to reflect on the possible deeper import of the questions asked in Psalm 8:4.

(6) In Genesis 1 the divine speech is performative in character. It does not describe, but enacts what it says. Yet the enactment is not, after all, purely unilateral. It is implicit in the *imperative* (not indicative) character of the address, such as "let there be light," that what the divine speech does is to pose a possibility which for its realization presupposes the response of the potential creature to the divine word. (The same logic informs Rom. 4:17–21 with its center in v. 17*b*, a logic in which the creating call seeks the response of faith and obedience.) Similarly, in Genesis 2 the divine injunctions in 2:16–17 are performative, insofar as they open up a region of multiple possibilities calling for decision enacted in freedom. In Job 3, Job has responded to his calamities with language reminiscent of Genesis 1; but his performative speech there (the curse), taken by itself, tends to enact a refusal to participate in existence on the terms and under the conditions offered him in his experience. By chapters 29—31, Job's oath (his second, after 27:1–6) shows him enacting a profound intention to participate loyally in existence. That intention is offered in the face of every indication that it will not be reciprocated, yet in the hope that perhaps it may. (In hope, we may suggest, Job believes against hope.) In chapters 38—41 we may take the divine speech as again performative, in its positively ironic undertone opening up for Job a possibility for transformed self-understanding.

(7) In the prologue, the divine question about Job was "addressed" to him in the form of two types of calamity; and Job's response accordingly came in two stages. In 38:1—42:6 the vertical dialogue implicit in the prologue becomes explicit and again takes the form of a two-stage divine address and a two-stage human response. In the prologue, Job's first response displayed all the marks of conventional submissive piety, while the second response was seen to be irreducibly ambiguous. In 40:3–5, we will find Job's first response to continue the tone of ambiguity, whereas in 42:1–6 we will hear, at last, the unambiguous tone of confessional affirmation.

The First Divine Address (38:1—40:2)

The Voice from the Whirlwind (38:1). "Then Yahweh answered Job from out of the whirlwind." As has been indicated in the Introduction, Frank Moore Cross interprets the storm language of this verse to indicate *El* or *Baal* (the Canaanite storm-god) as speaker. We need not repeat here our disagreement with this view. We may note in this context that the imagery of 38:1 continues the imagery to which Elihu's lengthy speech has brought him in 36:24—37:24 (cf. also 26:14 and our interpretation). The language of 38:1 identifies a voice which Israelites might be expected to recognize as properly credentialed to be Yahweh.

Design of Darkness? (38:2). "Who is this that darkens counsel or [design] by words without knowledge *[da'at]*"? The "counsel" here is *'eṣa*, which has reference to design, plan, scheme, or purpose. It is the word used, for example, in 12:13. There Job characterized God's "purpose" *('eṣa)* as *dark*. As we have suggested in our interpretation of that chapter, Job has taken "let there be light," and the rise of human consciousness, thereafter, as serving God's purpose of bringing to light the depths of reality; and those depths have been disclosed through Job's experience as having the character of deep darkness *(ṣalmawet)*. Such a divine purpose, for Job, can itself be characterized only as dark. God's design is a "design of darkness to appall," to borrow a phrase and a conclusion from Robert Frost's Joban sonnet "Design."

It is to the charge implicit in many of Job's words, and explicit in 12:22, that 38:2 is a direct rebuttal. In characterizing God's creative purpose as a design of darkness, Job has obscured God's creative intent; and therein Job's words are devoid of knowledge. Now, we may note the implications of the divine response of 38:2 for our assessment of the role of irony in the Book of Job. It is in the nature of universal human sensibility that the words "let there be light" come primally as good news. Consequently, when Job in 12:22 accuses God of bringing light into existence for the purpose of disclosing the dark truth at the heart of things—a purpose which becomes clear only through experience such as Job's—he in effect accuses God of a cosmic irony in the worst possible taste. By the divine response to that accusation in 38:2 we are to gather that, whatever purposes

231

irony may serve in the rest of the divine address, it is not intended to subvert the human sense of the good news implicit
in the words "let there be light."

The divine strategy in 38:2 may further be illuminated by
observing that Yahweh calls in question Job's *words*. (Similarly,
Job had said to his wife, "You speak as one of the foolish women
would speak.") By challenging Job at the point of his words—
and exclusively at the point of his words concerning the divine
creative intent—Yahweh calls upon Job to assess the propriety
of these *words* against the character of his *experience* of God as
a whole.

Answer Like the Man You Were Called to Be (38:3). "Gird
up your loins like a man *(geber)*, /I will question you, and you
shall declare to me *(hodi'eni)*." Job is not asked to debase himself; he is called to present himself in all his vigor (as a *geber*)
for the interchange, in which God will question and Job will
respond. The final verb in this verse is suggestive. In the previous verse God has characterized Job's words as "devoid of
knowledge *(da'at)*." The point of Yahweh's new questions will
be to elicit from Job a response in which Job will, literally,
"make me to know" *(hodi'eni)*. What should Yahweh expect to
learn from Job now that Yahweh has not already heard? One
could, to be sure, take the question of 38:3b as tantamount to
an abasement of Job. But such an interpretation would forget
the divine concern disclosed in the prologue—a question about
Job from which everything since then has occurred. We may
take the question in 38:3 as intent upon the same object as that
in the prologue: the concern to find out who Job is in relation
to God. In Exodus 33:13 we find the sentence "make me, now,
to know your ways *(hodi'eni)*, that I may know you." Precisely
this, it seems, is the tone of 38:3b. Having posed his questions,
Yahweh will await that answer which alone can disclose to God
who and what Job will choose to be in response to the divine
address. Thus verse 3 ends on the concern with which verse 2
began: "Who is this? . . . Make me to know (who you are)." At
the burning bush, the first effect of the divine self-disclosure to
Moses was the latter's question "Who am I?" A question offered
in rhetorical self-defense but which opened onto a transformed
vocational self-understanding (See Janzen, Interp 33:227–39).
Similarly here, the first thing the divine theophanic address
does is to pose the question of who Job is. By its position of
priority in chapters 38—41, this question is the chief question

232

of the divine address, one which all subsequent questions only provoke Job to consider ever more deeply and comprehensively. It is part of the way in which 42:1–6 resolves the drama of the Book of Job, that, in that response to God, Job recurs again and again to this word "know."

Foundation of the Earth: Rejoicing of the Stars (38:4–7). "Where were you when I laid the foundation of the earth"? The first specific question is similar to parts of Isaiah 40:12–26. The latter passage portraying creation comes in response to, and as a rebuttal of, the Job-like charge of Jacob-Israel (40:27): "My way is hid from Yahweh [cf. Job 3:23a], and my right *(mišpat)* is disregarded by my God." One may compare especially Isaiah 40:12–14 with Job 38:4—5. In 12:12–25 Job had presumed to know the divine purpose and to be privy to the divine understanding *(bina, 38:4b)*. In that case, says Yahweh, he should be able to answer a series of elementary questions, of the sort posed in verses 5–6. The series is nicely concluded by verse 7, whose phrase "sons of God" forms a contrast with the "Where were you?" of verse 4.

By the contrast between Job (v. 4) and the "sons of God" (v. 7), it is easy to take verses 4–7 as an abasement. The matter is not so simple. In his commentary on Isaiah 40—66, Claus Westermann has argued that the re-use of old cultic forms of praise in Second Isaiah serves to enlist the deep-rooted old energies of Israelite piety in the cause of reorienting the exilic community toward eschatological hope. Elsewhere, Westermann has argued that the form of the creation narrative in Genesis 1 betrays a background in the traditions of Israel's worship of God as Creator. May we not see in Job 38:4–7 a rhetorical strategy similar to that of Second Isaiah, whereby the themes of praise for creation are sounded in order to touch sensibilities still running deep within Job? Moreover, what does it mean to stand in the cult and to praise God for the divine goodness in creation? Does it not mean that, in some sense, one stands with the morning stars and the sons of God in such praise? This, surely, is the import of passages such as Psalm 29, Psalm 89: 5–18, and the like. Though such worship is subsequent to the creative act, yet the deep import of such worship is an affirmation of creation, such that the congregation participates with God in the divine "it is good," and to that degree at least is drawn into the creative act.

The reference to "morning stars" singing together and

233

"sons of God" shouting for joy sounds the unambiguous note of the good news of light which opens the divine creative activity. Such a celebration, however, implies an acknowledgment of the darkness *vis-à-vis* which that foundation was made. The latter element in the light-darkness polarity leads naturally to verses 8–11.

The Sea Swaddled and Hedged (38:8–11). "Or who shut in the sea with doors, . . . ? Elsewhere, in Babylonian creation myths as well as in Genesis 1 with its reference to the firmament, cosmic creation is portrayed as arising in part through the erection of a barrier which restrains the primordial waters and so clears a living space for the denizens of the world. In 38:10a (as in Ps. 148:6) this barrier is termed a *ḥoq*, which word means both a boundary (or "bound") and a decree or statute. In all such contexts the Sea appears as a chaotic energy threatening destruction; and cosmic order with its life-giving and meaningful forms presupposes the effective limitation of this energy. This primal mythic theme is clearly alluded to in Job 7:12; 9:8; and 26:12 and probably is echoed also in 28:14 (cf. 28:22) and 38:16. In view of these allusions earlier in Job, it is unlikely that (as some suppose) the sea is presented in 38:8–11 in demythologized fashion, that is, as simply a natural region. The overtones of primal chaos are unmistakable.

What is remarkable about the present treatment of this standard theme is its ambivalence. On the one hand the Sea is restrained by bars and doors. On the other hand the birth of this same Sea is attended by God as by a midwife who carefully swaddles the infant in protective wrappings. This ambivalence, in which the Sea is surrounded by an action at once restraining and sustaining, is reflected in the structure of the passage. Verse 11 comes as the actual content of the speech of verse 11, the narration in verses 8–10 displays an inclusion—the "doors" of verse 8a and the "bars and doors" of verse 10 enclose and, as it were, "bound" verse 9 with its birth imagery and its positive imagery of swaddling bands and clothes. The ambivalence of this imagery is continued within the direct speech setting forth the decree. For if that decree says ". . . no farther, / and here shall your proud waves be stayed," it also says "thus far you shall [or may] come." In view of this thoroughgoing ambivalence, we are led to a re-valuation of the motif sounded in verse 8a, "shut in." For the Hebrew verb here literally means "hedged in," as

234

in 3:23 and 1:10. The ambivalence with which this motif of the hedge is presented in verses 8–11 means that the sea in its mythic overtones is not viewed in simply negative terms. The sea, even as primal chaos, is limited to, yet given, a place in the scheme of things.

In this respect there is a deep unity of conception between the portrayal in 38:8–11 and the scenes in 1:6–12 and 2:1–6. For one thing, in one passage Yahweh *addresses* the Satan, and in the other passage Yahweh *addresses* the Sea. For another, the content of the divine address is similar: The Satan and the Sea are given just so much room and no more (cf. 1:12 and 2:6 with 38:11).

Too often, interpreters are tempted to resolve this ambivalent conception in straightforward terms. Such resolutions lose the richness and the adequacy to experience of poetic presentations such as we have in verses 8–11. For instance, a key term in this passage is Hebrew *ḥoq* which, as we have noted, indicates both a boundary and a decree. It is a standard term in the biblical vocabulary of law and justice. All systematic attempts to read existence (or to exegete the Bible) according to a principle of justice involving strict recompense or retribution break themselves against the fact that the sea is given a place in the cosmos. All attempts to exegete the Book of Job in such a way as to arrive at the conclusion that God there is indifferent to matters of justice overlook the fact that the place of the sea in the cosmos is delimited by divine decree. Perhaps the issue can be stated only in the modes of poetry. As for Job, he must come to terms with the brute fact of the place of the sea in the scheme of things; yet he is not to interpret it in such a way as to imply God's disinterest in law or justice. This is underscored by the imagery of the following section.

The Light Which Exposes the Wicked (38:12–15). "Have you commanded the morning . . ."? While not all the details of the imagery are clear, especially in verse 14, the general idea is that the coming of morning light removes the mantle of darkness under the cover of which the wicked have pursued their schemes (cf. 24:13–17). In this section the image of darkness as covering (v. 13*a*, "skirts"; v. 14*b*, "garment") echoes the image of clouds and thick darkness as garment/swaddling band in verses 8–11. The image of the primal lawless sea is matched by the figure of the lawless and high-handed wicked humans.

Just as the sea is bounded and yet given its place, so the night time with its lawless deeds is bounded by the day and yet has its time. Is it, then, that God gives a time to the wicked as though somehow beaming approval on their schemes (cf. 10:3 and commentary)? No; when the light comes it exposes them to judgment. Yet the world is so made that it is possible for wickedness to arise.

Into the Dark Depths (38:16–18). "Have you entered into the springs of the sea, . . ."? Yahweh now draws Job's attention to the underworld and the regions of death. ('eres in v. 18a is probably to be translated "underworld," for RSV "earth.") On the face of it Job might be supposed to have to answer Yahweh's questions with a "No, I have not; nor do I know all this." Closer consideration suggests the appropriateness of quite a different answer. The speeches of Job are liberally strewn with references to his entry into the regions here described. Though he has not yet died, he portrays the regions of death with such imaginative vividness, and he portrays his own bodily and spiritual sufferings in such a way, as to entitle him to some sort of claim to have experienced the regions here indicated. Or is it the other way around? Is it possible that the apparently rhetorical taunts of verses 16–18 in fact intend and convey a solicitation which, adopting as it does the imagery of Job's own portrayals of his current plight and imminent destination, seeks to draw Job into an affirmative response? The language of verses 16–17, of deep, revelation, and deep darkness, so resonates with the terms of 12:22 (not to say 10:21–22) that one finds oneself leaning forward in the posture of a kibbitzer, self-involvingly wanting to say, "Say yes, Job, say yes! You *have* been there, as your own words attest."

The Relation of Light and Darkness (38:19–21). "Where is the way to the dwelling of light," . . . ? This section concludes the two previous sections on light (vv. 12–15) and darkness (vv. 16–18). This is doubly indicated: by the announcement of the twofold theme in verse 19 and by the way in which "your days" in verse 22b forms an inclusion with the same phrase in verse 12a. Verses 19–20 display a chiastic structure which may be indicated in this way:

236

"Where is the <u>way</u> to the dwelling of light,
    and where is the place of darkness,

that you may take it to its territory *(gebul)*
    and that you may discern the paths to its home?"

This chiastic structure tells us that the fourth line, like the first, refers to light, while the third line refers, like the second, to darkness. The *place* of darkness is its territory, its *gebul*—its proper region as marked off by decision and decree. The clause "that you may *take* it to its *gebul*" nicely evokes the overtones of Genesis 1:3–5, wherein the once undifferentiated and apparently limitless darkness now is bounded by light and "taken to its proper place" by God's creative action. The structure of verses 19–20 informs the thematics: For darkness (vv. 19*b*, 20*a*) is bounded by light (vv. 19*a*, 20*b*) and thereby given its place.

Verse 21 then picks up, in an apparently taunting tone, the questions which Eliphaz had posed to Job in 15:7–8. Yet the very way in which Yahweh seems here to side with that friend may warn us that there is more here than meets the eye. *Is* it the case that Job in no sense has ever taken darkness to its territory and delimited its sway through an act which images what God did in Genesis 1:3–5? Even if the exegesis offered above at 17:11–12 is judged to be dubious, one cannot gainsay the fact that Job's periodic imaginative ventures of hope toward God—as well as his persistent affirmations of his own innocence and integrity and his reiterated oaths—do in fact delimit the darkness in which his life is engulfed. At least in these ways Job has seen the gates of darkness and from there has commanded a morning.

The Weather and the Constellations (38:22–38). "Have you entered the storehouses of the snow, . . ."? The first four sections described the four regions of the cosmos: the earth (vv. 4–7), the sea (vv. 8–11), the sky (vv. 12–15) and the underworld (vv. 16–18). Now the questioning shifts to a consideration of the creaturely phenomena inhabiting these regions. This phase of the questioning begins with phenomena of the heavens: astral bodies and meteorological activity. If in 38:2 Yahweh responds to Job's words in 12:22, 38:22–38 comes perhaps in response to 12:15. In chapter 12 Job ironically characterizes the divine "wisdom" and "understanding" as generally frustrating and overturning human needs and aspirations. For instance (12:15), God's control of water leads either to drought or to flood. (The theme of arbitrary divine action is, of course, prominent in non-Israelite versions of the flood story.) Floods destroy all that

237

has grown up from the earth or has been built up by human effort; drought renders growth impossible and removes the conditions requisite to the rise of human culture. Job shares with the biblical tradition generally a negative view of desert and wilderness as a place where life is not possible, so that the earth is divisible into good land (the "sown" or sowable) and badlands (desert). This negative view has come to most vivid expression on his lips in 30:1–8, 29–31 and (according to our interpretation) 31:38–40.

The line of questioning in verses 22–38 goes to show God distributing precipitation according to times and seasons subordinately determined by the stars. These stars rule (as in Gen. 1:14) according to season (v. 32) and ordinance (v. 33). On the one hand the stars rule through weather in such a way as to influence the outcome of human military action (vv. 22–23). One thinks of the battle of Megiddo (Judg. 5:19–21) and, less directly, of Joshua 10:12–14. On the other hand, the stars rule in such a way that the weather bears upon matters having nothing to do with immediate human concern—the welfare of the desert (vv. 25–27). If one works within the conventional categories of desert and cultivable land, God's control and distribution of water makes no sense. Just as elsewhere it is said that the rain falls on the just and the unjust, so here the rain is shown falling on the human and the non-human, with a generosity and life-giving care which renders human measures of appropriateness penultimate. All this, God asserts, displays a wisdom and an understanding (vv. 36–37) which may properly be so termed, though they may not conform to Job's valuations and definitions as reflected in chapter 12.

At two points this section is reminiscent of Second Isaiah: The naming of constellations in 38:31–32 exemplifies Isaiah 40:26, "calling them all by name," and the portrayal of the wilderness as becoming verdant through God's rain sounds a note which pervades Second Isaiah from 40:6–8 through 55:10–13 and which comes to striking expression in 43:19–21. In both Second Isaiah and Job, then, God's control of rain is not purely retributive but freely creative and redemptive in the divine wisdom.

238

Verse 36 is of uncertain meaning, since the word-pair concluding the two lines may designate "clouds/mists" (RSV), "Thoth/Sekwi" (Pope), or "ibis/the cock" (Gordis). Since the ibis is the symbol of Thoth as the Egyptian God of wisdom, the latter two alternatives need not be mutually exclusive. Gordis points out that "The ibis was believed to foretell the rising of the Nile, and the cock was popularly believed to forecast the rain . . . or to announce the dawn . . ." (p. 453). He goes on to say, "The poet has been describing meteorological phenomena with which the ibis and the cock are familiar, but not man." And he concludes, "The implication for man's pretensions to wisdom is not lost on the Hebrew reader." The implication, presumably, is a deft abasement. But one should read verses 36–37 against the background of Job's words in 12:7–8. There Job had satirized the so-called hidden wisdom of God (11:5–9) as something known to beast and bird, plant and fish. Now Yahweh takes up Job's point, accepts it, and by affirming it in the positive context of 38:22–38 provokes Job with the contrast between what Job has been saying about divine wisdom and what ibis and cock can say. Are the implications of this provocation what Gordis supposes them to be? If ibis and cock can forecast life-giving rain, the prophet of Second Isaiah does likewise, as Elijah had done much earlier. Moreover, Job himself has been known to speak a wisdom which comes down as rain to the needy (29:21–25). What appears as a taunt concerning Job's ignorance and inability once again sounds motifs which may convey a different and more positive undertone. Such an undertone becomes even more evident in the following section.

The Realm of Animal Life: (38:39—39:30). "Can you hunt the prey for the lion, . . ."? In this section we find God delighting in the existence of what Gerard Manley Hopkins called "All things counter, original, spare, strange" (in his poem "Pied Beauty"). Lions hunt for their young; the raven seeks prey to feed its starvelings; and God is in the hunt with them. Mountain goats give birth, raise their young, and see them no more; and God sees it all. The wild ass roams freely on the steppe, free at God's hand from domesticating bonds and driver's shout, free to search steppe, salt land, and mountain for greenery (cf. 38: 27). The wild ox also is blissfully free of Job's harness. The ostrich is most wierd, acting in a God-given way that is devoid of humanly recognizable wisdom and understanding. The horse alone in this catalogue is domesticated. Yet, even so, the horse is hardly a drudge of field and yard, but is at home in the midst of the turbulence and danger of war. Finally, hawk and eagle soar high, build their nest, and hunt prey for

239

their young. Thematically, 39:26–30 forms an inclusion with 38:39–41.

Several things may be noted concerning this celebration of the animal kingdom. First, all the animals (except the horse) are wild and exult in their wild free ways. Second, they do nevertheless constitute a kingdom. For their activities proceed under the eye and with the help of God, executing divine commands (39:27) and exemplifying divine wisdom (39:26). Now, it is with conventional valuations of the animal kingdom as it is with valuations of desert and habitable land: Humans typically relate to those species on the principle that the only good animal is a dead one or a domesticated one. Wild animals are a source of danger and anxiety—danger, because of the possibility of attack; anxiety, because they display modes of existence other than those familiar to humans. In this perspective, the portrayals of human-animal relations in Genesis 1:26, 28; 2:18–20 and Psalm 8, in which a divine commission is given humankind to have dominion over the animals, might well be interpreted as ideological rationalization of human actions undertaken from other motivations such as physical fear and cognitive/existential anxiety. In such a view, Job 38:39—39:30 may be read as a critique of such ideological distortions of the place of humankind in the cosmos. But another possibility presents itself.

We may begin with the observation that in Genesis 1 the commission to rule the animals goes hand in hand with the limitation of human diet to vegetation. Not until Genesis 9:3 is humankind portrayed as becoming carnivorous and, significantly, not until then (9:2) is the fear and dread of humankind felt by the animals. The implication is that the rule in Genesis 1 would have been experienced by the animals as benign (perhaps after the fashion exemplified by Yahweh in Job 38:39—39:30).

Such a protological vision in Genesis 1 finds an eschatological counterpart in the Isaianic tradition (a tradition, we may note, in which Davidic and eventually Israelite royal function is thematic). At Isaiah 11:6–9, under the aegis of the wise and effective rule of the Messianic king, the relations between animals, and between animals and humans, is so peaceable that no longer will humans *drive* animals (Job 39:7b; on the verb cf. 3:18b), but a *child* shall *lead* them. It is as though the vision of Isaiah 11:1–9 includes a portrayal of a different sort of dominion over the animals—a wise dominion—than has been the case in

240

history. This vision is picked up again in Isaiah 65:25; and it may be incipient in such places also as Isaiah 43:20. Within the schema of the canonical text, then, we may and indeed must speak of protological and eschatological counterpart visions. For that matter, in Genesis 1 (read as an affirmation of hope by the priestly writer of the exile) we may also hear 1:26, 28 as a veiled eschatology, similar to the way in which we are accustomed to read Genesis 2:1–3 as an anticipation of the institution of the Sabbath at Sinai.

Now, with these priestly and Isaianic visions in view, one begins to suspect that more is going on in Job 38:39—39:30 than just a confounding of conventional human views of the animal kingdom. Insofar as conventional views embody a fixed understanding of how human rule of the animals should realize itself, they are indeed being confounded or "deconstructed." We recall that deconstruction is a function of irony which may serve reconstruction. We may take it that the catalogue of the animal kingdom in its beautifully wild freedom has as its aim to challenge Job at the point of his conventional self-understanding *vis-à-vis* the animals. If human lordship over the animal realm is part of the realization of the divine image, then the portrayal here of God's divine rule of the animals offers Job an opportunity to re-conceive himself in that image. Once again, then, what appears to be a rhetorical "impossible question" designed to put Job in his place turns out to be a question enticing Job into a transformed understanding of his vocation as lord of the animal kingdom.

Conclusion to the First Divine Address (40:1–2). "Shall one who argues with the Almighty instruct? /Shall one answer as an adjudicator of God"? The first divine speech gathers all the preceding questions into a summary challenge with this parallel pair of questions. Often in the Hebrew Bible, God is said to have a *rib*, a cause for dispute or "argument ' with Israel. In Jeremiah 12:1 the situation is reversed: The prophet has a dispute against Yahweh, very much in the same vein as Job (cf. Jer. 12:1–4). Interestingly, in that context Yahweh responds to the faithful prophet in the same taunting fashion as in Job chapters 38—41:

241

"If you have raced with men on foot, and they have wearied you,
    how will you compete with horses?
And if in a safe land you fall down,
    how will you do in the jungle of the Jordan?" (Jer. 12:5).

The point of this divine response is not to put the prophet down with an impossible question, but to express surprise over the quickness with which the prophet succumbs to discouragement and disillusionment and to challenge the prophet to a deeper loyalty and vocational endurance. Where such endurance founders on mistaken views as to God's ways of working they must be eschewed (cf. Jer. 15:15–21). It is the same with Job. Does he suppose that he will instruct God? The same verb occurs at 4:3 to refer to how Job once instructed many. Similarly, in 9:33 Job longed for an umpire (mokiah), the same Hebrew word which occurs in 40:2b where we have translated it "an adjudicator." Does Job now suppose that he will adjudicate God for himself?

Job's dilemma is one that is intrinsic to the human status as divine image. This dilemma consists in the fact that the image or symbol in some sense participates in the reality which it symbolizes but is not that reality. The temptation, in this dilemma, is for the human to seek literal clarity—to literalize. To do so, however, is to act against one's own nature as image. In Job's situation, to literalize means to apply to God, directly and exactly, human conceptions of justice—or, where God does not act according to such conceptions, to "instruct" God in the ways of true justice. God then becomes the dispenser of rewards and punishments according to a human calculus of virtue and evil. This literalizing temptation manifests itself in another "fall" from the human vocation as divine image, when such attempts to instruct God shatter themselves against the stubborn facts of experience. For the same literalizing view concludes that if God does not display justice according to human conceptions then God is indifferent to justice altogether and is "above" such earthly human concerns. The dilemma of Job points to the challenge and the difficulty in the human vocation to live as the image of God—which, in this connection, means to take our human concerns for justice and conceptions of justice seriously, as imaging divine concerns, and to recognize that God's justice is not reducible to our conceptions of it.

Job's First Response (40:3–5)

242

Job's response at first glance seems disappointingly submissive, a regression to the piety of 1:21, or worse, since it is a retreat from the honesty of the anguish of the dialogues. After the boldness of such utterances as 13:13–16; 23:10; and 31:35–37, one might have hoped for something more feisty than a meek "Behold, I am of small account." A closer reading discloses an irreducible ambiguity in his words. The opening word, *hen*, does indeed often mean "behold;" but it can also mean "if," introducing a hypothetical possibility as a ground on which a question is based. In such a case, the response may be translated, "Suppose/if I am of no account [as your questions all imply]; what shall I answer you?" Against the background of such earlier passages as 9:2–4, 13–16, 29–32, we may suspect Job of nuancing his response through an intentionally ambiguous use of *hen*, so that Yahweh can take it either way. For verse 5 can indicate either that Job gives up what he formerly said, or that, continuing in his former state of mind, he gives up on the attempt to make his point to such a one as God, resigned to harbor his convictions in the solitariness of his silence. Thus Job adopts the strategy which he used in his response to the second calamity in 2:10, offering words behind which he may keep his own counsel.

The Second Divine Address (40:6—41:34)

The Voice from the Whirlwind (40:6–14). Such a response will not do, so Yahweh begins all over again, reiterating (v. 7) the words of 38:3. Then comes a question (v. 8) which in its import closely parallels 38:2. In 38:2 Yahweh has objected to Job's inference from experience that God's creative counsel and purpose (*'eṣa*) is dark. Thereafter, the first divine address has gone to show the creative purpose as one which is meaningful, worthwhile, and evocative of exuberant celebration. As such, it proceeds not through the sheer elimination of darkness and wildness, but through the drawing of darkness and wildness into an emerging creative and redemptive order. At the beginning of this second address the point is made in a different way: "Will you overturn my justice *(mišpaṭ)?* /Will you make me out to be evil, to sustain your innocence?" This reversal of Job's argument is magnificently apropos. To Bildad's assertion that God does not pervert justice (*mišpaṭ*, 8:3), Job argues again and again that God in fact does so. In his first oath Job even swears by the God who has taken away his right (*mišpaṭ*, 27:2). It never occurs to him that in his accusations against God he may be doing to God what he accuses God of doing to him. This is because, up to now, Job is locked into a view of justice by the help of which he seeks to read God's character

243

directly from his own experience with the help of a theology common to him and his friends. Such a theology, Yahweh now implies in 40:8, gives no truer a picture of God than it gives of Job. A further implication of 40:8 is that Job does not need to violate or to deny God's justice in order to claim his own innocence.

Following the programmatic question of verse 8, the unit is once again demarcated by an inclusion: "Right hand" in verse 14*b* corresponds to "arm" in verse 9*a;* and "I will praise you" (for so the Hebrew reads) in verse 14*a* corresponds to "thunder with a voice" in verse 9*b.* Within this doubly constructed frame, in verses 10–13 Yahweh challenges Job to don the regalia of royalty (the word "splendor" in v. 10*b* is translated "honor" in Ps. 8:5) and to exercise that royalty appropriately. Can Job through sheer force eliminate every "proud" opposing power? Could he do so, he would have God's praise and homage. Gordis comments, "God concedes that the world order is not perfect, that the wicked have not been completely crushed, and that the problem of evil still exists in the world" (p. 566). His comment, otherwise to the point, presupposes that "perfection" of "world order" would involve the coercive crushing of evil and wickedness. This in turn involves the presupposition that the perfect reign (or royal rule) of order and justice would exemplify irresistible exercise of unilateral power, imposed "from the top down," a vision the totalitarian character of which should not be less odious for being projected upon God. Precisely such a vision is at the root of Job's false charges against God's justice. Job supposes (like the servants in the parable of Matt. 13:24–30) that a divine concern for justice should work itself out in a rigorous stamping out of all injustice. That, it appears, is how Job would do it. God here taunts Job with his inability to achieve that sort of royal rule. The implication is either that Job is no royal figure or that true royalty (divine or human) is of a different order. As has already been intimated in 38:39—39:30, and as will be intimated again in the two concluding portraits of Behemoth and Leviathan, true royalty engages "proud" power otherwise than by brute force.

244   **Yahweh's Concluding Challenge to Job (40:15—41:34).** The two creatures described in this section are presented as eminent instances of the sort of "proud" creature (40:11*b,* 12*a*) against which Job is challenged to exercise his dominion.

Named "Behemoth" and "Leviathan," these creatures are often identified as the hippopotamus and the crocodile (e.g., RSV notes). Alternatively, they may be identified as mythical figures, monsters of the land and the sea respectively. (The latter interpretation is argued at length by Pope.) The Canaanite mythic texts discovered in recent years inform us that "Leviathan" was one of the names of the chaos-dragon of the sea (cf. Isa. 27:1 and 51:9; also Ps. 74:14; but in Ps. 104:26 Leviathan is a non-mythic sea creature). If these two creatures convey at least overtones of mythic figures, then Leviathan at the end of the second divine speech balances the Sea in 38:9–11 and partakes of the same ambivalent character.

In line with our interpretation throughout this commentary, and in view of the royal imagery applied to Job in 40: 10–13, we interpret the presentation of Behemoth and Levia than against the background of Psalm 8. There, we may recall, human domain (Ps. 8:6b–8) is celebrated over the creatures of field, sky, and sea:

> thou hast put all things under his feet (cf. Job 40:12),
> all sheep and oxen,
>> and also the beasts *(behemoth)* of the field,
> the birds of the air, and the fish of the sea,
>> whatever passes along the paths of the sea.

Sheep and oxen are domestic field creatures; the beasts are, here, wild. Similarly the final, undefined "whatever passes along the paths of the sea" represents those marine inhabitants which haunt the fringes of human imagination. In our view, the creatures already described in 38:39—39:30 correspond to the creatures indicated in Psalm 8, in verses 7a and 8a, while the creatures of verses 7b and 8b are presented in amplified form in 40:15—41:34. It may be suggested, for example, that "whatever passes along the paths of the sea" is effectively elaborated into "He makes the deep boil like a pot; /he makes the sea like a pot of ointment: /Behind him he leaves a shining wake; /one would think the deep to be hoary" (RSV, 41:31–32).

The portraits of these two creatures are painted with all the exuberance and delight in their uncanny power and presence that one encounters in William Blake's poem on "The Tyger." To Blake's questions, "Did he smile his work to see? Did he who made the Lamb make thee?" as transferred to Behemoth and Leviathan, the answer implicit in the tone of the divine voice

245

in 40:15—41:34 is, Yes. God made them (40:15) and God owns them (41:11). The mystery of the divine rule is such that these are God's servants and playthings (41:4–5) without diminution of their awesomeness. What of Job? Can he, after all, thus rule over these creatures?

The issue is brought to an effective conclusion in the details of the final four lines of the divine address in 41:33–34. Yahweh concludes with what appears to be a challenging comparison: "Upon the dust *('apar)* there is not his like (Hebrew, "his *mosel*")." We recall Job's interpretation of God that "He has cast me into the mire, and I liken myself (using a form of the verb *mašal*) to dust and ashes" (30:19). Against such a background, and following the thematics of dust and royalty which has run through the dialogues, verses 33–34 appear to taunt Job with the royal eminence of Leviathan, such that there is no one upon the dust (let alone such a creature of dust as Job) who can be compared with him.

The same point emerges, though with even greater impact, and employing the word for dominion from Psalm 8:6, if we analyze 41:33a somewhat differently. Instead of translating the Hebrew phrase *mošlo* "his likeness, one like him," on the basis of the word *mošel*, "likeness," we may identify here the word *mošel*, "dominion," and translate "upon the dust there is not one to rule over him." In this reading, 41:33a and 41:34b would form a parallel pair, each containing the motif of royal rule. The statement in 41:33–34, then, apparently explodes the vision of human vocation in Psalm 8 as an empty piece of ideological rationalization. Or, by the way it echoes Psalm 8, the conclusion challenges Job to a renewed engagement of that vocation, in the spirit of Jeremiah 12:5. That Job hears the challenge in these last four lines, and this time responds to them worthily, is suggested by his own use of the word "dust" in his concluding words in 42:6.

Additional note. One other passage from a much later stage in the tradition curiously parallels both the form and the content of the divine challenge to Job's royal stature, as here interpreted. In Mark 10:35–45 two disciples come to Jesus and ask to be given positions of authority, in his "glory" (the royal connotations of this word are made explicit in Matthew's version of the episode [20:21]). Jesus' first words in response are "You do not *know* what you are asking." (One is reminded of

246

the emphasis on knowing in Job 38:2 and in 42:1–6.) Then Jesus goes on to ask, "Are you *able* to drink the cup that I drink, or to be baptized with the baptism with which I am baptized?" (author's italics). In view of Jesus' opening challenge to their knowledge, one might well suppose that he intended the question as a similar challenge to their powers, as an impossible question assuming the answer No. Undaunted, the two disciples assert, "We are able." To which Jesus replies: They not only are able but *will* so drink and be baptized. From this, the ironic character of Jesus' question emerges: apparently a rhetorical abasement, it veiled a genuine question. Further, from the conclusion to the pericope (10:42–45; cf. Matt. 16:13–28) it is clear that the human vocation to royal rule at one and the same time is both affirmed and redefined. Conventional human understandings of royal rule are to be inverted. God's rule, and the sort of rule enacted by God's servants, must take a different form. That form, according to the Gospels, is enacted eminently by the Anointed One who reigns from the cross. According to the reading of the Book of Job presented in this commentary, Job the royal sufferer is invited by the divine questions to enact the same form of rule. In such a view, one may appreciate the further significance of Frank Cross's suggestion that the Book of Job "belongs in the main line of the evolution of Israel's religion," a line, we may note, that runs also through Isaiah 52:13—53:12, where the righteous sufferer is presented as the *arm* of Yahweh (53:1).

Job 42:1–6
Job's Response to Yahweh: Confession as Covenant Speech

Since Job's first response to calamity, every instance of direct address has articulated the speaker's disagreement with what has been said. Finally, in Job's second response to Yahweh, direct address recovers the mode of speaking in agreement with what has been said. So to speak, of course, is to speak confessionally. Such confessional speech conveys the reconciliation between Yahweh and Job, a reconciliation in which they once again see eye to eye. Though the content of their agreement is not made explicit, it is perhaps intimated. What seems to be intimated is a transformed understanding of what it means to be dust and ashes before God and in the world.

* * *

Direct Discourse in Job as Confrontation and as Confession

Job's second response comes in reply not only to 40:6—41:34 but (as we shall see) to both divine speeches. This means that 42:1–6 comes as a replacement of 40:3–5. In that first response Job had resolved on silence. In this second response not only does Job speak, but his speaking has a specific character—the character of confessional speech. As the root meaning of "confession" indicates, Job now *speaks in agreement with* Yahweh. This is remarkable.

If we reflect on the Book of Job and consider all the direct speech which it contains, we find that the only speech which is not uttered in disagreement is Job's brief internal self-address in 1:5 and his response to the first set of calamities in 1:21. Otherwise, beginning with 1:9–11, direct speech in Job always has the character of disagreement. Thus, Job's wife opposes what she understands Job to be thinking (2:9); Job opposes what she proposes, yet internally is perhaps at odds with his own words (2:10); and Job's first extended outburst in chapter 3 comes as a comprehensive and vivid disagreement with God's intention and action in creating the world. If Eliphaz's first words are offered in relatively gentle disagreement, and as a kindly attempt to change Job's mind, thereafter the disagreement between Job and friends intensifies with each turn of the dialogue.

In this connection it may be noted that the speakers frequently draw attention to the character of each other's *words*. Eliphaz had diffidently said "if one *ventures* a word with you, will you be offended?" The italicized word *(nissa)* means "to test, try" something, as when David tried to fight with Saul's armor (I Sam. 17:39), or "to attempt, essay (venture)" something (cf. Deut. 4:34; 28:56). Eliphaz at the beginning sensed that he was in the presence of something for which common words and expressions are not adequate. The easy exchange by which people ordinarily traffic between language and experience, converting either into the other, slowed down as he searched for words. Yet his search, after all, found familiar patterns of

248

speech. Thereafter one large part of the dialogue has to do with
the relation between language and reality. The friends have
entrenched themselves in the conviction that their language is
soundly grounded in experience and observation, and therefore
they hear Job's words as so much wind (see 8:2; 11:2–3 [babble];
15:2–3; 18:2–3; 20:2–3 [spirit], chaps. 32—37 passim). Job likewise attacks their words (9:2 and commentary; 12:2; 16:2–5;
19:2–3; 21:2–3; 26:1–4). One of the most painful aspects of the
whole situation, for both Job and the friends, is this verbal
disagreement.

Primally, as the Bible would have it, people all spoke the
same language and meant the same things by the same words
(Gen. 11:1 and the JB trans.). Where there is the sort of deep
agreement between people that comes to expression in common speech—where there is *confessional* unity—then much
that is deeply difficult in experience can be borne and gone
through together. In fairness to the friends we may remind
ourselves that if Job could say "How long will you torment
me, and break me in pieces with words?" (19:2), Zophar could
reply to the same effect, that Job's words shake and jar his
whole being (20:2–3 and commentary). It is as though language itself is a hedge against chaos, a fragile fabric of agreed-
upon meanings, knit and woven together through
innumerable acts of individual good faith and communal consensus. The fabric is always in danger of rending and unravel-
ing. It is repaired and knit up again, and enlarged to fit
enlarged experience, through acts of affirmation and confession, wherein individual and community (as, e.g., in Pss. 66:16
or 116) testify to experiences in which chaos was overcome
and life and meaning were restored at Yahweh's hands. Now,
though, in the disagreement of words between Job and his
friends, the whole fabric of language threatens to come undone.

Each party strives mightily to keep the fabric intact. The
friends try to keep it intact in its communally agreed upon
form. Job's own pain, at its deepest, is his experiential knowledge that that fabric is torn down the middle and cannot be
repaired. His dilemma is disclosed in the fact of his own repeated efforts to repair it in a variety of ways. His search for
God as just is his search for One who will mend the garment
to its former state. Meanwhile, in his affirmation of his own

249

innocence, in his two concluding oaths, and in his final affirmation of his past experience (chap. 29) and his unblinking characterization of his present experience (chap. 30)—in and with all these words which are described in 31:40*b* as *tammu*, "ended, completed, finished"—Job attempts to salvage from the tatters of religious language a fragment which he can refashion and with which he can clothe himself in his solitary integrity.

Then comes Yahweh. The divine words begin the way Job and his friends began, with a subversion of the words to which God responds (38:2–3; 40:2, 7–8). What God says agrees with neither Job nor the friends. Again and again Yahweh uses words, motifs, and themes which previously appeared on the lips of Job and friends. Yet what is said by such means agrees with neither party, offering instead a vision which both sides have partially touched but which neither has embraced in its totality. In this fashion, it is as though the fabric of language, rent by Job's experience and tattered by the interminable arguments, is knit up again by God to display a new pattern. In 4:2 Eliphaz had ventured a word—unsuccessfully. In Deuteronomy 4:34 it is said that Yahweh ventured to go and take a nation for himself from the midst of another nation, and succeeded. In Job 38—39 a divine word was ventured which, from Job's response in 40:3–5, must be judged to have not yet succeeded. From Job's response in 42:1–6 it is seen that the total speech of chapters 38—41 has succeeded in gaining agreement and the fabric of language is once again whole.

Yet the wholeness that is achieved is a strange wholeness. It is like the ambiguous *hedge/swaddling bands* of 38:8–11, affirming more than either Job or friends had said and inviting both friends and Job to enter into and to inhabit the world of which it speaks. For in the divine speeches, Yahweh takes words as far as they can be made to go (words such as justice and wisdom, wildness and sea), says what can be said by means of them, and then leaves the rest to be gathered from what lies between the lines and the words.

Those who find the divine speeches unsatisfactory because they do not "solve the problem," want a language which provides a rigid and absolute hedge against chaos. The way in which the language of the divine speeches paints a picture of creation—at once moving and inviting and supremely worthwhile, and at the same time baffling and opaque—itself is part of the answer. As we shall see, Job's own response partakes of the same character.

Job's Confessional Response to Yahweh in 42:1–6

Full appreciation of the force of Job's second response calls for close attention to its literary features. The following translation seeks to focus significant details.

> 2.*a* You know that you can do all things,
>   *b* and that no purpose of yours can be thwarted.
> 3.*a* "Who is this that obscures design
>   *b* by words without knowledge?"
>   *c* Therefore, I have uttered what I have not understood,
>   *d* things too wonderful for me which I did not know.
> 4.*a* "Hear, and I will speak;
>   *b* I will question you, and you will make me to know."
> 5.*a* I have heard you with my own ears,
>   *b* and now my eye sees you!
> 6.*a* Therefore I recant and change my mind
>   *b* concerning dust and ashes
>
>   (author's translation).

Job's Confessional Response Begins (42:2ab). The opening verb is written in the Hebrew Bible as *Kethib/Qere,* in which the consonantal text indicates the second masculine singular form of the verb and the vowel signs indicate the Masoretes' judgment that we should read the first common singular form. The consonantal text is here followed because of the character of 42:1–6 as a confessional statement. In that context, "you know" is a stronger expression of agreement than "I know." Job's response to Yahweh thus is seen to resemble Ezekiel's (Ezek. 37:3). To say "I know" at the outset would still embed the affirmation in the context of the speaker's knowing. Here in Job (as in Ezek. 37:3), however, things have been proposed in question form which exceed what the hearer could have known but which offer a new basis on which the hearer's knowing may come to reconstitute itself.

To say "I know" is to imply the adequacy of a finite creature to assess the resourcefulness of the Infinite One. Either such a self-grounded "knowing" defines what is known too narrowly or, momentarily transcending its own settled structures of knowledge through the imaginative outreach of desperate faith (as in 19:25–27, "I know . . ."), it then falls back from such a height as from something unsupported and unsupportable in

251

the cold light of day (so 14:10–12 and 18–22, after 14:7–9 13–17).

To say "you know" is to confess one's agreement with that which is grounded outside the self, that which comes to one and solicits one's assent and one's trust. To say "you know" is to bring one's own views, one's own frames of reference and structures of understanding, under the judgment of another knowing which far transcends one's own. Yet at the same time, to say "you know" is to bind oneself covenantingly to the One who is affirmed as knowing. Job's continuing affirmation, "you can do all things, and no purpose of yours can be thwarted," is one version of the Yahwistic refrain which runs through the old and the New Testaments, "all things are possible." Here as elsewhere the refrain comes, not as a human assessment on the basis of a reading of worldly conditions, but as a human affirmation of the inexhaustible resourcefulness of the covenant God whose name is given at the burning bush as "I will be who I will be."

Yahweh's First Address Quoted and Job's Response (42:3ab). In Job 40:3–5 Job had responded to the first address by promising silence. Like Sir Thomas More in Robert Bolt's *A Man for All Seasons,* Job could offer that silence as public evidence for tacit consent, while perhaps harboring continuing dissent in the solitariness of his own heart. Now he takes the very words of God's speech on his own lips—the very words in which God has characterized Job's accusations as "without knowledge." This speaking of God's own words with his own lips enacts the speech-form of confession, of speaking-in-agreement-with. By such a use of words, such a taking into himself of God's words against him, he enacts already a change of mind. That enactment, implicit in 3*ab,* becomes explicit in 3*cd.* For though in 3*ab* Job utters God's words against himself, they still have the form of God's speech. In 3*cd,* with the shift in language, the internal agreement with God is made complete, as Job "owns" what God has said to him.

Yahweh's Second Address Quoted (42:4ab). The first line of the second quotation does not actually occur in either divine address but comes here in place of "Gird up your loins like a man," which at 38:3 and 40:7 precedes the line quoted in 42:4 *b.* Why this substitution? While gathering up the import of the two divine speeches, it appears to set the stage also for a proper construal of 42:5. Job is to *hear* while Yahweh speaks. Yahweh will question and then Job is to make Yahweh know.

In passing, one should note that the Hebrew root *yd'*, "to know/knowledge," occurs in each of the four couplets making up verses 2–4. Moreover, by the way it opens verse 2 and closes verse 4, this root brackets these three verses in an inclusion, before the climactic words in verses 5–6. One may hazard the suggestion that the frequency of occurrence of this verb "to know" fittingly characterizes the climactic speech of Job, following so many chapters of confused questions and conflicting opinions.

Job's Concluding Words Begin (42:5). In the conventional reading of verse 5, Job's new insight gained through the divine speeches is contrasted with what he had been hearing about God from his friends or with what he had been taught about God in his earlier life or both. Hearsay religion, in this interpretation, now is superseded by immediate encounter with the divine. This may well be the correct reading. As such it hardly needs exposition here, so deeply is it embedded in the western religious consciousness. Yet one wonders if this is the most natural reading.

Again and again Job has sought God's presence, but in vain; all he has found for his pains is darkness and silence. In 9:16 he said "If I summoned him and he answered me, I would not believe he was listening to my voice;" and in 9:11 he said "Lo, he passes by me, and I see him not; he moves on, but I do not perceive him." Similarly, in 23:5 he said "I would learn what he would answer me, and understand what he would say to me." And in 23:8–9 he said "Behold, I go forward, but he is not there; and backward, but I cannot perceive him; on the left hand I seek him, but I cannot behold him; I turn to the right hand, but I cannot see him." All this comes in stark contrast to the momentary conviction that " . . . from my flesh shall I see God, whom I shall see on my side, and my eyes shall behold, not as a stranger [RSV: and not another]" (19:26–27). On the one hand, then, 42:5 comes in contrast to the negatives of such passages as 9:11, 16 and 23:5, 8–9, and in one sort of fulfillment of 19:26–27; on the other hand it comes in response to what after all is its proximate context in 42:4a: "Hear and I will speak." To the divine address which he has just referred to, Job responds: "I have heard you with my own ears!" The same rhetorical connection is thus seen to exist between verses 4 and 5 as was seen to exist between verses 3*ab* and 3*cd*. In the earlier instance, words first spoken by God, and then quoted by Job as God spoke them, are finally re-phrased in Job's own terms. Specifically, the "words without knowledge" of 3*b* are echoed in the "uttered . . . things . . . which I did not know." Similarly, the "Hear" of 4*a* is echoed in the "I have heard you." We may remind ourselves that chapters 38—41 are not in the technical sense a theo-*phany*, but a divine answering (38:1) and speaking. All this is to say, then, that verse 5 brings to a positive conclusion the question which Job has posed in great anguish throughout the dialogues: Will the silent God *speak*, that Job may *hear?* and will the absent God *appear*, that Job may *see?*

Job's Concluding Words (42:6). The first quotation of Yahweh in verse 3*ab* was followed by Job's confessional affirmation beginning with "therefore." While verse 5 begins to signal Job's response to verse 4, it serves also momentarily to delay the climactic affirmation introduced by the second "therefore" in verse 6*a*. That affirmation, finally arrived at, concludes the rhetorical shift which has been taking place throughout verses 2–6: in verse 2 the focus is all on what God knows; in verse 3*ab* (the first quotation) the focus is on God's calling in question what Job knows; in verse 3*cd* Job's first response is to affirm God's charge that Job did not know; in verse 4 (the second quotation) the focus is on God's claim on Job to hear, after which Job is to make God to know (see commentary on this line, at 38:2); in verse 5 Job's second response answers to verse 4, "hear;" but it leaves the second half of verse 4*b* unanswered. What is thus left incomplete by verse 5 is completed in verse 6. What God has sought from Job in the words "make me to know," by way of Job's self-revelation to God, is given in the words, "I change my mind." Though the root "know" does not occur in verse 6, yet the idea of Job's making himself known to God through self-disclosure is implicit. The shift, then, is from the other-directed "you know" of verse 2 to the "I change my mind" of verse 6. What, now, is the content of this change of mind?

254

The translation "I loathe *myself*" is interpretive; in Hebrew there is no direct object. Recently the unexpressed object has been taken to be Job's own words. (Thus, JPS "I loathe *my words;*" cf. Pope, "I recant.")

Two other possibilities may be mentioned: (1) The two verbs in 42:6 may occur as a *hendiadys*, in which one adverbially modifies the other: Job utterly changes his mind. (2) The verb in question may not be *ma'as I*, "to loathe, abhor," but *ma'as II*, "flow run," a close cognate of *masas*, "to dissolve, melt." The verb then describes a typical first response to divine revelation and presence. Like Job, Habakkuk had challenged Yahweh's apparent indifference to the sufferings of the righteous. Then God made visionary response. Following his own visionary awareness of God's theophanic presence, Habakkuk says "I *hear*," and then graphically confesses how he is "undone" (3:16a) before going on to loyal affirmation of patient trust. It is perhaps the same with Job. Yahweh has spoken; Job has said "I *hear . . ., I see!*" (42:5). Now all his questions and charges are dissolved. His structures of understanding are melted down ("I dissolve") in the presence of Yahweh, in such a transformation as both requires and enables him to give up what he had formerly thought. The question remains: What had he formerly thought, and concerning what had he formerly thought it?

This brings us to the line which more than any other determines our understanding of the book: 42:6b. This line, unaccountably, has generally been translated *"in* dust and ashes." The facts of Hebrew usage are these: In every other instance where the niphal (middle or reflexive) form of *nhm*, "change the mind," is followed by the preposition *'al*, translators uniformly render the expression "to repent *of, concerning"* (e.g., Jer. 18:8, 10). What would lead to a different (and otherwise unexampled) rendering of the idiom in the present instance?

Two or three factors may have conspired to produce the conventional rendering. First, there is the partially related expression in 2:8, where Job is said to sit *amidst (betok)* the ashes, presumably in mourning and perhaps in self-abasement. The respective expressions, however, are not synonymous. For in 2:8 the preposition "amidst" is clearly spatial-locative in its reference; whereas in 42:6 the preposition is part of a consistent idiom in which its force is not spatial-locative ("upon") but relational ("concerning"). Second, there is the practice, variously described, of the use of dust or of ashes in acts of mourning or

255

self-abasement. These materials are vivid symbols of human finitude and mortality as creatures deriving from and returning to the earth. As such, these materials fittingly function in acknowledgment of one's finitude and mortality and in repudiation of one's acts of presumption. It would be easy to assume that 42:6b sets forth such an acknowledgment and repudiation. A third factor may lie not so much in textual usage as in the religious sensibilities of translators and interpreters. There is an almost universal tendency (as attested already in the friends of Job) to view Job's words and actions up to this point as presumptuous and proud. Similarly, there is a predisposition on the part of readers to expect a resolution in which Job repents of this presumption and abases himself before God. The question, of course, is whether the author of this book intended to present Job in such a fashion as to confirm and reinforce such conventional expectations and predispositions. Two textual features suggest otherwise: (1) If usage determines meaning, then general usage is all against the meaning "repent *in* dust and ashes" and in favor of "repent *concerning.* . . ." (The preposition is so construed, now, also by Dale Patrick [VT 26:367–71] and by John Briggs Curtis [JBL 98:497–511]; and according to L. J Kaplan [VT 28:356–58] it seems to have been so understood already by the great medieval scholar Maimonides.) (2) The phrase "dust and ashes" occurs elsewhere only in Genesis 18:27 and Job 30:19. These two passages, and especially the latter, should guide us in our understanding of Job 42:6.

In Genesis 18:27, the phrase "dust and ashes" clearly is used to express Abraham's sense of his creaturely status before God, one who seems almost overwhelmed at the audacity with which he, as mere dust and ashes, should negotiate with the "judge of all the earth" (18:25) on matters of justice (that is, on matters closely similar to those which have exercised Job). The fact remains, nevertheless, that one who is thus conscious of his finitude does so negotiate. What we see, then, is not one who is self-abased before God in repentance, but one who, fully conscious of being dust and ashes, boldly claims a hearing with God. That such a stance is appropriate is suggested by the context. For, before it was changed by one of the rare intentional alterations of the scribes, Genesis 18:22 depicted Yahweh as standing before Abraham. What troubled the scribes who altered the text, apparently, was the picture in which the "judge of all the earth" stood in attendance upon "dust and ashes" to

256

see what Abraham would say. We may hazard the suggestion
that the alteration of the text defaced a passage in which the
divine image was being enacted.

As for the occurrence in Job 30:19, it is not necessary to
repeat here the comments made on that passage. As we have
tried to show, it comes as a kind of nodal point around which
cluster all the references to dust and clay and ashes in Job. As
such it functions pivotally in the service of the critique of Israelite anthropology which the Book of Job offers us. The Israelite
vision of humankind—of *'adam,* the earthling—came to one
kind of expression in Genesis 1 and 2, as well as in Psalm 8. On
the one hand Job's experience caused him to question and to
doubt that vision (cf. e.g., 29:25; 19:9; 30:19; and 7:17–18 with
Ps. 8). On the other hand, in spite of his despair concerning the
implications of his experience, not only for himself but also for
humankind as a whole (7:17–18), he repeatedly returned to
such affirmations as those in 23:10 (cf. 22:23–25) and 31:35–37.
His dilemma lay in his inability or his unwillingness unilaterally
to draw his fears and his hopes together into some kind of
resolution grounded in a steady vision of God.

It was into this dilemma that Yahweh spoke out of the
whirlwind. In that speech nothing was said to thrust Job further
into the mire. All that was done was to portray Yahweh as a
cosmic creator who delights in a world sufficiently ordered
to make life possible and worthwhile, but sufficiently free to
allow for the possibility of bilateral participation. Humankind
is not painted into the picture as one creature among many,
but is addressed by the Creator in a series of questions, the
response to which will disclose the human decision for self-
understanding in such a world: solely as a creature; or as a
creature (as "dust and ashes") challenged to take up the divine
image through engagement with the partly determinate, partly
indeterminate character of the world.

In the latter alternative, self-understanding as "dust and
ashes," with all the suffering to which it is vulnerable, is not
incompatible with royal status but now may be accepted as the
very condition under which royalty manifests itself. Henceforth, to affirm oneself as "dust and ashes" *need* not be an act
of self-abasement. In specific and appropriate contexts, to be 257
sure, it may continue so to function powerfully in acts of confession for sin and guilt. In other contexts an affirmation of oneself
as "dust and ashes" may also become an act in which the royal

vocation of humanity—the royal vocation to *become* humanity —is accepted and embraced with all its vulnerability to innocent suffering.

In Genesis 18:22 Yahweh the judge of all the earth stood in attendance upon Abraham to see what dust and ashes would say concerning the guilty and the innocent of Sodom and Gomorrah. There, Abraham's intercession both presupposed and enacted a freedom from strict retribution, as he (like Moses in Exod. 32) sought and participated in a deeper conception of divine justice. After the divine speeches in Job 38—41 (see particularly 38:3*b*; 40:7*b*), we may suppose Yahweh standing in attendance before Job, to see what dust and ashes will say concerning itself. What Yahweh hears is that dust and ashes no longer interprets its suffering in the manner indicated in 30:19 (or in 19:9).

How *does* Job now interpret his suffering? And how does he now understand his status before God and in the world? It is part of the character of the text that the precise content of Job's self-understanding is left unstated. On the basis of 42:1–6 as a whole, however, that self-understanding apparently is now affirmed confessionally, in agreement with God. As with the ending to the Book of Jonah, for example, the text ends in such an indeterminate way that the hearer or reader is drawn to complete the answer. That readerly act of completion will arise out of one's understanding of the book to this point and no doubt out of one's continuing engagement with the mystery of human existence and vocation in the world and before God.

The "act of completion" which has been adumbrated in this commentary is understood to bear a family resemblance to such portrayals as Mark 10:35–45; Matthew 16:13–28; and Philippians 2:5–11, not to speak of the portrayals of the servant in Second Isaiah. In these portrayals, the central figure is set forth as suffering in the service of God, and as serving God through suffering. In the three New Testament portrayals, that suffering servant also is a royal figure. In Second Isaiah, if the suffering servant is not presented prominently as a royal figure (though some evidence clearly points in that direction), nevertheless that servant is a redemptively central figure within the eschatological community which itself is set forth in royal terms (Isa. 55:3–5).

Two considerations, perhaps, save such a vision from the charge of human presumption: it arises, not as a unilateral assertion, but in response to Yahweh's address across the field of the world (Job 38—41) and it entails actions which display human participation in the dialectic of order and freedom manifest in creation. To be dust in God's image is to enjoy and to be responsible for the order manifest in creation; it is to enjoy and to be responsible for the freedom which is also manifest in the events of the world and which resides by God's gift in the human soul. This last comment brings us to a consideration of the epilogue.

PART SEVEN

Epilogue
Order and Freedom in Felicity

JOB 42:7–17

The drama of Job's life began under the energy of the question as to whether his piety was purely the piety of responsive gratitude or whether he freely worshiped God and turned from evil. The drama continued, in the dialogues, under the energy of the question as to whether Job's suffering was simply the suffering merited by him or whether it came upon him freely, without cause, in no discernible relation to his piety and his uprightness. In the divine speeches and Job's response to them, a universe is disclosed in which order and freedom both are inherent and Job responds to the creator of such a universe with a free confession of agreement. Now in the epilogue the vision arrived at through the dialogues is brought into the community—first to the friends, then to Job's family and acquaintances. It is a vision in which (characteristically for the Hebrew Bible) the most extraordinary disclosures and insights into the nature of things are embodied in life's ordinaries, thereby transforming them.

* * *

The Book of Job ends as it began, with narrative which includes some dialogue. But whereas in the prologue the dialogue explicitly transpires horizontally (among the parties in heaven and on earth respectively), leaving any vertical dialogue only implicit, now the explicit vertical dialogue, begun with the divine speeches of chapters 38—41 and continued with Job's response in 42:1–6, is extended to the friends (42:7–8). In this as in many other ways the epilogue recurs to elements first encountered in the prologue, but with such a shift in nuance as befits a conclusion. Among such common elements we may note the following: (1) In the single specific scene which balances the four specific scenes of the prologue, two elements are echoed: (a) Whenever Yahweh spoke to the Satan of Job, Job was

261

referred to as "my servant Job" (1:8; 2:3); similarly, in speaking of Job to the friends Yahweh uses the same phrase no less than four times (42:7-9). (b) Job's use of the term "foolish" in reference to his wife's speech (2:10) is echoed in Yahweh's words to the friends (42:8). (2) In the concluding narrative of 42:10-17, several elements from both 1:1-5 and 2:11-13 reappear. The assembly of Job's brothers and sisters (and acquaintances) to eat with him in his house is reminiscent of a similar assembly in the house of one or the other of Job's sons (1:4). On the other hand, the condolence and comfort shown Job by his own family (42:11) balances, while perhaps contrasting with, the condolence and comfort shown by his friends (2:11). Some other common elements will be noted below.

Job 42:7-9
Yahweh and the Friends of Job

In the commentary on 42:1-6 we have introduced the notion of language as a fabric of meaning and, as such, a hedge against chaos. It was there suggested that this fabric began to come apart with the first dialogue between Yahweh and the Satan and that thereafter it continued to fray and tatter until the exchange between Yahweh and Job in chapters 38—41 and 42:1-6, when the fabric of agreed-upon meaning was restored, though on a new basis.

Yet this new fabric—flexible and resilient, inclusive of the surd of non-meaning yet affirming ultimate meaning—is not yet fully restored. Or rather, its restoration is as yet only a private affair, between Job and Yahweh. To become more than a private language it must embrace also the friends. The Satan of course needs no reintroduction, for all along this figure was a loyal servant of Yahweh (in English parliamentary terms, "Her Majesty's Loyal Opposition") and not really *God's* adversary. It was the Satan's task to voice Yahweh's questions; and, those questions now fully answered in 42:1-6, there is no further task for the Satan to perform. Not only is the absence of this figure from the epilogue no problem, but it is a positive clue and signal of the resolution of the question raised concerning Job in the first place. If there is any merit in our interpretation of the Satan as the dramatic mouthpiece of Yahweh's own nascent question about Job, then the Satan's presence in the epilogue would in fact signal that Yahweh's question was not yet resolved.

Unlike the Satan, however, the friends cannot be allowed to fade unmentioned from the scene. The Job of 40:3–5 was not allowed to remain in the solitary counsel of his own silence but was drawn into participatory confession (42:1–6). All the more so, the friends must be drawn into some kind of statement (verbal or symbolic) indicative of their own change of mind. They too are deemed worthy—or rather, worthy or not, they are the recipients—of a divine word of direct address, though it is a word with a different content and (perhaps most humiliatingly) devoid of poetic elaboration. Yahweh speaks to them in the only idiom which their reward-punishment mentality allows them to hear:

A.a) "My wrath is kindled against you and against your two friends;

.b) for you have not spoken of me what is right, as my servant Job has.

B.a) Now therefore take seven bulls and seven rams,

.b) and go to my servant Job,

B'.a) and offer up for yourselves a burnt offering;

'.b) and my servant Job shall pray for you,

A'.a) for I will accept his prayer not to do folly with you (author's translation);

'.b) for you have not spoken of me what is right, as my servant Job has."

Why is Yahweh wrathful? Does this not smack of the old theology of reward and punishment? We may remind ourselves, however, that even in the midst of his deepest doubts as to God's concern for justice, Job himself could sustain some sense of the divine concern for truth about the nature of things (13:4–12; also 19:28–29). Moreover, it is simplistic to suppose that the truth about the nature of things is adequately articulated (in mutually exclusive fashion) according to *either* a doctrine of strict retribution *or* a doctrine of indeterminate freedom. Far from betraying the vision gained through the dialogues, the epilogue serves that vision (a vision in which, e.g., the Sea in 38:8–11 is both bounded and swaddled) by exemplifying how it works in human relations.

263

Yahweh is wrathful because the friends have not spoken of God what is right, as servant Job has. This statement could be taken, in a very general sense, to refer to the view of God and the nature of things as set forth by the friends and as set forth by Job. But it may also be taken to refer to how God would finally deal with Job. The friends have said that God will deal with Job in one of two ways: Either God will restore Job following his repentance for his sin and guilt, so that his latter days will be greater than his beginning (8:7; cf. 42:12), or God will judge Job inexorably if he persists in his sin. Job too has said that God will deal with him in one of two ways. They are not, however, alternatives which turn on Job's repentance. They turn, rather, on the question of God's disposition toward Job. If, as he fears, God is indifferent to the plight of the righteous, then Job will die at God's hands. In the midst of these fears, from time to time Job rises to expressions of hope which, however momentary, come as acts of free piety. Moreover, at the end Job freely binds himself to God by oaths. These oaths do not (as is sometimes said) coerce God into action. Rather, they present God with a free act of self-offering which invites a similar, felicitously free response from God. In and through such expressions of momentary hope, and such enactments of free self-binding, Job disposes himself toward the future in a stance of openness and vulnerable hope. In such acts he has spoken truly concerning God, even as in his accusations he has truly identified the fact that his terrible trials have transpired within God's world, a world for which God may properly and finally be held responsible.

Yahweh's rebuke to Eliphaz leads into a piece of often-noted and dramatically delicious irony. Eliphaz had promised Job that, were he to reconcile himself to God, he would even become an intercessor who could deliver the not-innocent from divine wrath (22:26–30). In this, for once, Eliphaz spoke truly —except that Job had no need to "lay his gold in ophir"! Eliphaz is to take the appropriate number of bulls and rams (such as would advertise clearly what he is about) and go to Job and offer a burnt offering. Job had once been accustomed to offer such sacrifices on behalf of his children, in case they had cursed God in their hearts. The friends are required, not simply to keep their own inner counsel while benefiting from such an act of Job's on their behalf, but to make public statement of their own repentance for what they have said openly concerning God. Yet their offering, by itself, will not suffice. Job must pray; it is his prayer which will incline God to deal graciously with them.

On the matter of Job's intercession (that part of v. 8 which is designated above as *A'a*), the interpretation turns on how one reads the idiom "not to do with you *nebala*." The expression is idiomatic, formally paralleling the idiomatic expressions "to do with someone *ḥesed*," that is, to deal *graciously* with someone, or "to do with someone *ṭob* (good)." Writing of the expression in 42:8, Gordis says, "in our passage, the phrase means, 'to exhibit you as *nebalim*, senseless, foolish, i.e., to expose you to disgrace." Yet Gordis gives no grounds for departing from the natural construal of the idiom "to do X with someone," where the X (whether *ḥesed*, *ṭob*, or *nebala*) characterizes the action done. (Translations such as AV, RSV and JB likewise are groundless.) In such instances, presumably, it is felt that "folly" cannot conceivably be attributed to God, not even in a hypothetical situation ("lest I . . ."). Pope's translation is idiomatically sound: ". . . so that I may not do *anything rash* to you." Yet the term "rash" (like the rendering "harsh" in NEB) does not capture the gravity of the Hebrew word, which in 42:8 echoes the connotations which it has in 2:10.

In a book which daringly probes moral and theological issues at a depth which transforms conventional frames of reference, the term *nebala* surely is to be taken with full force, and the expression in which it occurs likewise is to be given its proper meaning: ". . . not to deal foolishly with you." We may remind ourselves of S. R. Driver's definition of the term, as "moral and religious sensibility, a rooted incapacity to discern moral and religious relations, leading to an intolerant repudiation in practice of the claims which they impose." The key word in this definition is "sensibility." A "foolish" act does not simply contravene a specific moral or religious precept but, more deeply, betrays the primal sympathy in which moral and religious relations are grounded and of which rules and precepts are specific expressions. If this primal sympathy is itself not merely an automatic conditioned response to the situation of another, but is in part a display of moral and spiritual freedom, then we may be able to gain some idea of the tension between 42:7 *Aa* and 42:8 *A'a*, that is, between the wrath of God and the folly of God. Parenthetically, here we have an example of the importance of close attention to the *form* of the text: The elements in the first part of the speech, *A.ab* and *B.ab*, inversely are balanced by the elements in the second part, *B'ab* and *A'ab*. In part this implies that God's wrath against the friends would e an act of folly. But in what sense would this be an act of folly? To deal with the friends in wrath would be to deal with them according to their just desserts, as measured by a retributive conception of justice. But the justice of the creator of Job 38—41 (cf. the *mišpat* of 40:8, and of, e.g., Isa. 40:14) is not, finally, retributive. There is something about this creativity which properly has the character of a positive and life-giving *non sequitur*. It is a *non sequitur* (i.e., a truly free act), in the face of darkness to say "let there be light," whether the one so speaking be God (Gen. 1:1–3) or Job (17:11–12, and commentary). Just so, the justice of such a creative God has properly something in it of a *non sequitur*, such that, in comparison with creative justice, retributive justice would be an act of folly, an act devoid of the freedom and grace—the felicity—which is the mainspring of primal sympathy and of the moral and spiritual sensibilities by which relations are negotiated.

What we see in verses 7–8, then, is an attempt to lead the friends from where they are to where Yahweh would have them to be: from a view and a mode of relationship retributive in character—which in this instance would mean wrath for them—to a view and a mode of relationship grounded in freedom which in this instance calls for a change of mind on *everyone's* part. The dialectics of verses 7–8, then, may be summed up in this way: The friends do not have to repent, but may. Job does not have to intercede, but may. Yahweh does not have to forgive, but may. None of these actions *has* to occur. The logic by which any one of them, or all of them, may occur, is not the logic of necessity but the poetic (literally, the "making" or creative) logic of felicity. Yet if these actions do not occur, certain outcomes cannot occur: The potential for relations arising out of creative freedom will be diminished or lost altogether. If these actions do occur, the outcome will be a restored and enriched world, in which evil has been fully acknowledged by all parties, and yet overcome through acts of freedom in which Yahweh, Job, and the friends all participate. For it may be noted that Job's prayer to Yahweh appears in essence to be "O Yahweh, do not deal with them foolishly." Such a prayer means that, in interceding for his friends, Job's own spirit toward them displays a *non sequitur*, a freedom from vengefulness which is perhaps the irreducible and uncounterfeitable sign of participation in the covenant. Insofar as this prayer is in response to Yahweh's words addressed to the friends, we may see that while

266

all parties are invited to act toward one another in freedom, that freedom originates in Yahweh.

Job 42:10–17
Restoration and More

What then of Job's restored fortunes, in 42:10? The precise placement in the narrative of this verse is crucial for its proper interpretation. Coming where it does, it cannot be supposed to be the basis of Job's grateful prayer for his friends. The latter prayer remains an act of freedom toward them, arising out of the freedom characterizing his exchange with Yahweh in chapters 38—41 and 42:1–6. Similarly, it cannot be supposed to be Yahweh's reward for Job's change of mind in 42:6. For that matter, the text explicitly connects the restoration with Job's prayer for his friends. This is to suggest that the restoration comes as an act of divine freedom enacting itself in felicity. To argue (as many commentators implicitly do) that as a result of the message of the dialogues God cannot and must not bless Job on any account is itself to reinstate a rigorous logic admissive of no *non sequiturs,* no felicitously poetic acts.

The proper way to approach the restoration of 42:10–17, in our view, is as follows: In light of the dialogues we may no longer interpret any specific aspect of experience—positive or negative—in terms of a strict law of reward and punishment. Very well, then. When we see Job blessed, in the end, we are invited to interpret this as arising out of God's freedom enacted toward Job.

Commenting on the "twice as much" of verse 10, Francis I. Anderson writes, "It is a wry touch that the Lord, like any thief who has been found out (Exod. 22:4), repays Job double what he took away" (*Job,* p. 293). The connection with Exodus 22:4 cannot be overlooked. Yet one may ask whether the direction of the connection should not be reversed. As we are arguing, the epilogue is governed not by law but by freedom enacted felicitously. This may be seen also in the fact that, in contrast to the otherwise universal custom in Hebrew birth narrative, none of the sons are named; whereas, remarkably, all three daughters are named and commented on. Moreover, in

267

contrast (one is tempted to say, in deliberate contrast) to the provisions of the law in Numbers 27, by which daughters inherited only when there were no male heirs, here the daughters are given inheritance freely alongside their brothers. These last two features of the narrative impart to it an overtone of free generosity which is the clue to how we should take the "twice as much" of verse 10. If there is a hermeneutical connection between the latter verse and Exodus 22:4, then, it may be such as to suggest that law itself has its basis in freedom and, if it is deeply understood, is itself a felicitous enactment of freedom.

At first glance, verse 11 seems to interrupt the connection between verse 10 and verses 12–13. However, it does not really do so. Like the scene in verses 7–9, the narrative in 10–17 portrays the interweaving of free acts combining toward the reinstatement of the world of divine and human relations in felicity. In verses 10–17 this interweaving is presented as follows:

10 divine action toward Job;

11 human community's action toward Job;

12–13 divine action toward Job;

14–15 Job's action toward his daughters (and toward the community through his dowry of full inheritances bestowed on the daughters);

16–17 summary of divine action toward Job (in the form of a long and full life).

Structurally, then, verse 11 has its place in the alternating pattern of the narrative. Thematically, as we have noted, the scene of Job's brothers and sisters coming to eat with him in his house answers to the scene set out in 1:4. If the customary scene in 1:4 was connected with birth celebrations (see commentary), then ever so lightly the scene in 42:11 prepares the reader for the generative theme in verses 12–13.

In verse 11, the sentence "they showed him sympathy and comforted him" (RSV) in Hebrew exactly reproduces 2:11 "they came to condole with him and comfort him" (RSV). Does the author here offer us one more gentle irony? Are we invited to imagine that, like the friends who came for that purpose and stayed to lay on Job all sorts of conventional language that was completely beside the point, so these brothers and sisters and acquaintances, oblivious to what had gone on to this point, gave him the benefit of all their clichés? How realistic a touch this would be! If such is the case, did Job gently set them straight? Or, foregoing the dubious pleasure of three more cycles of debates with these three groups (brothers, sisters, acquaintances), did he quietly forgive them in his heart, resolving to get up early in the morning to offer burnt offerings on their behalf?

The foregoing may, however, misread the clues in the text. The recollection of 2:11 in 42:11 may serve rather to set up a contrast between the friends and the family. The friends followed their head-shaking sympathy, eventually, with the dubious gift to Job of their wordy attempts at wisdom. The family followed their head-shaking with material gifts to help him rebuild at least that part of his life. Perhaps they were relatively unconcerned with theological analysis of what Job had just been through—or somehow possessed the theological wisdom to leave explanations of his suffering in the mystery in which Yahweh left it—and were more concerned with the practical solution of his resulting condition. In what they *do,* without benefit of the dialogues in 3:1—42:9, one may identify an unselfconscious version of the felicitous freedom and primal sympathy of which we have spoken in connection with 42:7–9. In that case, it is salutary to end this commentary on the observation that the enactment of such freedom and sympathy, and the mediation of the grace of life out of which they arise, occurs where it occurs and exists in no *necessary* relation either to the intense debates and the divine speeches of the dialogues, or to the reading (and the writing) of commentaries on the Book of Job.